Collaboration and Resistance Reviewed

Alan Morris

This volume examines the renewal of interest in, and extensive re-evaluation of, the wartime occupation of France by the Nazis. The author places the phenomenon in its literary and historical context, revealing how, until 1970, a collective and predominantly Gaullist 'myth' of the resistance was able to establish itself in France. The subsequent undermining of this 'myth' is discussed through a survey of the works of prominent writers and through more detailed studies of some of the younger of these writers, showing how, in the effort to escape a problematic heritage, new myths are created.

Alan Morris is in the Department of Modern Languages at the University of Strathclyde.

Berg French Studies

General Editor: John E. Flower

John E. Flower and Bernard C. Swift (eds), *Francois Mauriac: Visions and Reappraisals*

Michael Tilby (ed.), *Beyond the Nouveau Roman: Essays on the Contemporary French Novel*

Richard Griffiths, *The Use of Abuse: The Polemics of the Dreyfus Affair and its Aftermath*

Alec G. Hargreaves, *Voices from the North African Immigrant Community in France: Immigration and Identity in Beur Fiction*

Colin Nettelbeck, *Forever French: The French Exiles in the United States of America during the Second World War*

Bill Marshall, *Victor Serge: The Uses of Dissent*

– Forthcoming –

Malcolm Cook, *Fictional France: Social Reality in the French Novel, 1775–1800*

Nicholas Hewitt, *Intellectuals and the New Right in Postwar France*

David Looseley, *Culture and Politics in Contemporary France*

Alan Clark, *Paris Peasant: Francois Mitterrand and the Modernisation of France*

Collaboration and Resistance Reviewed

Writers and the *Mode Rétro* in Post-Gaullist France

Alan Morris

BERG

New York/Oxford

Distributed exclusively in the US and Canada by
St Martin's Press, New York

First published in 1992 by
Berg Publishers Limited
Editorial offices:
165 Taber Avenue, Providence, RI 02906, USA
150 Cowley Road, Oxford, OX4 1JJ, UK

Library of Congress Cataloging-in-Publication Data
Morris, Alan. 1955–
Collaboration and resistance reviewed : writers and the "mode rétro" in Post-Gaullist France / Alan Morris.
p. cm. — (Berg French studies)
Includes bibliographical references and index.
ISBN 0–85496–634–X
1. World War. 1939–1945—Collaborationists—France. 2. World War, 1939–1945—Underground movements—France. 3. France—History—German occupation, 1939–1945. I. Title. II. Series.
D802.F8 M68 1992
940.53′163—dc20 91–23611
CIP

British Library Cataloguing in Publication Data
Morris, Alan
Collaboration and resistance reviewed: writers and the "mode rétro" in post-Gaullist France.
– (Berg French studies)
1. Title II. Series
944.081

ISBN 0–85496–634–X

For my parents

La mode 'rétro' appliquée à la collaboration nationale mériterait déjà une étude spécifique.

Pascal Ory

Il s'agit des années noires qui demeurent, pour les Français qui les ont vécues, une période chargée de passions toujours vivaces et dont les plus jeunes n'ont, habituellement, qu'une image déformée.

Jean-Pierre Azéma

La guerre n'était pas toujours sur les champs de bataille. La facture était alourdie par les infirmes, la jeunesse déboussolée et surtout la France divisée.

José Giovanni

Contents

Acknowledgements

A number of people have assisted me considerably in bringing this project to fruition: Mr I. Higgins and Dr D. Gascoigne, both of whom, over the years, have been a constant and invaluable source of encouragement and advice; Professor J. E. Flower, Mr H. R. Kedward and Dr W. Kidd, whose general comments and suggestions have helped shape the text into its present form; my colleagues at the University of Strathclyde, who, for the first semester of 1990, took over all my teaching duties and allowed me to concentrate on producing the final draft; and last but not least, Miss A. Abercrombie, whose patience and support have been almost boundless. I gratefully record my thanks to them all, and hope that the work which follows is worthy of the interest they have taken in it.

Finally, thanks are also due to the University of Strathclyde and, especially, to the Carnegie Trust for the Universities of Scotland; without the generous financial assistance of these two institutions, the research expounded by this book could never have been undertaken.

List of Abbreviations

BBC	British Broadcasting Corporation
BOF	*Beurre, Oeufs, Fromage* (applied to those who became rich selling such goods during the war)
CNE	Comité National des Écrivains
EFR	Éditeurs Français Réunis
FFI	Forces Françaises de l'Intérieur
FTP	Francs-Tireurs-Partisans
LVF	Légion des Volontaires Français contre le Bolchevisme
NRF	*La Nouvelle Revue Française*
ORTF	Office de la Radiodiffusion-Télévision Française
PCF	Parti Communiste Français
PPF	Parti Populaire Français
PUF	Presses Universitaires de France
RPF	Rassemblement du Peuple Français
SS	Schutzstaffel (Protection Squad)
TF1	Télévision Française 1
TSF	Télégraphie sans fils (wireless)
VE Day	The day on which the Allies achieved victory in Europe (8 May 1945)
VIP	Very important person

Introduction

Of all the various fashions which have preoccupied the French over the last two decades or so, perhaps the most evident and most sustained has been the all-embracing *mode rétro*, that remarkable renewal of interest in, and extensive re-evaluation of, the wartime occupation of France by Adolf Hitler's Germany. Dominant at virtually every level of cultural activity for most of the 1970s, and surviving into the early 1980s, this vogue left embers so incandescent that their presence can still be detected today. The extradition of Klaus Barbie from Bolivia (1983), his subsequent trial and conviction (1987), the posthumous indictment of Jean Leguay (1989), the arrest of Paul Touvier (1989), the *cinquantenaire* of de Gaulle's *appel à la résistance* (1990) – these are just some of the events which, right up to the present, have kept the *années noires* of 1940–5 firmly fixed in the public eye. And with more fiftieth anniversaries to come, the 'dark years' are not likely to be forgotten for some time yet.

In spite of this enduring relevance, however, the *mode rétro* seems not really to have received the critical attention it deserves, for although its importance from an historical point of view has been examined and assessed,[1] its literary expression has scarcely been studied in any depth at all. The present book will therefore seek to remedy this neglect, the twofold aim it will set itself being first to analyse and characterise this *mode* – in its written manifestation for the most part – and second to spotlight the contribution made to it by four young authors, each of whose work can, in terms of both thematic content and literary quality, quite rightly be viewed as exemplary.

The structure of the text which follows will reflect this double objective. Part I will concentrate on the fashion as a whole and attempt to shed light upon it from three different angles: chapter 1 will place the phenomenon in its literary, social and historical context, revealing how, up until about 1970, a predominantly Gaullist 'myth' of the Resistance was able to establish itself in

France, with the result that the national response to invasion was accepted to be one of widespread heroism and revolt; chapter 2 will study the reaction to such *résistancialisme* (as I will henceforth call it),[2] and show exactly how the orthodox interpretation of events was undermined in the 1970s, while chapter 3 will offer explanations of the timing and direction of the new view of the Occupation. With the characteristics of the *mode rétro* as a trend thus firmly established, Part II will then switch from the general to the particular, and the spotlight will be placed upon Pascal Jardin, Marie Chaix and Evelyne Le Garrec (in chapter 4) and Patrick Modiano (in chapter 5). As each of these four authors will be seen to create an individual account of the past, an account which, although running counter to the prevailing orthodoxy, will be no less mythopoeic in nature, it will be the notion of myth which will link the five chapters of the book together, and hence give the work its overall unity.

This extensive reliance on the concept of myth is, of course, not without its possible pitfalls, since there is no unanimous agreement about what myths actually are, even if there is consensus that they can be of many different types. Indeed, in the pages which follow, I myself shall refer to two different kinds of myth: collective and personal. What I shall call a collective myth will be a partial view of history which, for one reason or another, is formed in the consciousness of a whole nation, and is accepted by most members of that nation.[3] By a personal myth, I shall mean a unique version of past events, a fabrication designed to serve therapeutic ends, meaningful mainly to an individual anxious to escape the reality of his or her position. Such differentiation of two types of myth may, at first glance, appear somewhat confusing, but this is not really the case: ultimately, as will be shown, there is only one process of mythification involved, for the personal myths will arise as specific counters to the collective myth which developed around the Resistance. They will, in other words, embody both the phenomenon that I shall call demythification (the destruction of an existing myth) and that which I shall term countermythification (demythification by the use of another myth, frequently the exact opposite of the original one). Now this is all very well, it might be said, but why choose to employ imprecise words like 'myth' and its derivatives in the first place? Why not seek out less ambiguous alternatives? My reply to such questions is that, in a sense, the decision was taken for me, for whatever other characteristics myths may have, one of the most fundamental, it seems to me, is that they are accepted as such by later generations, and when the young writers of the *mode rétro* re-evaluate the Occupation they do not talk of attacking a legend, nor do they talk of deflating an epic; what they actually talk about, with virtual unanimity, is *demythifying* the *années noires*. This, then, is why I utilise the vocabulary I do – no matter how problematic it may be, it is, in my opinion, by far and away the best available.

In addition to this problem stemming from the use of the term 'myth' and its compounds, a further difficulty in a survey of this sort relates to the way in which texts are selected for analysis. To mention every piece of prose which contributed to the *mode rétro* would, quite obviously, prove unfeasible if not impossible, so to help me decide what to include and what not to include in this book I have applied the criteria of variety and representativeness. As regards variety, the very nature of the trend under consideration demands that all kinds of literary expression be acknowledged, so reference will be made not only to novels, *récits* and short stories, but also to biographies, autobiographies, memoirs, essays, histories, book reviews, journalistic articles, and so on and so forth. As for representativeness, although there are countless other books on which I could have drawn to provide further illustrative material, I have endeavoured to discuss only those texts which, to my mind, convey the essence of the fashion most visibly. The pick of these, that is to say the most resonant of all, have in turn been singled out for more detailed study in Part II, and that these spotlighted works should also be of the highest literary standard is by no means coincidental, for what gives them their supreme quality and what makes them absolutely typical are most manifestly one and the same thing – an intense authorial sensitivity, a sensitivity which makes every facet of the response to the Occupation as acute as can be.

Before concluding this introduction I should perhaps say a final word about how my title is to be interpreted. To appreciate fully what I mean by 'Collaboration and Resistance Reviewed', it will be necessary to bear in mind that there were, in a manner of speaking, two Collaborations and two Resistances prior to 1970: the real, wartime phenomena, which tended to be ignored by the vast majority of French people, and the later, partial re-presentations of these phenomena by the postwar myth-makers, which were far more widely accepted. It was only these latter, peacetime constructs – the myth-based Collaboration and Resistance – that the *mode rétro* called into question, only these highly simplistic re-creations that, consequently, were regularly and radically 're-viewed'. Or at least that was the case in the first instance. In the longer run, sadly, things were not quite so clear-cut, for the more demythification established itself, and the more it slipped over into countermythification, the more an unintended side effect of the process began to make itself felt – the real Collaboration and the real Resistance, albeit indirectly, were soon being reappraised as well. Little wonder, therefore, that the fashion was to prove controversial. And little wonder either that, as noted right at the start, its consequences should still be absorbing the French even today.

Notes

1. See e.g. Henry Rousso, *Le Syndrome de Vichy, 1944–198. . . .* Full publication details of this, and other works mentioned hereafter can be found in the select bibliography. The editions given there are the ones referred to in the text.
2. Regarding my use of this term, cf. Rousso, *Le Syndrome de Vichy*, pp.20–1. (See also p.39.)
3. My use of the phrase 'collective myth' here can be compared to the definition of classical myths given by Christopher Nash: 'Myths are regarded as attempts at *history*, in the course of which the confused memory and imagination of early peoples have transfigured human leaders into "gods" and the record of their acts into theology' ('Myth and Modern Literature', in *The Context of English Literature, 1900–30*, edited by Michael Bell, p.161).

PART I

La Mode Rétro: New Myths for Old

On a tendance à ne rien croire de ce qui est écrit sur un sujet interdit. Et sont interdits la plupart des sujets inconfortables.

François Nourissier

Évoquer des souvenirs, c'est déjà faire de la littérature; on noircit ou on embellit malgré soi.

Jacques Peuchmaurd

Les vaincus doivent se taire. Comme les graines.

Antoine de Saint-Exupéry

–1–

The Heritage 1940–1969

Quoi qu'il arrive, la flamme de la résistance française ne doit pas s'éteindre et ne s'éteindra pas.

General Charles de Gaulle

Ils n'étaient que quelques-uns / Ils furent foule soudain.

Paul Éluard

Les livres étaient plutôt décevants. Côté résistant, les héros étaient tous sublimes et les traîtres semblaient avoir été marqués dès le berceau pour la trahison. Trop facile.

Gilles Perrault

In August 1944, Paris is finally liberated, and General Charles de Gaulle, the Head of the Temporary Government, is at long last able to return to the capital of France. The crowd which turns out to greet him is in a state of complete euphoria, and understandably so, for the troubles born of the *années noires* now seem to be well and truly over. But are they really? Sadly, time will show that they are not. Decades pass, but the old war wounds irritatingly refuse to heal. Indeed, a good twenty-five years after the peace treaties have been signed, there is still no trace of scar tissue forming. Jean-Pierre Azéma explains why: 'La Collaboration laissa des séquelles suffisamment traumatisantes pour ne sécréter qu'une histoire *post-mortem* âpre, confuse, complexe dont la mode "rétro" est l'aboutissement ambigu.'[1] It is this 'mode "rétro"' – the widespread reassessment of the Occupation that took place from 1970 onwards – which will be the prime focus of the present work. However, if a full understanding of the phenomenon is to be achieved, it will initially be necessary to examine the social, political and historical bases from which the fashion grew. This introductory chapter will therefore attempt to turn the clock back and do precisely that.

Any review of French society since 1939 must inevitably centre on the figure of de Gaulle, and must equally inevitably spotlight the month of June 1940, a formative time for him as things turned out. On the eighteenth, he made his now famous *appel* from London, and in so doing, in the eyes of many, he single-handedly created the Resistance. Furthermore, over the next few days, he established the persona with which he would forever be associated: that of 'soldat et chef français',[2] protector of *la patrie*, and guardian of national honour. In short, he set himself up as Hope incarnate, and this for the very good reason that 'il faut qu'il y ait un idéal. Il faut qu'il y ait une espérance. Il faut que, quelque part, brille et brûle la flamme de la résistance française.'[3] This was all very well, and quite comprehensible in the circumstances, but the problem with his embodying an ideal in this way was that an idealised view of the situation tended to be put forward, especially with regard to the extent of his support and influence. To give just one example, on 15 November 1941, he confidently observed: 'Pour quarante millions de Français, l'idée même de la victoire se confond avec celle de la victoire des Français Libres.'[4] This was manifestly untrue. Most French people at that moment were *attentistes* if not *pétainistes*.[5] Of course, the need to boost morale, the attempt to impress the Allies and the very recourse to rhetoric encouraged such exaggeration, as is only to be expected in wartime. What is perhaps more surprising, in retrospect, is the fact that a partial account of the *années noires* seems to have been widely expressed long after the war had ended. In other words, using the term as defined in the Introduction, a *myth* would appear to have grown up around the Resistance, and principally around de Gaulle.

The events of 1944–6 are particularly revealing in this respect. One of de Gaulle's first acts on returning to Paris at the Liberation was to move back into the War Ministry, to which he had been appointed on 5 June 1940 in the last Cabinet reshuffle before Pétain came to power. Such a symbolic gesture served to underline the legitimacy of his refusal to give up the fight, and was reinforced by his walk down the Champs-Élysées, during which he received enthusiastic acclaim: 'De Gaulle s'enfonce dans un hommage populaire qui légitime le 18 juin 1940 et les combattants de l'ombre.'[6] This popular acceptance had far-reaching implications, for in addition to justifying the general's belligerent stance, it also lent credibility to his utterances from London, not least of which was his contention that the whole of France supported him in his struggle. Because of this, he was now able to suggest, with scant acknowledgement of his allies' efforts, that the French had liberated themselves, as illustrated by his address to the Parisians on 25 August 1944:

> Paris! Paris outragé! Paris brisé! Paris martyrisé! mais Paris libéré! libéré par lui-même, libéré par son peuple avec le concours des armées de la France, avec l'appui et le concours de la France tout entière, de la France qui se bat, de la seule France, de la vraie France, de la France éternelle.[7]

By thus evoking extensive involvement in the Resistance, de Gaulle could minimise the degree of collaboration which had occurred, and could therefore paint a picture of national unity. His line of reasoning emerges particularly well from the speech he made on 31 December 1944:

> Sauf un nombre infime de malheureux qui ont consciemment préféré le triomphe de l'ennemi à la victoire de la France et qu'il appartient à la Justice de l'État de châtier équitablement, la masse immense des Français n'a jamais voulu autre chose que le bien de la patrie, lors même que beaucoup furent parfois égarés sur le chemin. Au point où nous en sommes et étant donné tout ce qu'il nous reste à faire pour nous sauver, nous relever et nous agrandir, les fureurs intestines, les querelles, les invectives sont injustes et malfaisantes.[8]

This sense of unity was essential for de Gaulle, since it allowed him to redeem his fellow countrymen retroactively, as Jean Touchard agrees: 'Le gaullisme de gouvernement [. . .] emporte l'adhésion confuse et souvent ambiguë d'un pays victorieux sans avoir beaucoup combattu, et dont de Gaulle est la bonne conscience.'[9] Moreover, on the basis of this consensus, the general could proceed to insist that France remained great, using her now massive participation in the war to ensure that she took her rightful place alongside the other victorious powers of the day – the United States of America, the Soviet Union and the United Kingdom. This too is a point which Touchard recognises, and it is not without cause that he says of de Gaulle's speeches from 1944 to 1946: 'Le thème fondamental est celui du rang, le rang de la France dans le monde.'[10]

There is one obvious danger with the procedure outlined above, however: true Resistants are likely to have the value of their *engagement* nullified by the welcoming of virtually everyone into the ranks. Well aware of this pitfall, no doubt, de Gaulle took great care to distinguish between an elite of active, heroic *résistants*, and the mass of rehabilitated passive ones, one of his clearest expositions of this distinction coming in his speech of 16 June 1946:

> [Le salut] vint, d'abord, d'une élite, spontanément jaillie des profondeurs de la nation et qui, bien au-dessus de toute préoccupation de parti ou de classe, se dévoua au combat pour la libération, la grandeur et la rénovation de la France. Sentiment de sa supériorité morale, conscience d'exercer une sorte de sacerdoce du sacrifice et de l'exemple, passion du risque et de l'entreprise, mépris des agitations, prétentions, surenchères, confiance souveraine en la force et en la ruse de sa puissante conjuration aussi bien qu'en la victoire et en l'avenir de la patrie, telle fut la psychologie de cette élite partie de rien et qui, malgré de lourdes pertes, devait entraîner derrière elle tout l'Empire et toute la France.
>
> Elle n'y eût point, cependant, réussi sans l'assentiment de l'immense masse française. Celle-ci, en effet, dans sa volonté instinctive de survivre et de triompher, n'avait jamais vu dans le désastre de 1940 qu'une péripétie de la guerre mondiale où la France servait d'avant-garde. Si beaucoup se plièrent, par force, aux circonstances, le nombre de ceux qui les acceptèrent dans leur esprit et dans leur cœur fut littéralement infime.[11]

Given that this was merely one speech amongst many which dealt with exactly the same themes, it can be assumed that the Gaullist view of events was imposing itself quite strongly at this time.

In fact, to confirm that this was the case, one has simply to consult the contemporary press. There, Raymond Aron for instance can be found acknowledging the general's exceptional status (even though his main aim in writing is to call for greater democracy):

> A la fin du mois d'août 1944, le général de Gaulle prit le pouvoir avec l'assentiment unanime de la nation. De l'extrême-gauche à l'extrême-droite, tous les partis, toutes les familles spirituelles acclamaient le premier Résistant de France, l'homme qui symbolisait l'honneur de nos armes, qui avait maintenu la patrie dans la guerre et dans la victoire.[12]

Similar statements abounded in papers and journals elsewhere. Apparently, then, the message was indeed getting across.

While the Gaullist myth was establishing itself in this manner, an equally simplified account of the Occupation was being put forward by the Communist Party. Building on the sacrifices of its members, and deliberately forgetting its ambiguous position prior to the German invasion of Russia in 1941, the self-styled *parti des fusillés* sought to present the Resistance as a rising of the masses, and not as the work of a limited elite.[13] Accordingly, de Gaulle was quite openly attacked for his appropriation of the movement: 'Il s'attribue indûment à lui tout seul le mérite de la Résistance tout entière [. . .]. Il feint aujourd'hui d'oublier que [le gouvernement] fut poussé et imposé par tout un peuple.'[14] The conclusion to be drawn from this argument is clear: such a popular uprising could only be truly represented by the party of the working classes – that is to say the Parti Communiste Français (PCF).

Both branches of the Resistance therefore offered the French people a share of the victory and a clear conscience in return for their support.[15] But here the similarity ends. Whereas the Gaullists called for unity and for the reacceptance of the less tainted collaborators, the Communists seemed set on the extermination of the whole political class to which they were opposed. The extent of the difference is reflected in the newspapers of the day. On the one hand, there was *Le Figaro*, which presented well-reasoned, often legalistic arguments in favour of moderation of judgement and leniency of sentence.[16] On the other hand, there was the Communist-dominated *Lettres Françaises*, whose outlook and style can be gauged from the following extract:

> Pour nous – nous le crierons sans nous lasser – il ne saurait y avoir de 'frères ennemis' ni 'd'adversaires fraternels'. Mais seulement, d'un côté, les innocentes victimes et de l'autre les bourreaux; d'un côté l'immense majorité des écrivains patriotes et de l'autre cette poignée de misérables, le 'honteux petit troupeau' qui s'est vendu à l'ennemi. Entre nous et eux, il n'y a pas il ne peut y avoir de commune mesure.[17]

Such condemnation of 'le "honteux petit troupeau"' was not confined to *Les Lettres Françaises*, though. It also materialised in a whole host of books, all as blatantly propagandist as the collection of short stories which Jean Fréville published under the title of *Les Collabos* (1946). Despite the author's claim that 'ce ne sont ni une caricature, ni un pamphlet, mais des histoires vraies, des témoignages qu'on ne peut récuser dans leur ensemble' (p.5), the exact opposite would be nearer the truth. The characters are mere mouthpieces because of their distinct lack of psychological depth, and a black-and-white moral standpoint leaves no extenuating circumstances for any of the collaborators portrayed. It is quite patent that literary concerns have been abandoned in the aim of settling scores.

Be that as it may, the review of the work in *Les Lettres Françaises* was, not unnaturally, extremely favourable (Fréville was soon to become a contributor himself). And not only did the reviewer make a point of praising the short stories, he used the platform this gave him to add to the burgeoning Resistance myth himself, albeit on a more general, apparently non-partisan level:

> Le livre de Jean Fréville, qui nous déprime bien souvent en soulignant le caractère odieux des collaborateurs, nous oblige, par un retour sur nous-mêmes, à nous souvenir de ceux qui ont sauvé l'honneur de notre pays humilié et qui ont compensé par leur sacrifice bien des crimes de la collaboration.[18]

With texts like these to sway national opinion, it is no great surprise that the passion for vengeance momentarily swept aside reason and legality. Law courts passed sentences with little respect for justice, personal vendettas were pursued, and summary executions followed outbursts of public indignation.[19] What is more, the Resistance began to be shamelessly exploited by numerous opportunists and outsiders. Thus, the *épuration*, which was intended to cure France of her ills, managed only to increase her divisions, and the consequences of this state of affairs were not long in coming: the general euphoria rapidly turned into disenchantment.

Nowhere is this upsurge in disillusionment better seen than in two pieces written by François Mauriac. In 1944, joy and expectation abounded:

> La Résistance doit devenir, nous sommes persuadés qu'elle est déjà devenue une pépinière d'hommes de gouvernement. La France [. . .] espère voir surgir de ses rangs une race, digne héritière de celle des grands commis dont on peut dire que la disparition a précipité la ruine de la Troisième République. [. . .]
>
> La Résistance n'exploite pas un passé glorieux, elle est une force de l'avenir: en elle repose le destin futur de la République.

A mere eighteen months later the tone had changed dramatically:

> A peine osons-nous aujourd'hui parler de Résistance, comme si entre ces héros et nous s'accumulaient trop de réputations menteuses, trop de fausses gloires, comme si nous n'arrivons plus à discerner ceux d'entre eux qui se démasquèrent, le moment venu, à l'heure du plus grand péril.
>
> Ils ont existé pourtant, et beaucoup parmi ceux qui ont survécu étaient dignes de parler en leur nom. Que s'est-il donc passé? Toutes les

impostures, tous les crimes, toutes les usurpations de certains ouvriers de la dernière heure ne suffiraient pas à expliquer ce discrédit. Sans chercher les responsables d'un côté plutôt que de l'autre, reconnaissons simplement que l'esprit de la Résistance a été contaminé sans remède par la politique.[20]

The spirit of the Resistance had indeed been contaminated in the way that Mauriac suggests. Unable to unite the country behind him, de Gaulle had resigned as Head of the Temporary Government in January 1946, and since his departure the political parties had once again been fighting amongst themselves. But if the general was down, he was certainly not out. Denouncing the divisive behaviour which was threatening to destroy France's resurgence, he continued to promote national reconciliation. He refused to form a party of his own, believing such a grouping to be too restrictive, and chose instead to endorse an all-embracing *rassemblement*, the Rassemblement du Peuple Français (RPF). In this fashion, he was able to safeguard his reputation and remain the 'chef dont toute la politique, depuis qu'il s'est éloigné du pouvoir, tient dans la conscience qu'il a d'incarner cet esprit auquel tant de Français sont devenus infidèles et que la surenchère des partis a disqualifié'.[21] And to consolidate this privileged position, he endeavoured to distance himself from the Communists, indicating that they alone were responsible for the predominant disillusionment. His allusiveness on 23 October 1949 was intended to puzzle nobody:

> Ainsi qu'il arrive toujours des grandes actions, de celles du moins qui ont réussi, la Résistance, une fois victorieuse, a donné lieu à des surenchères. Sans doute, parmi ceux et celles qui y prirent part effectivement, beaucoup – les meilleurs souvent – enferment-ils en eux-mêmes le trésor de leurs mérites et de leurs souvenirs comme s'ils voulaient le préserver des flots de boue qui déferlent. Mais certains – vous savez lesquels – cherchent à accaparer, pour soutenir leur mauvaise querelle d'à présent, le sens et la gloire du grand combat qu'ils contribuèrent à mener.[22]

By the end of the 1940s, then, if the overall image of the Resistance was tainted, de Gaulle's individual prestige had suffered less than might have been expected. He was still renowned as the Saviour of France, even though the element of hagiography had not gone unnoticed: 'Depuis la Libération, les livres sur les Français libres n'ont pas manqué. Mais se réclamant en général de l'orthodoxie gaulliste ces écrits taisent ou déforment ce qui ne cadre pas avec la légende.'[23] To illustrate just how widely expressed this 'orthodoxie gaulliste' seemed to be as the 1950s approached, one could do much worse than to quote Jean-Paul Sartre who, in an article first published in London in 1945 and reproduced in *Situations III* (1949), proved himself to be just as committed to the notion of national redemption by the few as the general himself was: 'Mais d'abord, il faut comprendre que la Résistance active devait, par nécessité, se limiter à une minorité. Et puis, il me semble que cette minorité qui s'est offerte au martyre, délibérément et sans espoir, suffit amplement à racheter nos faiblesses' (p.42). Given that Sartre was not naturally inclined towards de Gaulle, the above statement appears to show that the myth (or at least the laundering of consciences which it embodied!) could appeal to people from a whole variety of social and political backgrounds. This is, no doubt, why it was to enjoy such a long life.

The extensive promotion of an heroic *France résistante*, or, to employ the term used in the Introduction, the phenomenon of *résistancialisme*, did not go ahead unchallenged after the Liberation, however. Many of those who had compromised themselves during the Occupation had an entirely different story to tell, and tell it they most certainly did. In a collection of articles published *Au nom des silencieux* (1945), for example, Alfred Fabre-Luce single-mindedly set out to demythify de Gaulle and the Resistance, and did so, in part, by complaining that the law was being exploited to cover political crimes, and by bemoaning the lack of free opposition in the country:

> Il existe bien des journaux qui s'expriment en sens divers sur les nationalisations ou le Bloc Occidental. Il n'en a été autorisé aucun qui fût capable de mettre en question la sagesse de la politique de guerre du Général de Gaulle. En d'autres termes, le sujet essentiel est *tabou*. Une religion d'État, connue sous le nom de 'Résistance' donne pour critère au patriotisme la condamnation de l'armistice. (p.11)

Fabre-Luce refuses to accept that the armistice was shameful, and so abuses its critics with gay abandon: the Temporary Government is castigated as anarchic, 'un fascisme renversé, qui montre tous les vices du fascisme sans avoir la noblesse d'exprimer une croyance, l'excuse de répondre à une nécessité, l'avantage d'assurer l'ordre, et qui ne serait même pas capable de triompher d'une presse d'opposition, comme le fascisme hitlérien de 1933' (p.31). On a more positive, if no less provocative note, he then goes on to distinguish two types of Vichy follower – the hard-line collaborationist and the *maréchaliste*; only the former is deemed to be a traitor, the latter being categorised as a different kind of patriot.

Claude Jamet was another writer who had grounds for complaint when the *années noires* ended – he found himself in prison for condemning the Allied bombing raids on France. He was eventually acquitted, but out of his experience grew *Fifi Roi* (1948), a powerful work of demythification, the essence of which is captured in the publishers' preface:

> La Collection 'Témoignages Contemporains' a été créée par LES ÉDITIONS DE L'ÉLAN dans le dessein de contribuer à rétablir la vérité historique devant une opinion publique à qui elle échappe trop souvent, particulièrement en ce moment où des courants multiples et des propagandes abusives déforment, dans bien des cas, le jugement du citoyen.

The text is every bit as controversial as this foreword implies, bringing to light the infighting to which the Resistance was prone, and showing how the Liberation was used to launch people into careers in politics. It also exposes the lack of justice and the disrespect for legal procedure at trials (portrayed as glorified *règlements de compte*), and boldly states that not all members of the Milice and the Légion des Volontaires Français contre le Bolchevisme (LVF) deserve to be executed. In short, it pleads the case for national reconciliation. Obviously, such heresy was unlikely to be well received in the prevailing climate, but Jamet remained hopeful:

> Ce n'est pas ma faute si ce que j'ai vu ne s'accorde pas tout à fait avec les mythes somptueux et les belles légendes en images d'Épinal, sur lesquels le grand public a vécu depuis trois ans. Un seul témoignage vrai, je n'y peux rien, c'est peut-être assez pour que tout l'échafaudage du Mensonge officiel s'écroule; on verra bien. (p.13)

As it transpired, this one *document* had no effect at all on the 'Mensonge officiel'.

Nevertheless, a certain current of dissent was visibly establishing itself as the 1950s drew near. Books were appearing on the former head of the wartime régime at Vichy, Philippe Pétain, indicating that he had played the role of 'bouclier' in support of de Gaulle's more combative 'épée';[24] Maurice Bardèche was active and productive in defence of the Collaboration, as his *Lettre à François Mauriac* (1947) shows; and *Les Temps Modernes* was regularly publishing articles by unrepentant *réprouvés* like Yves Lebreton and Paul Delas.[25] In striking fashion, then, the fundamental quarrel of the past dragged on.[26] The *collabos* were plainly more numerous than the myth would allow, and as a group they seemed determined to speak out and justify themselves, for only by remaining true to their beliefs could they prove their sincerity and maintain the value of their initial *engagement*. Moreover, they knew that the 'wrong' side was often chosen with the best of intentions, so they saw it as vital to combat those who labelled them traitors and/or criminals. In the words of Paul Delas: 'Libérés, nous tenons à crier le message qui nous hantait captifs, le message de nos amis qui ne peuvent pas encore parler, et que nous avons à cœur de ne pas trahir.'[27]

Whilst it was only to be expected that the collaborators would react in this way, their retort is nonetheless significant, for it tends to consist of just two basic manoeuvres: either the Collaboration is rehabilitated, being presented in an excessively favourable light, or the Resistance is unduly blackened, because its crimes and misdemeanours are over-emphasised.[28] Bardèche's *Lettre à François Mauriac* provides a perfect illustration of both these procedures, and also demonstrates another significant point, namely that this two-pronged attack generally results in countermythification. As a contemporary reviewer recognises:

> Il serait, en effet, facile et inutile de dresser en regard de ce tableau idyllique de la collaboration un tableau non moins touchant de la résistance. Reconnaissons d'ailleurs que ce n'est pas Bardèche qui a commencé. Il démolit d'une manière très réjouissante une certaine mythologie de la résistance; mais s'il est bon de la dénoncer, il ne faut pas que ce soit au profit d'une autre. C'est pourtant ce qui se passe.[29]

It is well worth noting that the myth/countermyth cycle was in evidence soon after the Liberation, for this was to be a key feature of the heritage passed on to the young writers of the 1970s and 80s.

Yet it was not simply the *réprouvés* who went against the grain in the late 1940s. Many novelists too ignored the pressure to conform, as some of the best-known works of the period testify. Roger Vailland's *Drôle de jeu* (1945), for instance, depicts the Resistance not as a valiant enterprise, but rather as a game of chance. Incident upon incident attests to the power of Fate, and there is shown to be little to differentiate heroes from traitors (Annie observes that a Communist can have exactly the same background as a *milicien*). Fittingly, play draws to a close when Frédéric, by a strange series of coincidences, goes into a café and is arrested in Marat's place; not for the first time in the book is it evident that 'le destin n'a pas de morale' (p.257).

A similarly unorthodox stance was taken by Marcel Aymé who, true to his nature, held nothing sacred after 1945, being as ready as ever to expose hypocrisy and baseness. In *Le Chemin des écoliers* (1946), he offers an insight into the workings of the black market (which is shown to be fairly widespread and especially appealing to *écoliers*), and uses footnotes indirectly to admonish the institutions and attitudes of his day. More interestingly, perhaps, he openly links himself to Vailland, because Paul agrees that destinies are frequently sealed by accidents and not by ideological choices:

> On m'a parlé ces jours-ci d'un noyau de volontaires armés qui serait en voie de se constituer quelque part dans le centre de la France. Il s'agirait de former des hommes pour l'attaque des convois allemands et des postes isolés. C'est un genre de vie et de société qui me plairait beaucoup. Mais depuis tout à l'heure, je me sens tenté par la LVF. Faire la guerre en Russie avec des hommes dans le genre de Malinier, ça ne doit pas être mal non plus. L'ennui, c'est que pour s'engager dans ces formations-là, il faut probablement l'autorisation paternelle et je sais que mon père ne me la donnera pas, tandis que pour rejoindre les autres, je n'ai besoin de la permission de personne. (p.193)[30]

This heretical line is repeated in *Uranus* (1948), when Watrin reflects that Archambaud would do well to act like him:

> En regardant son propre fils, il penserait avec un sourire attendri: 'Dire qu'il a en lui de quoi faire un assassin, un voleur, un traître, un satyre, et qu'il sera très probablement un brave type comme tout le monde, et peut-être un héros ou un saint . . .'. Il se garderait d'éplucher sans fin les intentions et de dresser des bornes entre des nuances, voyant trop clairement que les bonnes actions sont aussi troubles que les mauvaises. (p.110)

But *Uranus* does not merely take up where *Le Chemin des écoliers* leaves off; it goes much further, being a far more virulent text than its predecessor. The Parti Communiste Français in particular comes under heavy attack: Aymé does not shirk from portraying a collaborator who compares sympathy with Germany to the Communists' leanings towards Russia, nor does he desist from showing how the Party has people arrested on spurious charges. In fact, the post-Liberation society he presents is one in which the PCF is dominant, and where manipulation, crime and insincerity are rife. It is a society which bears no resemblance at all to the reassuring *France résistante.*

Jean Genet is another writer who takes an unconventional approach to the Occupation, for in *Pompes funèbres* (1947) he both praises the grandeur of the doomed German and collaborationist cause, and implicitly suggests that there was little to choose between the Milice, the French Gestapo and the Resistance (Paulo tries to join all three). Coming from Genet, of course, such heresy is scarcely astounding, since perversity and scandal are essential to the universe he seeks to create. Yet in spite of this, his choice of subject is still significant – his very intention to shock says a great deal about the collaborators' standing in 1947.

The year of 1947 also saw the publication of Jean-Louis Curtis's *Les Forêts de la nuit* (1947), which can be likened to Jean-Louis Bory's *Mon village à l'heure allemande* (1945). Both novels use a small community to represent France as a whole, and every reaction to the Germans – collaborationist, resistant, *attentiste*, profiteering, *pétainiste*, egoistical, etc. – is given expression. Of the two books, it was *Les Forêts de la nuit* which was the more controversial, for Curtis, without ever entirely neglecting the positive side of the Resistance, openly put a spotlight on the bad side, revealing the movement to be split into two main ideological factions. Moreover, he acknowledged that the Liberation and the *épuration* were mere mockeries of what they should have been, since opportunism and injustice abounded:

> Après la contrainte monstrueuse des années d'occupation, après ce long bain de boue, de sang et de bêtise, on était en droit d'attendre un sursaut magnifique, des châtiments vraiment exemplaires, le meurtre rituel des vrais coupables, le ruissellement des eaux lustrales de la joie et de l'espérance. On avait eu un discours en bon vieux style électoral, le guignol de la tonte, une basse jubilation mêlée de hargne et d'inquiétude. (p.367)

As has already been seen, such disillusionment was quite typical of the late 1940s, but unfortunately for Curtis, it was not typical enough to unite all his readers behind him. Numerous literary critics did readily acclaim his novel, it is true.[31] But many others took a more negative view of the work. Louis Parrot, for example, felt obliged to complain in *Les Lettres Françaises*:

> De fait, si l'on va jusqu'au bout de la pensée de J-L Curtis, la résistance n'a été le fait que de pauvres bougres, que d'illuminés sans grand caractère, ou de politiciens sans scrupules, alors que les collaborateurs, ou, pour être plus mesuré, les vichyssois, ont toujours été des gens de bon sens, et, en fin de compte, les seuls vrais patriotes. Ce rajustement, très sensible vers la fin du livre, est assez déplaisant.[32]

In *Le Figaro Littéraire*, the reception was no less chilly: 'A la Résistance trahie, bafouée, il manquait encore de recevoir ce que le fabuliste représente par le coup de pied de l'âne. Maintenant c'est fait.'[33]

These two criticisms of *Les Forêts de la nuit* are extremely noteworthy, for they embody an evident *parti pris* which says much about the journalistic concerns of the day. But it was not simply by means of such 'patriotic' book reviews that the press fostered a spirit of *résistancialisme*; the serialisation of heroic tales of resistance played its part as well. This being the case, it may be helpful to recall what Archambaud thought of the situation in *Uranus*:

> Que la presse entière feignît d'ignorer qu'il existait des millions d'individus tenant pour telle opinion ou en réduisît le nombre à quelques dizaines de milliers d'imbéciles et de vendus, il y avait là, songeait-il, un mensonge colossal. Il en arriva ainsi à conclure qu'une partie de la France manœuvrait à donner le change sur ses convictions, l'autre partie affectant de croire que certaines façons de penser n'avaient d'existence ni dans le présent ni dans le passé. (p.28)

Reference could also be made here to Roger Nimier's *Les Épées* (1948). Although irony and cynicism make all Sanders's statements as suspect and as problematic as those of Genet's narrator, the following remark nevertheless seems to support Archambaud's observations: 'Pendant trois ans [les Français] avaient affiché une photo du Maréchal: geste grivois, mais qui n'était pas sale. Au lendemain de la libération, les journaux et le cinéma leur avait fabriqué une solide conscience de résistants' (p.156).

The comment on the cinema deserves to be taken up, because

after the Liberation it was indeed true that many films contrived to celebrate a *France résistante.* René Clément's *La Bataille du rail* (1946), for example, focused on the valiant combat and sacrifices of a group of railway workers, and was a great success on its release. But not all *cinéastes* dealt with the Resistance as skilfully or as artistically as Clément. More often than not, the Occupation was evoked in an excessively simplistic fashion, as Jacques Siclier indicates: 'La "France de Pétain" resta dans l'ombre. On ne vit plus sur les écrans que la lutte manichéenne de la majorité des Français contre les nazis et les collaborateurs (minorité honnie).'[34] There were, admittedly, some directors who tried to avoid this moral polarisation, but their deviation from the norm was usually condemned as scandalous. To quote Siclier once again: 'Il ne fallait pas, alors, poser des questions "dérangeantes". Il fallait entretenir le mythe d'une France presque unanimement résistante, gommer "l'État français" au profit d'une union nationale contre l'occupant.'[35] The French cinema of the late 1940s thus had little room for manoeuvre. Mythification was the order of the day, and those who refused to comply generally did so to their cost.

It may now be apparent that certain creative talents like Vailland, Aymé, Genet and Curtis successfully retained their independence when dealing with the *années noires* after 1944. However, this handful of dissidents was never likely to prevent the birth and growth of *le résistancialisme.* Films, magazines, newspapers, memoirs, *témoignages*, children's comics and countless novels provided so many orthodox interpretations of events that anything which went against the tide soon sank in the swell – France was only too willing to convince herself she had resisted all along.[36] At the end of 1949, then, the Resistance myth was in relatively good condition. Even if the *épuration* had caused cracks to develop in its superstructure, its foundations remained intact and perfectly solid. So solid that something of an earthquake would be needed to destroy them.

The 1950s arrived and the *résistancialistes* once again found that their self-proclaimed superiority was under threat, as illustrated by Jacques Perret's *Bande à part* (1951). Perret is not taken in by the *images d'Épinal* normally associated with the *maquis*, and in this humorous account of his own wartime experiences, he actively sets about deflating them. He boldly mentions the 'saloperies qui se perpétraient sous le couvert de la bonne cause' (p.225), and he has no hesitation at all in recalling how few of his fellow combatants could be said to be stereotypical:

> Il y avait de tout sur cette montagne, depuis le grognard à trois poils et le glorieux candide jusqu'au sordide salaud en passant par ces riches natures qui peuvent mener de front une double carrière de héros et de bandit. En face, bien entendu, c'était pareil. Quel que soit le drapeau, il y a toujours, dans la piétaille, la même proportion de bons zigues et de salopards. Si tous les salopards se trouvaient invariablement dans le même camp, il y aurait beau temps que nous saurions à quoi nous en tenir sur les fondements de la morale. (p.65)[37]

A few pages later, he adds: 'Je n'ai jamais eu la pénible occasion de me trouver sous le tir des miliciens. J'aurais sans doute répondu coup pour coup, mais avec l'idée que nous étions d'accord sur l'essentiel et que l'accident nous séparait' (p.67). The moral question which Perret is raising here, of course, is precisely the one which Vailland and Aymé had posed some years earlier – the one which the myth totally ignores. This point is worth stressing. One decade may have finished and another one started, but continuity in dissent had been maintained.

Such continuity is further evidenced by Jean Paulhan's *Lettre aux directeurs de la Résistance* (1952), a text which builds on the past in a number of ways: it takes up old complaints concerning the undemocratic nature of the law courts; it re-emphasises that many postwar trials were mere travesties of justice; and it continues the criticism of the PCF.[38] Yet interesting though the content of this letter is, it is arguably the reaction it provoked which better captures the mood of the moment. Elsa Triolet, replying for the Communists, overlooked much of Paulhan's argument (which was often hard to refute) and concentrated instead on an emotive, personal attack:

> Tout cela signifie: mettons-nous ensemble, collaborateurs et résistants, ce gouvernement ou un autre, cours de justice ou pas, au nom de la loi, au nom d'une politique ou d'une idéologie, n'importe qui au nom de n'importe quoi, mais embastillons les communistes, et plus vite que ça!
>
> Tortures ou trente deniers, qu'a-t-on fait à Paulhan pour qu'il devienne un nazi?[39]

De Gaulle, on the other hand, responded less overtly – he declined to publish the *Lettre* in his ironically-named review *Liberté de l'Esprit.*[40] These two defensive reflexes are revealing, since they too underline a sense of continuity: the main body of influential *résistants* was still unwilling to admit that it could be wrong. In such circumstances, national redemption remained impossible.[41]

Amongst the first to realise this were those writers who dared to give the Collaboration a fair hearing in their fiction. One such was Pierre de Boisdeffre, whose novel *Les Fins dernières* (1952) actually has a collaborator – Jean de Courty – as its narrator. Although de Courty is seen to be tried, sentenced to death and shot as orthodoxy demands, the comments he is allowed to make during this procedure are anything but conventional, as typified by his declaration that 'Le ministre de de Gaulle qui se trouvait par hasard à Londres le 18 juin 1940 aurait tout aussi bien fait un ministre de Pétain s'il avait pu regagner Vichy' (p.145). And this insistence on the role of chance by no means marks the end of his controversial utterances. Equally inflammatory are his assessment of the jury chosen to judge him – 'ces hommes étaient des combattants et se souciaient moins de servir une justice abstraite que d'abattre un adversaire' (pp.54–5) – and his reflections on the *épuration*:

> En province, on ne fait pas tant d'histoires pour fusiller les collabos: on les lynche en plein air ou dans la cour de leur prison. Mais depuis quelques temps, les exécutions sommaires ne soulèvent plus tant d'enthousiasme. Sans doute a-t-on besoin de ces morts pour avoir tout à fait bonne conscience: mais on aimerait les tuer avec un peu plus de formes, l'approbation du code pénal et des grands principes. Cela s'appelle: rentrer dans la légalité républicaine. Après la justice du peuple, on réclame la justice des juges: plus de discours et moins de sang. (p.4)

Boisdeffre knew that such demythification was unlikely to be acceptable in 1952, so in his *avertissement* he took great care to justify his work, pointing out that he was not trying to rehabilitate the collaborators, but simply using the *années noires* to highlight an eternal problem – the human condition. He might just as well have said nothing, for his reassurances could not alter the fact that a *collabo* had been given freedom of speech, and this was more than enough to prompt a retort from the *résistancialistes. Les Lettres Françaises* led the way: *Les Fins dernières* was a 'méchant roman', 'un livre détestable' and a 'plaidoyer pour les traîtres'; in short, 'un livre qui défend l'indéfendable'. Because of this, Boisdeffre was advised to think long and hard about certain axioms before he wrote anything else:

> N'est-il pas impossible, matériellement impossible, de rien édifier de valable avec des matériaux pourris? de jamais peser sagement sur une

balance dont il [. . .] faut truquer les poids? Et s'il est courageux d'aller, parfois, à contre-courant de la littérature à la mode, n'est-il pas vain d'écrire à contre-courant de la vérité, de l'histoire?[42]

This was clearly intended to be the last word on the subject, but things did not turn out as planned. Over the next few years, many more novelists were to centre their texts on so-called *réprouvés*.

Roger Peyrefitte, for instance, constructed *La Fin des ambassades* (1953) around the character of Georges de la Sarre, a civil servant who is eventually *épuré* for serving under Vichy. Not unnaturally, such a focus again produced a favourable portrayal of the Collaboration, as the following depiction of the Liberation indicates:

Le général de Gaulle fit son entrée le lendemain et descendit à pied l'avenue des Champs-Élysées dans les acclamations de tout un peuple. Acclamations les plus enivrantes qui aient jamais salué un Français, acclamations qu'avait bien le droit de recevoir celui qui, le premier, avait refusé d'admettre même la défaite momentanée du pays. Son triomphe eût été complet, s'il avait pu descendre les Champs-Élysées, la main dans la main, avec le vieux maréchal qui, lui aussi, d'une autre façon, avait sauvé la France. Les hommes de Londres et d'Alger la libéraient, mais les hommes de Vichy leur permettaient de la retrouver encore debout, riche encore, jeune encore: ses épreuves physiques, matérielles et morales avaient été grandes, mais infiniment moindres que si, avant d'être délivrée par le général de Gaulle, elle avait été piétinée par un gauleiter. (p.351)

Unfortunately for Peyrefitte, the myth-makers were no less vigilant than they had been when Boisdeffre's book came out, so *La Fin des ambassades* stood absolutely no chance of being widely acclaimed, whatever its merits. As one contemporary reviewer sadly opined: 'On se prend à regretter que les commentaires qui l'attendent n'aient rien à voir – Grands Dieux! – avec l'histoire des idées, ni – cela va sans dire – avec la littérature.'[43]

Jacques Laurent also fell victim to this climate when he published *Le Petit Canard* (1954), 'petit drame infini où la critique trouva de la politique parce que le jeune héros s'y engageait à la LVF'.[44] Yet it was not solely the *joining* of the LVF which gave cause for alarm; the very *nature* of the *engagement* was itself controversial. Laurent had created an ambiguous hero, and not only that, he had underlined his ambiguity in the interview which preceded the narrative:

> 'Votre héros alors aurait pu tout aussi bien combattre dans le maquis et être condamné par la milice?'
>
> 'Oui [. . .]. Pour moi, le romancier est celui qui trouve les circonstances atténuantes et qui reconnaît ce que l'homme de science ou le justicier peuvent ignorer: le rôle du hasard. Le hasard est le collaborateur de tout roman. Si Antoine entre à la LVF c'est parce qu'un officier polonais a embrassé celle qu'il aimait.' (pp. X–XI)

What is more, it just so happened that the LVF recruiting office was virtually on Antoine's doorstep; it would have been a great deal harder for him to join the Resistance.

If Laurent and his colleagues were severely censured for basing their works on *collabos*, the real-life collaborators fared even worse – they were roundly condemned whatever they wrote about. Rebatet was released from jail and Céline returned to France, and both soon found an outlet for their thoughts in the novel. But the journalistic watchdogs were as attentive as ever. Every *auteur maudit* had to be castigated on principle, as Laurent knew only too well:

> Même un journal voué constitutionnellement au libéralisme comme *Le Figaro* permettait à André Rousseaux, lorsque Montherlant publia *La Rose des sables* (en 1954), de soutenir comme une evidence que si l'œuvre de Montherlant avait été admirable avant la guerre, elle avait été souillée par l'attitude de son auteur pendant l'Occupation, que la damnation qui s'en était suivie excluait pour celui qui en était frappé le pouvoir d'écrire jamais un livre réussi, donc que *La Rose des sables* était forcément un roman raté, qu'il était superflu de l'entrouvrir pour s'en assurer.[45]

This peculiar logic encapsulates the dominant critical approach of the day – any text which could be construed as rehabilitating the Collaboration was, a priori, a bad text. Obviously, the myth of the Resistance had to be protected at all cost.

While journalists were thus suppressing heresy in the literature of the early 1950s, the cinema too was furthering the cause of mythification. 'Au début des années 50', Jacques Siclier notes, 'la France de Pétain était effacée derrière les images d'Épinal de la gloire militaire des "Français libres". [. . .] En somme le cinéma français réussit, par des fictions "rassurantes" inspirées d'une réalité mythifiée, à éviter la réalité prosaïque vécue dans la France de Pétain et de l'occupation allemande.'[46]

There were, understandably, exceptions to this general rule, and one of the most notable of them was Alain Resnais's *Nuit et brouillard* (1955), a harrowing documentary about deportation and the death camps. This painful re-enactment of the past was anything but *reassuring*, and it instantly reopened wounds that had barely healed – in a shot of the *camp de rassemblement* at Pithiviers, Vichy's contribution to the holocaust was displayed for all to see, because a *gendarme* in frame could plainly be identified as French from his *képi*. However, as in the novel, such unconventional treatment of the *années noires* could not be pursued with impunity. Resnais had to cover up the offending headwear with a dab of gouache.

Another exception to the rule, and another work which therefore had to be amended, was Claude Autant-Lara's *La Traversée de Paris* (1956). Based on Marcel Aymé's short story, this film bravely cast off the straitjacket of heroism and dealt instead with black marketeering, fear, baseness and cowardice. Rarely before had the realities of life in occupied France been so strikingly spotlighted, and rarely before had *le résistancialisme* been flouted with such aplomb. But Autant-Lara was not permitted to break the mould entirely. His producer insisted that there should be an optimistic ending, so an optimistic ending there eventually had to be. Once again, then, powerful defensive forces had come into play to limit the impact of demythification. In fact, it is perhaps these selfsame forces which explain why things rapidly returned to normal after 1956, as Jacques Siclier indicates: '*La Traversée de Paris* n'eut pas de suite immédiate. A la fin des années 50, on vit renaître les mythes romanesques de l'espionnage, de la Résistance, du sursaut français contre l'occupant.'[47] In other words, the mythifiers quickly won back the initiative they had momentarily surrendered. The challenge of Resnais and Autant-Lara was defeated.

As may now be clear, the 1950s saw little improvement on the late 1940s, since free discussion of the Occupation remained problematic, and the nation was still as polarised as ever. This being the case, Jean Dutourd's humorous novel *Au bon beurre* (1952) provides a fitting conclusion to the present section, because it highlights precisely these points, and consequently captures the essence of the decade.

The story this text recounts is that of a family of *crémiers* who use wartime rationing to make enormous profits out of the suffering of others. Adapting their stance as the political climate changes, they come through the Liberation with the reputation of being true patriots, and later rise to become the prosperous kings of postwar France. Dutourd does not spare satire and irony in his depiction of these despicable profiteers, but in his preface he is visibly bracing himself for trouble, not expecting his book to be palatable, despite its comic intent: 'Il n'aura aucun succès et me mettra tout le monde à dos: les Résistants et les Pétainistes, les Communistes et les Juifs, les germanophiles et les germanophobes, les crémiers et les professeurs de lettres' (p.11).

Dutourd's concern was well founded. A remark by Félicien Marceau shows just how sensitive an issue the *années noires* continued to be:

> Avons-nous déjà digéré la guerre? En est-elle déjà à son âge du roman? J'en doute. L'autre jour, à propos du roman *Au bon beurre* que vient de publier Jean Dutourd, j'entendais reprocher à son auteur d'avoir 'décrit si gaiement une époque si sinistre'. Or, qui songerait à reprocher à un romancier d'avoir décrit avec bonne humeur un enterrement ou avec amertume un mariage? Cela montre bien à quel point la guerre est encore en nous prisonnière de toute son *aura* patriotique, politique ou sentimentale.[48]

Yet not everybody was averse to Dutourd's enterprise, and there were many who had nothing but praise for his frankness. François Mauriac, for one, readily confessed his admiration:

> Certains critiques m'avaient détourné de lire *Le bon beurre* [*sic*], laissant entendre qu'il existait, entre Jean Dutourd et le couple immonde qu'il a peint, une obscure connivence. Or, à mesure que, ces jours-ci, j'avançais dans le livre, j'éprouvais un sentiment de délivrance: 'Enfin me disais-je, tout de même, cela aura été dit. Ce couple à qui, plus ou moins, nous aurons eu tous affaire, pendant quatre ans, le voilà dénoncé, exposé sur un pilori qui désormais dominera l'histoire de ces années noires. Que l'auteur de ce beau livre soit un homme courageux, il faudrait pour le nier ne rien connaître de la lâcheté qui, aujourd'hui, incite tant de paupières à se baisser opportunément, scelle tant de lèvres.'[49]

These contrasting responses to Dutourd's work are worthy of the utmost attention, for their embodiment of opposing attitudes to the Occupation makes them doubly significant: not only do they represent the divided France of the 1950s in a nutshell, they quite clearly confirm that nothing had changed since the end of the war. In brief, they demonstrate that the French were still unsure whether to bury the past or resurrect it.

The period 1950–9 was thus a time when, to the delight of some and to the consternation of others, the myth of *la France résistante* was subjected to a fierce, unremitting attack, an attack which closely resembled the one conducted in the late 1940s, both by the heresies it expressed, and by the form it assumed (a two-pronged, countermythificatory thrust combining a downgrading of the Resistance with a rehabilitation of the Collaboration). However, troublesome though this onslaught proved to be, it was more than matched by the *résistancialiste* forces which rallied to confront it. Indeed, the longer the decade went on, the more and more exalted the Resistance became within the nation, so the harder and harder dissidents found it to demythify at all. This development is not difficult to explain, for it coincides with the return to prominence of a man who, by his very status, could spark off an upsurge in *résistancialisme* single-handedly. The man in question is, of course, General Charles de Gaulle, 'le premier Résistant de France'.

Although a new-found fame would not be long in coming, the 1950s began badly for the general. Unavoidably caught up in the enduring polemical exchanges between former Resistants, and recognising that his personal prestige was consequently under grave threat, he continued to try and distance himself from the quarrels in order to preserve his purity. 'Vous avez une position très forte dans le pays', André Malraux reassured him, 'votre mythe y est puissant et vous ne pouvez le sauvegarder qu'en maintenant à tout prix la pureté, donc en refusant de vous compromettre.'[50] But such optimism was quite blatantly misplaced. Much of the mud thrown had inevitably stuck, and so adhesive was it that Claude Mauriac could come to an entirely different conclusion when assessing the situation: 'Le mythe de Gaulle est très atteint', he noted in his diary on 18 March 1952,[51] and if asked for their opinion at this time, many others would surely have agreed.[52]

De Gaulle had thus been unable to protect his image by remaining *au-dessus de la mêlée*, and further evidence of his declining popularity came in 1953 when the local elections ended in disappointment for the RPF, the political group with which he was associated. But if his *traversée du désert* had clearly begun, his support had not disappeared entirely, for a whole host of 'official' works came to his aid as he tried to limit the damage to his credibility.[53]

One such work was André Frossard's *Histoire paradoxale de la IVe République* (1954). At first glance, this *Histoire* is deceptive, because Frossard's prime objective seems to be to demythify. Using humour and irony, he manifests his sadness at the level to which the

Resistance has sunk, and directly subverts the myth-makers' view of a France liberated by the French:

> Le mythe fracassant de l'auto-libération n'était pas aussi inoffensif qu'il en avait l'air.
>
> Ce n'était pas une image d'Épinal, mais un excellent instrument de répression.
>
> Le crime de non-résistance devenait en effet sans excuse, dès lors qu'il avait suffi à quelques hommes résolus de se former en 'réseaux' pour chasser l'occupant, et de prendre un nom de guerre pour la gagner. (pp.81–2)

In addition to this perennial complaint, other well-worn criticisms are also repeated. For example, the Resistance is again shown to be a springboard launching people into high positions (pp.92–3), and the workings of the judicial system are once more presented as being anomalous, if not farcical: 'Au sommet de la hiérarchie judiciaire, les hauts magistrats se disculpaient en public de leur serment de fidélité à Pétain en expliquant qu'il s'agissait d'un faux serment, ce qui donnait d'ailleurs entière satisfaction aux faux-juges qui siégeaient à leurs côtés pour appliquer, à faux, l'article 75 du Code pénal à des accusés qui se déclaraient de faux collaborateurs' (p.95).[54]

Such statements would appear to establish Frossard's work as a standard heretical text, and this is why confusion is possible, for on the whole it is just one aspect of the Resistance which is being demythified – the involvement of the 'communistes abusifs' (p.75). The Communist Party is blamed for many things in the book, but a particular source of irritation for the author is its rapid about-turn during the war:

> On nous avait dit que le parti communiste, déchu en 1939, avait brillamment gagné son procès dans la clandestinité: russe et suspect de germanophilie jusqu'en mai 1941, il était français en juin de la même année, et français au point qu'il fût possible, par la suite, d'identifier l'anticommunisme et la trahison.
>
> Ce fut sans doute le mensonge le plus onéreux de la collection. (p.84)

Underlining the consequences of such behaviour, Frossard goes on to accuse the Communists of destroying his beloved notion of *la patrie*, and this allows him to emphasise the superiority of de

Gaulle, whose actions and conduct are deliberately shown to contrast with those of the PCF. Indeed, it is in its all-too-apparent 'Gaullism' that the book reveals itself to promote – and not to denounce – mythification, as can perhaps be judged from the dismissal of the collaborators as 'quelques douzaines de Français démunis de sens national, de fierté ou d'argent' (p.52). It is in the conclusion, though, that the myth-making is at its most flagrant:

> La France a besoin de vérité pour vivre, comme d'autres peuples ont besoin de musique.
>
> Avec son amour très humble et très fidèle de la patrie, de Gaulle est le dernier Français à nous faire entendre une note juste, en harmonie avec notre Histoire. Mais ce rassembleur paradoxal a la vocation de la solitude, il se fait de son pays une idée trop haute pour son temps, pour les siens, et pour un peuple qui a perdu trop de gloire, trop de sang, et trop d'espoirs. Ce n'est plus qu'un témoin désobligeant de nos médiocrités, le signet – géant – d'un Livre auquel, après lui, nous n'ajouterons peut-être plus une seule page. (p.147)

It is obvious from this that the myth of 'The Great Man' is not simply being accepted – it is being enthusiastically perpetuated as well.

While books like *Histoire paradoxale de la IVᵉ République* undoubtedly did much to further the Gaullist cause, the general was by no means reliant on the pens of others to record his achievements in print. During the mid- to late 1950s, he once again led from the front, and actively contributed to his own rehabilitation by publishing his *Mémoires de guerre* (3 vols, 1954–9), a work in which he reiterates the inspiring view of the Occupation he had first expressed a decade earlier. As in the past, France is portrayed as a nation of Resistants totally united behind his leadership, and typical of this continued mythification are his comments on 1942:

> La France avait choisi d'elle-même. Les renseignements qui en arrivaient chaque jour démontraient, en effet, que la résistance ne cessait pas d'y grandir, qu'autant vaut dire tous ceux qui y prenaient part avaient moralement rallié le général de Gaulle et que tout gouvernement bâti en dehors de lui serait rejeté par la masse dès l'instant de la libération. (II, p.36)

The basis of the myth has thus changed little. What is new, however, is the reference to the *épuration*, which is portrayed in such a way as to ease consciences and remove worries. In particular, the official purge is said to have been marked by restraint: 'L'épuration par la voie des tribunaux comporta autant d'indulgence que possible' (III, p.108). Even the unofficial action is deemed not to have tarnished the Resistance's purity: 'Peu à peu, cessent les représailles où la résistance *risquait* d'être déshonorée' (III, p.38 – my italics).[55] Such comforting observations perhaps illustrate that these memoirs should be approached with care, for they are not impartial. They do not give a series of memories of the Second World War, they comprise a personal *interpretation* of the period, as the famous first sentence suggests: 'Toute ma vie, je me suis fait une certaine idée de la France' (I, p.1).[56] This partial stance is also confirmed by the end to which the author puts his manifest stylistic skills. Deliberately portraying himself as a prophet, a chosen man of destiny, he plays on the patriotic emotions of his readers, and hence encourages them to rally behind him, albeit retroactively:

> Trêve de doutes! Penché sur le gouffre où la patrie a roulé, je suis son fils, qui l'appelle, lui tient la lumière, lui montre la voie du salut. Beaucoup, déjà, m'ont rejoint. D'autres viendront, j'en suis sûr! Maintenant, j'entends la France me répondre. Au fond de l'abîme, elle se relève, elle marche, elle gravit la pente. Ah! mère, tels que nous sommes, nous voici pour vous servir. (I, p.261)

On the basis of this survey of the *Mémoires de guerre*, one is inescapably driven to accept the conclusion reached by *Les Lettres Françaises*, namely that the work reads like the cult of de Gaulle's personality.[57] Nevertheless, when all three volumes were published in the 1950s, few unappreciative voices could be heard. Indeed, most reviewers seemed to seize on the opportunity to make their own contribution to the myth. André Rousseaux, for example, opined that

> le portrait le plus grandiose des *Mémoires*, nulle part dessiné mais partout visible, est celui de ce sauveur de la France qui s'est senti appelé et que le destin a élu. Des malveillants ne manqueront pas de dire que l'auteur de ce livre y sculpte sa propre statue. Et c'est vrai qu'il y a une statue. Mais un homme vivant s'en est senti devenir le glorieux captif.[58]

Marcel Arland agreed:

> De Gaulle a su faire d'un mythe une réalité, ou plutôt [. . .] il a su donner à la réalité le prestige et la puissance d'un mythe.
>
> Le mythe d'un homme, ce serait peu. De Gaulle s'est cru de Gaulle, et il l'est devenu. Mais il s'est cru la France, et, pour un temps, il est devenu la France.[59]

In this way, then, the *Mémoires de guerre* regalvanised the press. But they also did something else besides – they provided abundant information and documentation on which historians could draw.[60] Consequently, they quickly became recommended reading for anyone with an interest in the war years. Their influential status was assured.

More than in the literary sphere, however, it was on the political front that de Gaulle's popularity increased as the decade wound down, because by 1958 France was in dire straits. The situation in Algeria was alarming, government after government had collapsed, and many Frenchmen were openly comparing the crisis to that of 1940 – once again there was a desperate need for a saviour. Not surprisingly, perhaps, this saviour soon emerged. Ever ready to serve his country, and hailed as 'le plus illustre des Français' by none other than President Coty, General Charles de Gaulle willingly stepped forward to form a new, all-powerful government.[61] When he was elected to a reinvigorated presidency on 21 December 1958, and finally installed there in January 1959, his remarkable resurrection was complete.[62]

As the 1960s began, the 'premier Résistant de France' was thus back at the head of the nation, and his personal view of the *années noires* had accordingly been legitimised for a second time. This was important, for it meant that the myth of the Resistance was now harder to attack than it had been before. Yet despite this worsening of the intellectual climate, many writers still tried their best to row against the tide. Alfred Fabre-Luce, for instance, dusted off many of the remarks he had made in *Au nom des silencieux* and reiterated them in *Le plus illustre des Français* (1960). As its title suggests, this work deals primarily with de Gaulle, but no compliment should be read into the use of Coty's epithet here, because Fabre-Luce is employing the phrase ironically. His preface leaves no room for doubt in this respect:

> Dès le début de ma carrière d'écrivain, j'ai eu à contester des légendes officiellement répandues. Il s'agissait des origines de la première guerre

> mondiale. Les faits dont la révélation faisait alors scandale figurent aujourd'hui dans les manuels d'Histoire de mes enfants. Il en sera de même pour les tabous de la guerre II et le plus tôt sera le mieux. En travaillant à cette démystification, je pense faire œuvre, non seulement d'historien consciencieux, mais de bon Français. Les vertus du mensonge patriotique sont illusoires [. . .]. Celui qui confère un caractère criminel à l'armistice de 1940 a divisé, donc affaibli, la France. (pp. 8–9)

From this starting point, Fabre-Luce proceeds to destroy the Gaullist persona bit by bit. He instantly dismisses the general's self-styled gift for prophecy; he boldly proclaims that the wartime broadcasts from London were ineffective: 'Il semblera plus tard que les discours de Gaulle ont mis en mouvement la résistance. C'est une construction *a posteriori*' (p.74); he questions the motives which lay behind *la France libre*: 'De 1940 à 1944, l'action du général de Gaulle a été essentiellement une conquête du pouvoir' (p.152); and he re-emphasises the excesses of the *épuration*, alleging that the French have deliberately been misinformed on the matter. On top of all this, he has harsh words to say about the *Mémoires de guerre*, mainly because, for him, they reveal much about the concerns of their author: 'Sa principale occupation est de tisser lui-même le linceul de pourpre où, mort, il sera roulé par la patrie reconnaissante et l'Histoire déférente.[. . .] Il n'écrit d'ailleurs pas une Histoire, mais sa Légende. Il y a dans l'esprit de l'auteur une vérité idéale à laquelle les faits doivent se conformer' (p.170). And as if this demolition of de Gaulle were not heretical enough, Fabre-Luce laces it with a quiet rehabilitation of Pétain. All in all, then, *Le plus illustre des Français* is scarcely a book for those seeking orthodoxy.

Claude Jamet was another writer who returned to the fray in the 1960s, publishing *Le Rendez-vous manqué de 1944* (1964). Resolute in his belief that neither the Resistance nor the Collaboration could claim to have a morally superior position, patriotism and barbarity having coexisted in both camps, he had long dreamed of bringing authentic documents from both sides together in one work. He had even approached René Julliard with his plan shortly after the Liberation, only to be met with incredulity, as he now recalls:

> Mais en 1946! Tout de même! En France! Au lendemain de la Libération! Je n'ai pas le sens du sacré. Je ne me rendais pas compte, c'est vrai, du sacrilège que ç'aurait été de confondre ainsi dans le même volume, et sous les mêmes caractères (d'imprimerie), les bons et les méchants, amis et ennemis, les héros et les traîtres [. . .]. Et de rappeler ainsi que ces ennemis d'hier sont, en effet, des frères, qu'ils le veuillent ou non; qu'ils

se ressemblent; et de rendre évidente cette scandaleuse ressemblance, par le rapprochement même; qu'ils se ressemblent? Et donc qu'ils se valent peut-être. (pp.10–11)

Undeterred by this early setback, he thought that his countrymen might be prepared to sign a Franco-French peace treaty in the 1960s, and so finally went ahead with his project, inviting old campaigners of all political colours to participate in a round table. But although personalities as opposed as André Frossard and Maurice Bardèche did actually come together at the meeting, it was only in terms of their physical proximity to each other. Frossard quickly turned on the ex-collaborators who faced him, making no attempt to understand their motivations, and the famous Colonel Rémy went one better – he refused even to enter a forum which included his previous adversaries. *Le Rendez-vous manqué de 1944* thus did little to reconcile the various factions invited, and Jamet was left to salvage what he could from the wreckage by producing an accurate account of the proceedings. The book he eventually compiled shows that his idealism had emerged intact from the gathering: 'Ce livre, enfin, est pour qu'on cesse d'enseigner la haine à nos enfants. Qu'on désarme les manuels. Qu'on fasse taire les menteurs. Que l'on déchire enfin ces images d'Épinal, idiotes et féroces, sur lesquelles nous vivons – et dont beaucoup sont morts – depuis vingt ans' (p.28). In short, 'Bien que je n'aime guère ce mot, dont on abuse, il s'agit bel et bien d'une entreprise de *démystification*' (p.305).

Yet for all the tireless determination of Jamet and Fabre-Luce, *le résistancialisme* continued to flourish throughout the 1960s, and this is hardly astounding in retrospect, for the promoters of *la France résistante* had some extremely effective means of defending themselves. The lawsuit brought against Jacques Laurent is an obvious case in point. Laurent's troubles began when, unhappy with the hagiographical nature of François Mauriac's *De Gaulle* (1964), he felt obliged to riposte with *Mauriac sous de Gaulle* (1964), a controversial essay which earned him few friends and countless enemies. Indeed, so intense was the hostile feeling he aroused that a counter-reaction became inevitable, and it duly arrived in swift and decisive form: he was taken to court on twenty-four charges of *outrage au chef de l'État*, tried, found guilty, fined and informed that about twenty pages of his work would have to be cut.[63] What this signified, of course, was that as long as de Gaulle remained at the Élysée Palace, no serious demythification could take place, for it would represent an unpatriotic attack on the President of France and hence be liable to legal action. Put another way, the Gaullist myth had been raised to the level of a sacrosanct national institution, so respect for the Resistance was now almost compulsory.

Further evidence of this pressure to conform can be found in the French cinema of the period, because here too any attempt to stray from the recognised path invariably led to isolation. Jacques Laurent was again amongst the first to realise this when he and Jean Aurel made *La Bataille de France* (1964), a documentary which started with the Munich Agreement and ended with the débâcle of 1940. Although such a focus provided numerous opportunities for the revealing of unpleasant home truths, it was not so much what the work said that gave cause for concern as what it did *not* say. No mention at all was made of 18 June 1940, and François Mauriac in particular seized on this fact to accuse Laurent of neglect. The lesson was not lost on the writer-turned-*cinéaste*: years later he would still be aware that, in 1964, 'omettre de se référer à de Gaulle était coupable en soi'.[64]

But it was not just critics like Mauriac who had firm views about what should be shown on the silver screen. The general public also knew what it wanted from directors, as the experience of Alexandre Astruc illustrates. In the mid-1960s, Astruc made *La Longue Marche* (1966), a wartime drama in which he portrayed the Occupation in all its complexity, highlighting a cross-section of opinions and attitudes, very few of which could be called heroic. Unfortunately for him, however, his immense efforts were all in vain. The cinema-goers of the day would only pay to watch acts of bravery and derring-do, so he was condemned to suffer the most emphatic of rebuffs: his film was a resounding commercial failure.

Interestingly enough, a similar fate had already befallen another study in anti-heroism, Jean Dewever's *Les Honneurs de la guerre*, but in this case there was a more disturbing reason for the lack of success. Completed in 1960, the picture was not distributed until 1962, and when it finally did come out, it was released uniquely in Paris (briefly), and solely during the low-season month of July. Such deliberate sabotage speaks volumes about the spirit of the time, and when translated it can mean but one thing: demythification was in no way a saleable product, and so had to be stifled at all cost.

Yet important though the works of Laurent, Astruc and Dewever undoubtedly are, it would be wrong to imply that the French cinema of the 1960s was a hotbed of dissidence which needed to be damped down from the outside. This was most definitely not so. There was actually little support for rebellion within the industry from 1960 to 1969, and the vast majority of film-makers still tended to be strong proponents of *la France résistante*, as Jacques Siclier once again recognises. Throughout the decade, he asserts, 'Le cinéma français suivit cette mode des années 40, revues par un recul historique confortant, en fait, l'idée d'un élan national pendant la guerre et l'Occupation et la gloire de la France libre légitimée par le général de Gaulle.'[65] Not even Jean-Pierre Melville could distance himself entirely from this trend: although his impressive *L'Armée des ombres* (1969) sought, for the most part, to highlight the more mundane aspects of life in a *réseau* (admittedly a relatively rare event), so too did it emphasise the traditional heroic values of loyalty, comradeship and ultimate self-sacrifice. All things considered, then, the prevalent view of the *années noires* had scarcely changed since 1945. *Le résistancialisme* continued to thrive unabated.

The above analysis would now appear to have demonstrated that, in the twenty-five-year period from the Liberation to 1969, a collective myth of the Resistance came to dominate the French cultural and social scenes, largely because Gaullists from the general downwards consistently put forward partial accounts of the Occupation, accounts which relied heavily on four basic propositions: first, that the actual number of collaborators was minimal; second, that the vast majority of French people were patriotic at heart, no matter how confused or misled they might have been; third, that the real interests of France were actively pursued by an elite of heroic freedom fighters; and finally, that the Resistance was led and personified by Charles de Gaulle, 'le premier Résistant de France'. (The Communists, of course, whilst accepting and propagating points one and two, totally rejected points three and four; for them, the underground movement was a popular uprising which only the PCF could represent.)

What seems to have made this mythification so effective is undoubtedly the fact that, throughout the quarter-century in question, the gospel was spread not simply in one or two isolated media, but over much of the entire literary and artistic spectrum – in novels, memoirs, *témoignages*, newspaper articles, book reviews, political speeches, official biographies, historical studies, popular films, and the like.[66] Indeed, it is hard to imagine a genre which was not, at some stage or another, transformed into an eloquent vehicle for the cause.

This is not to say, though, that the mythifiers had a complete and unopposed stranglehold over the country. Far from it. As has also been seen, many writers and *cinéastes* maintained their independence when dealing with the *années noires*, and deliberately set out to contest the pervasive *images d'Épinal*. It is true that they did not, at the end of the day, manage to turn back, or even to stem the advancing tide, but in spite of this they still achieved a certain measure of success: on the one hand, they established a critical consensus (exactly the same criticisms were made in exactly the same way across three decades), and on the other hand, they instituted a two-pronged countermyth (rehabilitation of the *collabos*, downgrading of the Resistance) as the standard riposte to the double-edged thrust of mythification (ostracism of the *collabos*, promotion of the Resistance). In other words, they created a tried and tested set of tools which future dissidents could utilise.

This well-worn stock-in-trade was ready and waiting to be taken up at a moment's notice, but before it could be exploited to the full, weaknesses needed to emerge in the mythifiers' defences. By the late 1960s, precisely such weaknesses were starting to develop. The *mode rétro* was about to commence.

Notes

1. *La Collaboration, 1940–1944*, p.9.
2. Charles de Gaulle, *Discours et messages*, I, p.4 (19 June 1940).
3. Ibid., I, p.8 (24 June 1940).
4. Ibid., I, p.134. Cf. his speech of 4 May 1943: 'Il nous a toujours paru que, dans le drame d'aujourd'hui, les grandes actions ne peuvent aboutir qu'appuyées sur une grande mystique. Or, il n'y a actuellement que deux mystiques parmi les Français: La croix de Lorraine pour presque tous, le vieux Maréchal pour quelques-uns' (I, p.286). Other Resistants too fostered this notion of massive support for de Gaulle. See e.g. 'Lettre ouverte à Pierre Laval', *Libération*, 23 (1 February 1943), reproduced in Dominique Veillon, *La Collaboration: textes et débats*, pp.166–7.
5. See e.g. Robert Aron, *Histoire de l'épuration*, I, pp.281–2.
6. Jean-Pierre Rioux, *La France de la Quatrième République*, I, p.7.
7. *Discours et messages*, I, p.440.
8. Ibid., I, pp.493–4. Regarding the stated level of collaboration, cf. General Weygand: 'Permettez-moi de sourire quand on parle de quelques hommes qui ont fait de la résistance. Ce sont tous les Français qui ont fait de la résistance, sauf quelques traîtres, et les traîtres, les vrais collaborateurs, sont l'exception' (cit. in Henri Amouroux, *La Vie des Français sous l'Occupation*, p.548).

9. *Le Gaullisme, 1940–1969*, p.353.
10. Ibid., p.86. A striking feature of this Gaullist scenario is the fact that much of the vocabulary and many of the ideas on which it is based had already been popularised by Pétain, as Dominique Veillon's *La Collaboration: textes et débats* demonstrates. In 1941, the 'Victor of Verdun' was advising the nation: 'Gardez confiance en la France éternelle' (p.81); in 1944, with defeat looming, he re-emphasised his preoccupation with national honour, unity, *salut* and *grandeur* (p.112); and even in the High Court in 1945, he continued to maintain that he had enormous support: 'Des millions de Français pensent à moi, qui m'ont accordé leur confiance et me gardent leur fidélité' (p.402). For further insights into the Pétainists' and the Resistants' battle over words and concepts, see Ian Higgins, 'Tradition and Myth in French Resistance Poetry: Reaction or Subversion?' and H. R. Kedward, 'Patriots and Patriotism in Vichy France', pp.189–92. It should be noted, however, that in *Occupied France: Collaboration and Resistance, 1940–1944*, Kedward denies that there was a Gaullist myth of the Resistance (p.80), although he does accept that Pétain was a mythical figure. This only goes to show that myths are different things to different people, and a source of constant disagreement.
11. *Discours et messages*, II, p.6. By defining his elite of active *résistants* in these terms, de Gaulle is, of course, relegating the Communists to a minor role. This is hardly surprising, for anti-Communism was another characteristic of his postwar *prise de position*.
12. 'Les Désillusions de la liberté', p.77. Cf. Georges Bernanos, *Français si vous saviez, 1945–1948*. Here, in an article entitled 'Le Poids de l'exil' (first published in *Le Figaro* on 2 February 1946), Bernanos enshrines de Gaulle as 'le Libérateur de la Patrie' (p.131).
13. For the origins of the term 'le parti des fusillés' see Elsa Triolet, *Le Premier Accroc coûte deux cents francs*, pp.15–17. The Communists' redemption is illustrated by the words of Judge Didier at the trial of the *Je suis partout* team, quoted in Pierre-Marie Dioudonnat, *'Je suis partout', 1930–1944*: 'Si le parti communiste s'est trompé durant les premiers mois de l'occupation, il s'est racheté par le nombre de ses morts' (p.406).
14. 'Premier Maurrassien de France', p.2.
15. Many recent historical works have come to the same conclusion. See e.g. *De Munich à la Libération, 1938–1944*, in which Jean-Pierre Azéma examines the *années noires* and highlights 'l'image qu'ont donnée de ces années à la fois communistes et gaullistes, celle de Français remontant très vite leurs défaillances passagères et se rassemblant – à l'exception d'une poignée de "collabos" et d'une minorité de vichyssois abusés – pour la Libération, autour de la classe ouvrière et de son parti d'avant-garde, disent les premiers, autour de l'homme du 18 juin, rétorquent les seconds' (p.356). Cf. Rioux, *La France de la Quatrième République*, I,

p.79, and Rousso, *Le Syndrome de Vichy*, p.319.

16. See e.g. François Mauriac, 'Justice', p.1; François Mauriac, 'L'Année de la réconciliation', p.1; Maurice Garçon, 'La Juste Mesure', p.1.
17. Claude Morgan, 'L'Armée du crime', p.1. (Note how the collaborationist writers – typically – are reduced to a 'poignée de misérables' and distinguished from 'l'immense majorité des écrivains patriotes'.)
18. Louis Parrot, 'Les Livres et l'homme: documents', p.5.
19. For a detailed account of legal injustices, see Aron, *Histoire de l'épuration*, II, pp.98–116.
20. 'La Vocation de la Résistance', p.1; 'L'Esprit de la Résistance', p.1. Cf. Claude Mauriac who, in *Un autre de Gaulle: journal 1944–54*, is similarly afflicted by 'ce malaise qui, après avoir empoisonné lentement notre euphorie première, oblige les plus lucides d'entre nous à un redoutable débat intérieur' (p.94). Cf. also Frédérique Moret, *Journal d'une mauvaise Française*, p.244. (Although published in 1972, this diary was actually kept during the Occupation.) For poetic expressions of post-Liberation disenchantment, see Ian Higgins, *Anthology of Second World War French Poetry*.
21. François Mauriac, 'L'Esprit de la Résistance', p.1.
22. *Discours et messages*, II, pp.317–18.
23. Louis de Villefosse, 'Les Petites Iles de la liberté', p.869.
24. Pétain himself popularised these terms when defending his actions in a *proclamation* on 18 August 1944. For a transcription of this speech, see Veillon, *La Collaboration: textes et débats*, pp.111–12.
25. See Yves Lebreton, 'Les Silencieux parlent', Paul Delas, 'Fresnes 1948', and Paul Delas, 'A propos de "Fresnes 1948"'. The significance of this unorthodox trend did not go unnoticed at the time. See e.g. Claude Mauriac, 'Nous n'avons pas voulu cela': '*Les Temps Modernes* ont pu se permettre sans imprudence excessive de donner publiquement la parole à un hôte de Fresnes. [. . .] le fait qu'un tel témoignage puisse être sans danger imprimé au grand jour avec sa signature (Paul Delas) montre, une fois de plus, que notre société n'a pas bonne conscience quant à l'épuration' (p.1747). See also Jean Pouillon, 'Offres de collaboration'.
26. Cf. Paul Delas, 'Fresnes 1948': 'La plaie ouverte par l'occupation n'est pas près d'être refermée, [. . .] les Français n'ont pas la mémoire courte' (p.315).
27. 'A propos de "Fresnes 1948"', p.766.
28. Cf. Simone de Beauvoir's recollection of 1948 in *La Force des choses*: 'Une profusion de livres parurent alors, excusant ou justifiant la politique de Pétain, ce qui eût été inconcevable, deux ans plus tôt [. . .]. Dans certains milieux, on parlait avec ironie des 'résistantialistes', assimilant la Résistance à un calcul et à une mode. [. . .] Ce grand cadavre derrière nous, la guerre, achevait de se décomposer, l'air en était empuanti' (pp.168–9).

29. Jean Pouillon, 'Notes: *Lettre à François Mauriac*, par Maurice Bardèche', p.951. For another warning against anti-Resistance countermythification, see Jean-H. Roy, 'Les Deux Justices'.
30. For a real-life illustration of the power of destiny in side-taking, see 'Vie d'un légionnaire'.
31. See e.g. Jacques Tournier, 'Lectures: Jean-Louis Curtis: *Les Forêts de la nuit*'. The book also won the Prix Goncourt.
32. 'Prix littéraires', p.5. Simone de Beauvoir helps to place this review in its context. Speaking of the Communists' standpoint at roughly this time (1946–7), she comments: 'Ils avaient de la littérature une conception tranchée [. . .]. Ils réclamaient des œuvres exaltantes: de l'épopée, de l'optimisme' (*La Force des choses*, p.129).
33. André Rousseaux, '*Les Forêts de la nuit*', p.2.
34. *La France de Pétain et son cinéma*, p.242. For fuller details of the French cinema's treatment of the *années noires* after the Liberation, see pp.241–54 of this work (I draw on them myself extensively throughout the present study). See also Albert Zissler, '*Le Chagrin et la pitié*' and Jacques Siclier, 'Depuis trente-cinq ans le cinéma raconte le nazisme'.
35. *La France de Pétain et son cinéma*, p.243. According to Siclier, two films in particular were condemned for their unorthodox nature: Christian-Jaque's *Boule de suif* (1945) and Louis Daquin's *Patrie* (1946).
36. Cf. François Nourissier, 'Les Français étaient-ils des veaux en 40?': 'Les moyens d'expression, ces années-là [1945–55] furent mis au service d'une mythologie et d'une consolation. Quoi de plus explicable? Bien que la France n'ait jamais été experte à chanter ses grandes heures nationales, [. . .] tout se passa comme si la tentation nous était venue, insidieusement, de nous offrir alors une grande fable collective' (p.20). For the role of children's comics in mythification, see Cavanna, *Bête et méchant*, pp.33–4.
37. Cf. Raymond Aron, 'De la trahison': 'Les Résistants n'ont pas tous été vertueux, les collaborateurs n'étaient pas tous intéressés ou bas. Les verdicts de la justice politique ne révèlent pas les mérites ou les démérites des individus' (p.65).
38. In publishing this *Lettre*, Paulhan was, moreover, simply pursuing the unorthodox line he had taken ever since 1945. See e.g. his earlier *Lettre aux membres du CNE* (1947) and his 'Trois notes à propos de la patrie' (1948). Interestingly enough, Paulhan, like Perret, is an ex-Resistant.
39. 'Jean Paulhan successeur de Drieu la Rochelle', p.1.
40. See Claude Mauriac, *Un autre de Gaulle: journal 1944–54*, pp.348ff.
41. Paulhan agreed. In *Un autre de Gaulle*, Claude Mauriac quotes him as saying: 'Rien ne s'oppose plus fortement à la réconciliation des Français qu'une certaine satisfaction pharisienne des Résistants dont Vercors offre l'exemple le plus éclatant (celle que je tâche justement de dénoncer)' (p.350).

42. All these quotations are taken from André Wurmser, 'Hommage au déshonneur', p.3.
43. François Nourissier, 'Roger Peyrefitte: *La Fin des ambassades*', p.721.
44. Jacques Laurent, *Histoire égoïste*, p.285.
45. *Histoire égoïste*, p.271. For first-hand reactions to the literary collaborators, see 'Après Céline Rebatet!' or Jean Roire, 'Après la mise en liberté de Lucien Rebatet'. Political collaborators like Pétain and Laval fared much better than their literary counterparts in the 1950s, because serious attempts were made to rehabilitate them. See Azéma, *De Munich à la Libération*, p.356 and especially note 2.
46. *La France de Pétain et son cinéma*, pp.245–6. Pages 246–7 of this work are the source of the information given in the two paragraphs which follow.
47. Ibid., p.247.
48. 'Plaies et bosses', p.148.
49. *Bloc-Notes, 1952–57*, p.366 (27 September 1957).
50. Cit. in Claude Mauriac, *Un autre de Gaulle*, p.368.
51. Ibid., p.368.
52. Cf. Bernard Frank, interviewed by André Rollin in May 1985 for *Lire*: 'A cette époque, au tout début des années 50, le nom de De Gaulle n'était pas beaucoup cité! [. . .] de très nombreuses personnes pensaient, à ce moment-là – nous n'étions pas encore en 58! – que le Général était fini' (*Écrire, lire et en parler*, p.254).
53. His first move in this respect was to abandon the ailing RPF.
54. In *Histoire de l'épuration*, Robert Aron reveals that the Resistance encouraged magistrates to take the oath of fidelity to Pétain so that they would not be replaced by hard-line *vichyssois* judges (II, pp.48–9).
55. Figures are provided to support these assertions: 'Parmi les Français qui ont [. . .] causé la mort de combattants de la résistance, il en aura été tué, sans procès régulier, 10 842, dont 6 675 pendant les combats des maquis avant la libération, le reste après, au cours des représailles. D'autre part, 779 auront été exécutés en vertu de jugements normalement rendus par les cours de justice et les tribunaux militaires' (III, p.38). Jean-Pierre Rioux, with access to the latest research into the matter, plumps for a slightly lower estimate: 'A quelques unités près, 9 000 exécutions sommaires, auxquelles il conviendra d'ajouter les 767 exécutions après verdict des cours de justice' (*La France de la Quatrième République*, I, p.54). Earlier, in *Histoire de l'épuration*, Robert Aron had claimed there were roughly 40,000 deaths (I, p.433), a figure which was accepted by Jean Touchard (*Le Gaullisme*, p.76).
56. Cf. Jean Touchard: 'Les *Mémoires de guerre* [. . .] ont parfois le caractère d'une recomposition a posteriori' (*Le Gaullisme*, p.53).
57. See Pierre Daix, 'Du culte de la personnalité'. Cf. Pascal Ory's assessment: 'L'ouvrage est une poursuite de la politique par d'autres moyens, et va amplement contribuer à l'enrichissement de la mythologie gaullienne' (*De Gaulle*, p.95).

58. 'Les *Mémoires* du général de Gaulle', p.2.
59. 'Sur les *Mémoires* du général de Gaulle', p.1073.
60. Such use of the memoirs was often uncritical. See e.g. Félix Garas, *Charles de Gaulle: seul contre les pouvoirs.*
61. The question of the legitimacy of this promotion was resolved predictably. See Jean-Pierre Rioux: 'Oubliés le Gouvernement provisoire et le RPF! D'instinct de Gaulle fonde sa légitimité sur le 18 juin 1940' (*La France de la Quatrième République*, II, p.154).
62. For de Gaulle's own (mythifying) account of this return to power, see vol. I, chapter 1 of his unfinished *Mémoires d'espoir.*
63. For Laurent's view of the affair, on which these details are based, see *Histoire égoïste*, pp.300–11. Note also Pascal Ory's comments on de Gaulle's presidency: 'Alors qu'en soixante ans la IIIe République n'avait jugé que six cas d'"offense au Chef de l'Etat", plus de cent furent soumis aux tribunaux dans les seules cinq premières années du règne' (*De Gaulle*, p.128). This massive increase in the number of cases is clearly a symptom of something quite significant – the Gaullist myth's inherent fragility and questionability.
64. *Histoire égoïste*, p.300. It was after this initial skirmish that Laurent attacked Mauriac's *De Gaulle*, and subsequently found himself in court.
65. *La France de Pétain et son cinéma*, p.248.
66. Regarding the historians' contribution to the myth prior to the 1970s, see Pascal Ory's comment in *L'Entre-deux-mai*: 'Héroïsation officielle, damnation de la mémoire: tout allait pour le mieux dans la meilleure des historiographies possibles' (pp.119–20).

–2–

The Mechanisms of Demythification

> On ne vit pas l'Histoire; il s'agit de bien l'écrire. Le Français adore les légendes; et c'est même par là qu'il commence. Il se chargera lui-même de les détruire. Il aime la vérité autant que l'illusion.
>
> *Jacques Chardonne*

> Ce qui intéresse aujourd'hui, ce n'est pas l'exemplaire, mais l'authentique. Pas l'héroïque, mais l'ambigu. Pas l'historique, mais le quotidien. Bref, pas le mythe, mais la réalité.
>
> *Pierre Billard*

> Oui, la collaboration – pardon, le collaborationnisme – est en vogue. Les rats sortent des trous où ils étaient restés terrés si longtemps. Écrivent, parlent, paradent à la télé.
>
> *Evelyne Le Garrec*

In the twenty-five-year period from the Liberation to 1969, the myth of a *France résistante* had been developed, nationally propagated, and assiduously defended. But by the mid-1970s the tide had turned. Re-evaluation of the *années noires* was now the order of the day, and the war against orthodoxy was being waged, unflinchingly, on two separate, but related fronts: the Resistance was being hauled down from its pedestal and the Collaboration was being rehabilitated. The reasons for this sudden growth in demythification will be examined in chapter 3, where one of the key factors will be shown to have been the demise of de Gaulle. But before considering the whys and the wherefores, there are two other aspects of the *remise en cause* which need to be discussed: exactly what did the demythifiers' two-pronged attack aim at, and just how significant can its occurrence be said to be? It is the aim of the present chapter to provide answers to both of these questions.

For many observers and commentators, the widespread reinterpretation of the Occupation, commonly referred to as the *mode rétro*, was sparked off in 1969 by the making of Marcel Ophüls's film *Le Chagrin et la pitié*.[1] It would be fruitless here to try and describe this four-and-a-half-hour documentary in any great detail; suffice to say that it uses the recollections of the war generation to undermine *le résistancialisme*. The past is relived and re-created, and where memory is failing, newsreels from the 1940s are utilised to redress the balance. As Ophüls explains: 'Pour nous, en effet, l'intérêt était de confronter la réalité historique – et tout le flou qui s'y attache – avec les souvenirs des gens d'aujourd'hui.'[2] In this way, he can show that 'les résistants actifs, sous l'Occupation, constituaient une infime minorité des Français'.[3] Moreover, he can remind his audience that Resistants had a bad reputation at the time, perhaps because many of them were social failures.[4]

The heretical nature of such an approach is by no means unintentional, for the avowed objective of Ophüls and his two producers, André Harris and Alain de Sédouy (political left-wingers all), was to oppose the view of the Occupation portrayed by most previous cinema and television films. 'Quant aux films faits par d'autres et relatifs à cette époque', the director confides, 'je dois avouer que ceux que nous avons vus nous semblaient surtout participer – plus ou moins consciemment – de ce que nous cherchions à éliminer, c'est-à-dire la mythologie.'[5] The starting point of the venture was thus a deliberate attempt to demythify contemporary opinion, as André Harris confirms:

> Cette espèce de mythologie un peu tricolore, un peu paranoïaque sur l'occupation m'agaçait depuis très longtemps. Comprenez bien: je ne sais pas comment vous réagissez vis-à-vis de cette période, mais moi j'ai l'impression que si j'avais été adulte, j'aurais fait de la résistance. Ce qui m'agaçait ce n'était donc pas la Résistance mais le résistancialisme qui ne représentait pas la réalité de l'Histoire et dont on a encombré la littérature, le cinéma, les conversations de bistrot et les manuels d'histoire.
>
> On a toujours besoin, après une période historique qui a fortement bouleversé les fondements politiques d'une société, de croire à certains ancrages mythologiques. En fait, beaucoup de Français savent bien qu'ils n'ont peut-être pas été spécifiquement brillants pendant la guerre. Mais la vie quotidienne s'est chargée d'effacer des souvenirs trop précis. Le besoin de justification et la bonne conscience (qui est une des grandes 'vertus' nationales) ont fait le reste.[6]

Such a controversial standpoint was not widely appreciated. In fact it is quite significant that the film, originally made for television, was to all intents and purposes banned by the ORTF, Jean-Jacques de Bresson (the director-general) arguing that 'ce film détruit des mythes dont les Français ont encore besoin.'[7] Only when the Socialists came to office in 1981 (whereupon André Harris became *directeur de programmes* at TF1) was the documentary allowed to be broadcast, although Ophüls remained convinced that it would have been screened, sooner or later, whatever the government.

In spite of its lengthy television 'ban', however, *Le Chagrin et la pitié* had played to packed houses in the Latin Quarter during a limited cinema release in 1971, and this is why it created such a stir. In the past, as chapter 1 has indicated, films which went against the official version of events had generally been commercial failures, so the *résistancialistes* had not needed to lose too much sleep. But from the moment the first 'House Full' sign went up on the Left Bank things began to change, not least because the assault which Ophüls had launched in the cinema was rapidly taken over by a multitude of writers. Initially, it was authors of Ophüls's own generation who lent their weight to the attack, but once they had begun to gain ground they were massively reinforced by their elders, who had direct adult experience of the war to call upon. And the consequences of this for the myth were catastrophic, as Pierre Daninos's *La Composition d'histoire* (1979) illustrates.

In this work, Daninos uses all his experience and knowledge to reassess History in the comic vein he has made his own, his aim being to demonstrate 'comment on apprend l'Histoire, comment on ne l'apprend pas. [. . .] Comment on la trahit, comment on la truque, comment on l'invente' (p.9). He turns his gaze to the legends of Joan of Arc, Attila the Hun and many others, but of all the examples he chooses, one particular period stands out as having been excessively misrepresented by the historians:

> On peut le parier sans risque: quelle que soit la manière dont l'Histoire sera écrite, elle sera maquillée d'une façon ou d'une autre.
>
> Preuve irréfutable, preuve par neuf tant l'événement est récent: le rôle de la France et des Français pendant l'Occupation et la fin de la Seconde Guerre mondiale.
>
> Ce n'est plus de maquillage qu'il s'agit, mais d'un monumental *lifting*: l'Histoire, telle qu'elle nous est contée, relève de la chirurgie esthétique. (p.70)

Having looked at most of the history books in use in the schools, Daninos shows surprise at the way a certain picture of France is being imposed on the young generation:

> Voilà. Voilà la France héroïque de l'Occupation; la France tout entière dressée comme un seul homme (une seule femme) contre l'ennemi; la France passant par bateaux entiers en Angleterre tandis qu'une poignée de traîtres à la solde des nazis collabore avec le gouvernement de Vichy (on préfère dire 'Vichy' que 'Pétain': avec les familles, on ne sait jamais. . .).
>
> Voilà l'histoire de France telle qu'elle va s'inscrire dans la cire des mémoires vierges, et de toutes les mémoires. (p.73)[8]

To set the record straight, Daninos produces extracts from school text books and makes his own comments on them. The result is a witty, and therefore appealing, yet extremely powerful demythification:

> 1 – *La France est écrasée par une force blindée supérieure.* Pas question de rappeler le manque total de combativité de la plupart de nos unités, ni le moral de la majorité des mobilisés. Cet état moral dont le symptôme pourrait se résumer en cinq mots: envie de rentrer chez soi. On lui trouvera des origines plus raffinées lorsque les exégètes de Vichy se 'pencheront' sur les causes de la défaite: les raisons de la débandade sont à la fois mécaniques et 'intellectuelles': pour avoir écrit *L'Immoraliste* et *Corydon*, Gide est tenu pour responsable de l'effondrement de l'armée. Les 'intellectuels' ont bon dos, surtout quand on attache le leur au poteau d'exécution, à la place des bâtisseurs du Mur de l'Atlantique.
>
> 2 – '*Tandis que le maréchal Pétain signe l'armistice, le général de Gaulle lance son appel. La Résistance s'organise.*' Pas question, là encore, de dire que l'armistice a été accueilli avec soulagement par 85% des Français et que l'appel du général de Gaulle n'a guère été entendu. Le jour où il a été lancé, on était occupés, ou occupés à autre chose.
>
> 3 – '*La France subit les tortures de l'Occupation*': Pas question de parler de la proportion – infime par rapport à l'ensemble de la population – des héros de la Résistance (48 000 médaillés, soit 1 pour 1 000 habitants); ou du fait que la France est le seul pays occupé (avec le Danemark) à avoir conservé un gouvernement légal sur son territoire.
>
> 4 – '*Les Anglo-Américains débarquent en Normandie*': Pas question des Canadiens, Australiens ou Néo-Zélandais qui, sans doute parce qu'ils sont morts pour du beurre, sont enterrés en Normandie. Des photos de De Gaulle, de De Lattre, de Leclerc, de F.F.I., de résistants – pas d'Eisenhower. [. . .]

> 5 – '*C'est le signal de l'insurrection nationale. Paris se soulève*': C'est le bouquet, si l'on ose écrire. Que ceux qui ont été témoins d'un tel événement lèvent la main: on pourrait les compter, comme il est facile de compter les Français qui ont pris part à cette insurrection dite nationale. Sur 42 millions de citoyens 41 800 000 se sont terrés chez eux, ont vaqué à leurs occupations, ou courageusement craché à la figure de quelques soldats allemands faits prisonniers par les F.F.I. (pp.74–6)

Daninos is making two basic assertions here. First, like Ophüls before him, he is stressing that there were precious few active *résistants* during the war. Second, by highlighting the tremendous debt owed to the Allies, without whose aid nothing could have been achieved, he effectively denies that the French liberated themselves (a topic he does not hesitate to expand upon).

These two criticisms are important, and it is not by chance that they characterise much more of the demythifying literature of the 1970s. In *Comme un verger avant l'hiver* (1978), for example, ex-*résistante* Brigitte Friang also refers to 'les quelque 0,7% (aux hautes eaux du printemps 1944) des Français qui avaient refusé un armistice honteux, honoré les engagements de la France et poursuivi le combat' (p.140).[9] In *Mon ami le traître* (1977) on the other hand, José Giovanni favours the alternative line of attack: 'Dans les Ardennes, les Américains faisaient les frais du sursaut allemand. Ils tombaient par paquets de milliers, les Ricains, ils tombaient pour juguler le monstre. Plus tard on leur cracherait dans la gueule. Il resterait quand même leurs cimetières' (p.136).[10]

Yet however much these statements contribute to the *mode rétro* they cannot, in all honesty, be said to break new ground. Jean Guéhenno, for one, had evoked the true source of his country's salvation as early as 1944. Writing in his *Journal des années noires* (1947) as the Liberation was still taking place, he recorded: 'Tous ces combats dans Paris, pour se donner l'illusion qu'on ne doit qu'à soi-même sa liberté, quand il est si clair que c'est aux autres que nous la devons, aux armées qui arrivent' (p.343).[11] As regards the limited nature of French resistance to the occupant, the evidence of the preceding chapter tends to confirm what Ophüls said on the matter: 'Cela s'écrit depuis longtemps, cela se dit un peu partout.'[12] Daninos is therefore in good company when condemning the myth on two counts.

The onslaught against *le résistancialisme* is not simply twofold, though. It is a great deal more wide-ranging than that, as can be seen from the three autobiographical novels which Alphonse Boudard has written on the *années noires*: *Bleubite* (1975), *Les Combat-*

tants du petit bonheur (1977) and *Le Corbillard de Jules* (1979).[13] Like Daninos, Boudard is a prize-winning author whose sense of humour adds to the appeal of his work, and he too uses his memories and experience to correct and oppose organised collective memory, a goal implicit in his revelation that 'l'époque où je vous ramène est mal connue, mal reconnue de ceux qui nous fabriquent l'Histoire' (*CPB*, p.72). Using a Célinian *style parlé* which gives a cutting edge to his declarations, he deflates the heroic concept of a *France résistante* in six distinct, yet related ways, the most incisive of which is surely his focus on the crimes and misdemeanours of the *armée de l'ombre*.

In *Bleubite*, the narrator and his two FFI friends, Gaspard and Herlier, are not the virtuous freedom fighters depicted in many other novels, but quite the contrary: none of them has any qualms about stealing the gold of a Vichy sympathiser; Gaspard enjoys rape, and remorselessly machine-guns two French peasants in order to requisition their lorry for The Cause; Herlier, it is soon disclosed, is a former member of the French Gestapo who has joined up to protect himself;[14] and that is not all. The principle of honour among thieves is not adhered to either, for when Herlier discovers that his colleagues know of his dark secret, he shoots Gaspard in the back during an offensive, and it is only his own demise which prevents him from killing the narrator as well. Yet surprising as this may seem, such criminality is by no means out of place, for the mood of the moment is shown to be one of anarchy, and normal social and legal practices have been abandoned by everyone: 'Un peu partout ça flinguait sec. . . la procédure accélérée. Quelques commérages sur votre compte. . . il était bon! [. . .] C'est le défoulement universel. . . toutes les passions, les rancœurs, jalminceries de clocher. . . les ressentiments distingués. . . et veuillez agréer, cher ami, ce coup de poignard entre les omoplates!' (*B*, p.66).[15] It is this atmosphere which causes captured *miliciens* to be unceremoniously hanged, or sadistically thrown under the tracks of passing Sherman tanks. It is also this atmosphere which allows Herlier's atrocities to be overlooked, with the result that he attains greatness despite himself: 'Aujourd'hui avec Gaspard et bien d'autres, il a son blaze sur le monument aux morts. Le sort le plus beau. . . comme dit la chanson. . . le plus digne d'envie!' (*B*, p.184). The irony hammers home Boudard's point.

Les Combattants du petit bonheur deals with the liberation of Paris, and the picture painted is again one of excess and barbarity. Collaborators who have no money and no protectors are executed without trial, while those who are highly placed easily escape reprimand; FFI armbands are handed out to all who ask for them; women are often *tondues* only for refusing to sleep with a Resistant;[16] and the crowd is frequently so quick to act as judge and jury that innocent people are killed by mistake, for no one is brave enough to face the throng and defend the victims. In short, 'on allait, durant un mois ou deux, jouer les émules de la Gestapo' (*CPB*, p.313).

This identification of *résistants* with collaborationist torturers recurs time after time in the 1970s, and Jacques Laurent is just one of the many who mirror Boudard in this respect. Evoking liberated Paris in *Histoire égoïste* (1976), he recalls that 'les officines pullulaient encore où des gens, pour qui un brassard tenait lieu de mandat, séquestraient leur prochain, parfois au petit bonheur, et le traitant à l'occasion avec l'acharnement qui avait été mis à la mode dans les caves de la Résistance et dans celles de la milice' (p.242).[17] A few pages further on, it is the law courts which give rise to his sense of injustice and outrage:

> Tous les jours, on faisait juger des gens par des gens qui étaient leurs ennemis et non des juges. L'assimilation de traîtres éclatants, de criminels de droit commun et de criminels de cauchemar avec des hommes honnêtes, loyaux qui s'étaient dévoués à ce qu'ils croyaient être un bien au temps de la peur du pire, avait pris la vertu durable d'un absolu. (p.246)[18]

Thus, probably without realising it, Boudard and Laurent act on the recommendation which Jacques Peuchmaurd made in *La Nuit allemande* (1967): 'Il est temps de dire certaines choses. Simplement, ce qui fut. Et, par exemple, tout bêtement, que les petits saints n'étaient pas tous d'un côté et les salauds de l'autre' (p.23). But this is not to imply that such a view had to wait until 1967 for an airing. Far from it. As has been seen, Perret said much the same in *Bande à part*, as did Aymé in *Uranus*, so Peuchmaurd is scarcely an innovator here. He is simply following a well-established tradition – as indeed are his successors.

Boudard's second assault on *le résistancialisme* relates to the exploitation and fabrication of war records, his observations on the subject leaving little doubt as to his disgust:

> Nous sommes juste après l'août glorieux 44. Ça se grade, se décore à tout va. Ça pousse à pleines manches, épaulettes, plastrons, képis. . . lieutenants, capitaines, commandants. . . et les colonels encore plus

> nombreux. Plus les Fritz s'éloignent plus ça brille. Même les flics, les pourris, qui se pavanent en fourragère rouge. C'est la grande quinzaine du galon, la vraie foire à la médaille. (*B*, p.18)

Accordingly, he now regrets not jumping on the bandwagon and pursuing a career in politics or business himself:

> Ma belle connerie, mais je ne m'en rendrai compte que beaucoup trop tard, ne pas m'être bombardé tout seul sergent puis chef. . . pour aboutir lieutenant Attila. . . capitaine Ouragan! Je me serais ensuite cloqué quelque part. . . inauguré les monuments, commémoré, congratulé les veuves, mes pairs héros. Aujourd'hui, au lieu de transpirer sur ce papelard pour amuser les divines lectrices, séduire un peu le carnet de chèques des éditeurs, je serais quelqu'un. . . député, blablateur d'estrade. . . homme d'affaires. . . je passerais toucher mes jetons de présence. . . j'irais, moi aussi, laper les pots-de-vin sous la table! (*CPB*, pp.150–1)[19]

In waging this campaign against opportunism, Boudard finds an admirable ally in Brigitte Friang. Her novel, *Comme un verger avant l'hiver* recounts how a *salaud* who betrayed his network during the Occupation (Gérard Bonhomme) is nevertheless able to capitalise on his past commitment and work his way up the postwar hierarchy of the Resistance, thanks to his money, his contacts and his heartless manipulation of all about him. His ambition, like his malevolence, knows no bounds, and by the end of the book his success is complete. Not only has he finally become a *commandeur de la Légion d'Honneur*, but a gathering of influential VIPs has been made aware of 'la vie exemplaire de ce grand résistant' (p.344).[20] The bitter irony emphasises Friang's contempt of her character, and reinforces the parallel with Darricade's rise to fame in Curtis's *Les Forêts de la nuit*. Yet although Gérard Bonhomme dominates the work, he is not alone in using the Resistance for personal advancement. Others see it as a means of self-promotion as well: 'Chaque groupuscule de vagues copains qui avaient héroïquement écouté la BBC et pointé sur une carte l'avance des armées alliées s'intitulaient réseau. [. . .] Des réseaux entiers, surgis tout armés du cerveau de quelques petits malins, avaient émergé de l'ombre. La vraie. La totale' (p.196).

It is at this juncture the Jean Paulhan's outburst springs back to mind. Paulhan too, it may be recalled, was irrevocably sickened by the way things developed after the Liberation, so much so that he eventually felt obliged to speak out against – and then part company with – his former *résistant* comrades. 'Il s'est trouvé quelques sots pour me reprocher d'avoir nié la Résistance, de l'avoir abandonnée', he remarked of the dispute.

> En fait, c'est tout le contraire. Je me fais de la Résistance une idée assez haute pour m'indigner d'avoir vu les Résistants servir de caution, non toujours malgré eux, aux tricheries et aux injustices de l'épuration. Mais il existe trop de soi-disant Résistants pour qui la Résistance n'a été qu'un moyen de se pousser dans le monde, d'obtenir des places et de la gloire et de l'argent. Évidemment, ce sont là des gens que je gêne.[21]

Clearly, it is to this ancient crusade that many writers now rally.

Not content with exposing misdemeanour and exploitation, Boudard singles out idealism as his third target foı destruction. Stressing the role of chance, he demonstrates that not all *résistants* consciously pledged their allegiance to The Cause. He himself, for instance, could so easily have joined the Collaboration, had he followed the lead of some of his schoolfriends:

> Je me demande aujourd'hui, au fin fond, ce qui nous a retenus d'aller dans leur direction. A ce moment on n'avait pas grand-chose à perdre en s'embauchant chez eux. La France, on va me rétorquer. . . Pour beaucoup elle avait les couleurs du vieux à Vichy. Je peux difficilement dire que j'ai imaginé la suite des événements telle qu'elle s'est déroulée. Il aurait suffi de quoi pour se tromper, se retrouver à la Libération parmi les traîtres? Que Stéphane ait une meilleure gueule, qu'il ne m'ait pas fait des misères à l'école lorsqu'il était le plus fort. Je m'interroge. . . s'il avait été sympathique, franc comme l'or et tout, il nous embarquait dans sa galère maudite. (*CPB*, p.93)[22]

Support for this observation on Fate would no doubt be voiced by André Pierrard, for he had stolen much of Boudard's thunder in *On l'appelait Tamerlan* (1970):

> Mais il demeure que notre vie d'alors n'avait pas l'exemplarité, l'unicité, la continuité que l'on nous prête.
>
> Ce fut parfois une circonstance hasardeuse qui jeta dans la lutte tel qui vivotait sans perspective; les héros se recrutaient dans le commun. (p.69)

But Pierrard is himself pre-empted here because, as chapter 1 testifies, Roger Vailland had already shown the Resistance to be a game of chance way back in 1945, in his meaningfully-entitled novel *Drôle de jeu.*

Boudard delivers a fourth blow to *le résistancialisme* when he announces that 'Au sein de la Résistance, il y avait des conflits sournois, surtout entre les gaullistes et les communistes' (*CJ*, p.36). Furthermore, in so saying, he articulates another key theme of the *mode rétro*, for while books rarely concentrate totally on the internal squabbles of the freedom fighters, time and again allusions are made, often only in passing, to strife within the ranks. This is the case, for example, in Jacques Laurent's *Histoire égoïste*:

> La discorde qui régnait dans le maquis inspirait des crimes qui bien souvent avaient moins pour motif l'élimination d'un collaborateur des Allemands que la suppression d'un adversaire politique en puissance. La Résistance n'avait pas effacé, même si elle y parvint en des moments et des lieux privilégiés, les compartiments politiques de la France d'avant 40. (p.233)[23]

As with virtually all aspects of the post-1969 revisionism, however, the points raised here are not new, since Boudard and Laurent are merely restating the ideas of predecessors such as Vercors. Vercors was a great defender of the Resistance (having clashed fiercely with Paulhan in the 1950s), but even he had been forced to concede in *La Bataille du silence* (1967) that 'la Résistance, unie à grand-peine par Jean Moulin [. . .] se délite de nouveau en groupes politiques rivaux, qui préparent leur accession future aux leviers du pouvoir, parfois même font le coup de feu les uns contre les autres' (p.330).[24] The most serious works of history had regularly broached the topic as well – works like Henri Amouroux's *La Vie des Français sous l'occupation* (1961):

> Il y aura donc, presque dès le début de l'aventure, un 'bon' et un 'mauvais' maquis. Division arbitraire, injuste peut-être, division qu'enregistrera cependant l'histoire et qui n'a pas fini de troubler, encore aujourd'hui, certaines de nos provinces. On verra donc les deux maquis, provisoirement unis, fondamentalement divisés, se disputer les armes parachutées, l'argent, les hommes et, bientôt, les postes et le pouvoir. (p.320)

Thus, now as previously, portrayals of a divided Resistance discredit the concept of French unity during the war.[25]

Boudard does not limit his demythification to the role of the active *résistants*, though; he extends his gaze to those whose hearts were supposedly in the right place and who are deemed to have rebelled 'in private'. Typical of his treatment of these so-called passive Resistants is his recollection of Pétain's visit to Paris, made barely a month before the Normandy landings. If this event is anything to go by, the France of the day was still unquestionably *attentiste*, if not *pétainiste*: 'Le Maréchal est venu spécial place de l'Hôtel de Ville réconforter ses populations en deuil. On l'a accueilli plutôt chaleureux. . . ça paraissait pas déjà que les Français soient si gaullistes enthousiastes! Ils cachent encore leur jeu' (*CPB*, p.149).[26] Daninos also seizes on this memorable occasion in *La Composition d'histoire*, and brings out its significance in an equally explicit fashion. Referring to two photographs taken in Paris in 1944, one of Pétain's reception in May, the other of de Gaulle's arrival in August, he claims that, with enlargements, at least four different people can be seen to figure amongst the crowd in both pictures, and from this he deduces that the masses always bend with the wind as far as History is concerned, leaving their rulers to pay for any mistakes made. This line of reasoning instantly links him to numerous other writers of the 1970s, for he and Boudard are not alone in suggesting that the welcomes given to Pétain and de Gaulle are revealing.[27] Yet no matter how effective such a consensus proves to be, the fickleness of the populace is not a recent discovery. Jean-Louis Bory had already recognised, in *La Sourde Oreille* (1958), that 'La vérité est *des deux côtés*: à Londres comme à Vichy. Mais n'aura raison que la vérité du vainqueur. Elle sera la plus vraie des deux. Puis la seule vérité vraiment vraie. Il suffit d'attendre' (p.180). Indeed, Jamet's *Fifi Roi* had set the tone as early as 1948: 'Pouah! Je n'attends rien de l'Histoire. C'est une putain qui couche avec tous les vainqueurs' (p.229). Once again, then, in more than the axiomatic sense, the *mode rétro*'s debt to the past is transparent.

As may be evident by this stage, the Resistance depicted by Boudard is not the same as the one embodied by de Gaulle. Gone are the cohesion and the discipline of the groups allegedly organised from London: 'Ce qui me paraît maintenant. . . après des années et puis aussi moult lectures sur les événements de la dernière guerre, que la plupart de nos réseaux, nos organisations avaient un côté amateur, improvisé. . . boy-scout' (*CPB*, p.166). Gone is the *levée en masse*, passive or active, which is said to have derived from the general's *appel* of 18 June 1940: 'Il intéressait pas encore grand monde en dehors des journaux pro-allemands. . . Eux les premiers qui lui ont fait de la propagande. . . je fus témoin' (*CPB*, pp.69–70).[28] Gone too are the idealism, the altruism and the respect which normally bind the *résistants* to their 'natural' leader: 'On a l'autre pour sauver la face, notre Charles qui plastronne en V, qui bouffe du micro, qui se sent la France à lui tout seul. Très chétive revanche. . . piètre cinoche! Autant tout de même en profiter!' (*B*, p.20). The discrepancy between the two standpoints is flagrant, and Boudard leaves his reader in no doubt that deliberate mythification is the cause. But more than this, he ensures that everyone knows exactly who the myth-maker is: 'Tout l'art du général de Gaulle fut de monter le blanc en neige, de nous faire croire qu'on était des lions alors que nous étions de pauvres clebs calamiteux' (*CPB*, p.257). Two years later, Daninos was to reiterate this remark in *La Composition d'histoire*, attributing the postwar orthodoxy to the 'grand maître du lifting, esthéticien hors classe, habile comme pas un à raffermir les chairs meurtries de Marianne et à remodeler son visage selon "certaine image" qu'il s'est toujours faite d'elle, incomparable magicien parvenant à faire admettre de nouveau la nation vaincue dans le Jockey Club des grands: Charles de Gaulle' (p.77).[29] Such a marvellous turn of phrase is extremely hard to follow, and it would be anticlimactic even to try. Suffice to say that the spirit of Fabre-Luce lives on.

Analysis of the representative works of Ophüls, Daninos and Boudard has now shown that, from 1969 onwards, the myth of a *France résistante* was subverted in a whole host of interconnected ways. Conveniently at this stage, many of these various lines of attack are summarised in *La Composition d'histoire*:

> Est-ce un péché mortel de rappeler que, sans l'avalanche des hommes et du matériel américains, anglais, canadiens, soviétiques, Paris croupirait peut-être encore sous la botte nazie? Et que la majorité de la population parisienne ne descendit dans la rue qu'au moment où l'ennemi était déjà parti? Est-ce un crime de dire que, s'il y eut une résistance héroïque, ses héros œuvrèrent non seulement dans l'ombre de l'occupant mais de tout un peuple passif, souvent courageux, quelquefois délateur, beaucoup plus préoccupé de chasser le bifteck que l'Allemand? Et que ces soldats des ténèbres enragent d'avoir vu leurs rangs grossir de tant de francs-tireurs entrés clandestinement dans la Résistance depuis 1945? [. . .]
>
> Pétainistes d'occasion, gaullistes de circonstance – parfois les deux dans le même mois – tels nous fûmes dans notre majorité, même si nous supportons mal cette image dans le rétroviseur de l'Histoire. (pp.79–80)

Four typically unconventional practices are in evidence here: the recognition of the Allies' efforts; the insistence that there were few active *résistants*; the revelation that most French people did not subscribe to any cause but naturally sided with the winners; and the assertion that involvement with the Resistance was often invented (if not exploited). When these heresies are added to Boudard's spotlighting of disunity, criminality and fortuitous commitment, the *mode rétro* can be seen to make seven different, but related assaults on *le résistancialisme*. In fact, perhaps an eighth can be appended, because de Gaulle is regularly exposed as the source of the threatened myth.[30] Yet none of these eight criticisms is actually new, for as has been demonstrated, all of them were originally made between 1944 and 1969. Be that as it may, it was not until a good twenty-five years after the Liberation that they began to be tolerated. This, then, was the novelty. If the nature of the contestation itself marked no departure from the past, the winning over of the French public most definitely did.[31]

Depreciation of *la France résistante* is only one aspect of the post-1969 offensive, however, for a second form of demythification was also utilised in the 1970s. This alternative manoeuvre aimed, primarily, to rehabilitate the Collaboration, and although it did so in part by redirecting many of the devices outlined above, overall it secured its objective by using three strategies in particular. Not least of these was the ploy adopted by grown-up children of real-life collaborators, a ploy which is consequently unique to more recent times: the restoration of a compromised father's battered reputation. The best-known exponents of such a venture are Pascal Jardin and Marie Chaix, two young writers whose work is discussed in chapter 4. Nevertheless, the general procedure is equally well illustrated by Jacques Bonny, son of the infamous Pierre and author of *Mon père, l'inspecteur Bonny* (1975).[32]

During the Occupation, Pierre Bonny headed a group of French *gestapistes* with Henri Laffont – the notorious *bande de la rue Lauriston* – and for this he was tried and eventually executed. Yet according to Jacques's book, he was nothing like the arch-villain he is widely believed to be: he was not a torturer; he did not know that people were tortured by his colleagues; and, unlike Laffont, he never wore the German uniform, because he loathed it. In short, he was only the administrative half of the partnership, a penpusher who was as shocked as everyone else by the gruesome stories told at his trial. And that is not all. The Americans had actually wanted to absolve him, we are informed, since he had used his position to save many allied parachutists, but de Gaulle, fearing a Communist backlash, had obstinately ignored their entreaties, leaving the orphan son to lament: 'La colonne "crédit" de mon père fut oubliée. On ne retint que la colonne "débit"' (p.261).[33]

If these disclosures already contrast radically with the prevailing assumptions of the day, then the anti-traditional stance is intensified when Jacques describes his own visits to the rue Lauriston. 'Les têtes que j'ai eu moi-même l'occasion de croiser là-bas, les rares fois où j'y suis allé voir mon père', he recalls, 'ne me parurent pas, je l'avoue, spécialement patibulaires. Et il serait trop facile, pour moi, de me dérober derrière ma jeunesse pour ne pas prendre la responsabilité – si c'en est une – de dire cela' (p.222). The implication here is that popular mythology has distorted the facts, transforming the visually unexceptional gang members into terrifying ogres and monsters. Indeed, Bonny considers the mythical view to be so well implanted that he deliberately targets his work at the virgin minds of the young generation, despairing of ever converting his older readers: 'Ce livre est moins écrit pour ceux qui vécurent cette période noire – dans l'un ou l'autre camp, aux extrêmes, leur siège est fait – que pour ceux qui sont nés depuis et qui diront d'abord devant ce titre: "Bonny? connais pas"' (p.263).[34] The uninitiated, of course, are less likely to react badly to what he says, and so will be more inclined to accept his flattering portrait of his father.

It is surely to foster this sympathetic response that the author resorts to a kind of fatalism. Pierre Bonny is presented as a luckless individual who, throughout his whole existence, has little control over what he does, being permanently in the grip of events which overwhelm him. Emerging from the First World War as a hero and a left-winger, he joins the police force and soars to fame during the Stavisky affair, when he recovers the missing cheque stubs. But although he is acclaimed as the 'premier flic de France' for locating the vital evidence, his career prospects do not improve. Quite the opposite. Many influential people are implicated in the scandal, and they unscrupulously strive to destroy him. He is hounded out of his job, his credibility in tatters, and is still unemployed when the Second World War starts.

It is at this stage that his ill-fortune is really underlined. In a chapter meaningfully entitled 'Ce qu'il peut résulter d'une vis platinée', the suggestion is made that he became a traitor simply because the family car broke down. Had mechanical failure not intervened, he would have caught the last boat to England; instead, being forced to remain in France, yet having no regular income, he felt obliged to take up Laffont's offer of a post at 93, rue Lauriston.[35] At the time, apparently, he did not realise what he was letting himself in for, and when the truth subsequently dawned on him, it was too late for him to leave: 'Il se rendit compte qu'il s'était laissé prendre à tel point dans l'engrenage qu'il n'était plus question pour lui d'y échapper: je crois qu'il y songea, mais on le "tenait" pieds et poings liés maintenant' (p.224). With the coming of the Liberation he paid a heavy price for this unwitting *engagement*, and it is quite fitting that his life should be seen to end as it was lived – according to the dictates of Fate.

In order to make this point more directly, Jacques faithfully reproduces extracts from his father's *carnets*, allowing the ex-inspector, at long last, to defend himself in public:

> L'occupation m'a trouvé à la recherche de moyens pour vivre et m'occuper.
>
> La destinée m'a conduit rue Lauriston.
>
> Les hommes érigés en juges n'ont pas cherché à comprendre. Ils m'ont frappé aveuglément comme tous les autres. Ils n'ont pas jugé des cas séparés. Ils ont jugé un ensemble. Je devais fatalement sombrer. (p.276)[36]

By emphasising the importance of chance in this manner, Jacques can convincingly plead that Pierre's story is hardly remarkable: 'Ce qui est arrivé à celui-ci aurait bien pu arriver à l'un ou l'autre d'entre nous' (pp.263–4). This being the case, the reader's sympathy is assured, and Bonny senior becomes less of a social outcast than before. The rehabilitation process is complete.

Jacques Bonny is by no means alone in homing in on the decisiveness of Fate, though. Acknowledgement of the power of destiny was tremendously popular in the 1970s, so popular in fact that it can be said to be the second major ploy used to raise the collaborators' standing. Denis Lalanne's humorous novel, *Le Devoir de Français* (1974), gives a perfect illustration of this widespread procedure:

> Mais je savais aussi de quoi il tenait souvent d'appartenir à un camp ou à l'autre: tout juste cette épaisseur d'orteil qui dépasse sur le soulier de l'autre lorsque les deux caïds du préau se partagent l'effectif de la classe, et dont il dépend que l'on soit gendarme ou voleur le temps d'une récréation. En août 1943, cependant que nous faisions les Zouaves à la ferme et à la plage, deux copains du lycée, peut-être parce qu'ils avaient

> échoué à l'examen, peut-être par répugnance pour les travaux des champs, avaient senti monter en eux une sève d'aventuriers. Ils avaient pris la direction de la montagne dans le projet de rejoindre Londres. Puis, n'ayant pu contacter à Barèges le fameux François Vignolle, champion de ski et des passages en Espagne, ils avaient rebroussé chemin, juste à temps pour tomber sur un troisième qui, celui-là, non moins résolument, courait s'engager à l'unité française de la Waffen SS, créée le mois précédent par un décret de Pierre Laval. L'affaire souffrant moins de complications, ils lui avaient vivement emboîté le pas. (pp.128–9)[37]

Further to highlight the arbitrariness of side-taking, perhaps, Lalanne breaks down the traditionally cohesive family unit, providing his narrator with two uncles, one a fervent Gaullist, the other an avowed Pétainist. The same technique is repeated and pushed to its logical conclusion in Michel Robida's *Le Déjeuner de Trieste* (1974), where it is twin brothers who go their separate ways, Sébastien into the Resistance, and Hugues into the Waffen SS, such an apparent anomaly forcing Edgar to observe:

> Les deux jumeaux inséparables revêtent des uniformes étrangers mais ennemis. [. . .] Voilà deux garçons qui ont joué aux mêmes jeux, épousé les mêmes causes et qui, soudain, se trouvent à l'opposé l'un de l'autre. Ce n'est même pas une situation tragique. C'est tout au plus une puérile affaire de collège. Les bleus ou les verts, comme à Byzance. Et on se tue pour cela! (p.204)[38]

All this serves to corroborate the sentiments of Roger Rabiniaux, who had succinctly summarised his colleagues' views in *Les Bonheurs de la guerre* (1973): 'En ces temps difficiles une même conception de la patrie pouvait conduire le même homme à des options bien différentes et mêmes contraires selon les climats et les hasards. Ce sont bien rarement *les idées* qui décident de nos choix essentiels' (p.216). This belief is one of the most fundamental tenets of the *mode rétro*.

Although the literature of the *remise en cause* strives hard to promote the omnipotence of chance, the most influential contribution to the trend here is arguably made by a film: Louis Malle's *Lacombe Lucien* (1974).[39] Lucien, the eponymous (anti-)hero of the work, is an uneducated country boy who is at his happiest when hunting wild animals, and it is possibly to be able to hunt bigger game that he tries to become a *résistant*. Sadly for him, he is turned down in no uncertain terms, but he does not have long to wait until adventure finally comes his way. A freak puncture leads him to be caught out after the blackout, so he soon finds himself in the nearby Gestapo building, where he is plied with drink and unsuspectingly encouraged to betray the local Resistance leader, which he does. In this unfortunate fashion, he joins the *gestapistes* without ever having consciously chosen to do so, and his moral ambiguity is established. As Malle himself says: 'Il n'y a pas de noir et de blanc. Nous sommes en demi-teinte. D'ailleurs, qu'il ait été dans la Résistance plutôt que dans la Gestapo n'aurait changé en rien le comportement fondamental de Lucien, cet enfant dont on ne sait s'il va ou non tuer un homme comme il traque poules et lapins.'[40] Because of this, Lacombe is extremely difficult to judge. Admittedly, the closing sequence of the film reveals that he was executed, but this does not necessarily imply that he ought to be condemned, for the death sentence raises more questions than it answers, not least because it is brought to the screen quite randomly, just as randomly as the original betrayal takes place. The orthodox verdict on the Occupation cannot accommodate such even-handedness, and Malle knows this only too well: 'Pour beaucoup, un garçon qui rentre dans la Gestapo en 1944 est un salaud. Il faudrait même, pour la mythologie, qu'il ait un pied bot, qu'il louche, que ce soit, en fait, un monstre que l'on extermine sans avoir à essayer de comprendre pourquoi de telles choses ont pu se produire.'[41] This explains why the myth is challenged: Lacombe Lucien and his novelistic counterparts demonstrate, as did Jacques Bonny's portrait of Pierre, that not all collaborators were the exceptional villains they are made out to be. They were often just *résistants manqués*.

Chance is thus a major characteristic of the *mode rétro*, invoked not merely to demythify the Resistance, but also to re-establish the credibility of the Collaboration. As was noted earlier, though, this theme is hardly a *trouvaille* of the 1970s. Ever since the Occupation ended, destiny has been exploited to help 'humanise' certain *collabos.*[42] In Georges Simenon's *La Neige était sale* (1948), for instance, Franck eventually compromises himself, but his life could so easily have turned out differently:

> Il aurait pu être chef de réseau.
>
> Il a tenté de s'engager, au début, quand on se battait encore avec des tanks et des canons, et on l'a renvoyé à l'école. (p.79)

Jacques Laurent, it may be recalled, paints a basically similar picture in *Le Petit Canard.* Yet it would be wrong to suggest that nothing has changed since 1969, for this is most patently untrue: the demythifiers' fatalism has at last been communicated to the country as a whole (as *Lacombe Lucien*'s programming in cinemas and, more recently, on television illustrates), so the French are now far more aware that collaborators can be ethically equivocal.

But not all the so-called *réprouvés* were seen in ambivalent terms after 1970. The longer the re-evaluation of France's wartime activities went on, the more noticeably thoroughly committed collaborationists – both real and fictional – began to come back into the spotlight, and this re-emergence of the once reviled figures was a third form of rehabilitation for them.

A good example of a fictional apologist for the Collaboration can be found in Pierre Serval's *Une boule de neige en enfer* (1980), which starts when Jean Duluc returns to Paris after twenty-five years' absence. Duluc was one of those *collabos* whose commitment to his cause actually increased as the Germans' victories diminished, so he has no qualms at all about reliving the past when interviewed by François Boulanger, the ostensible narrator of the work. Yet rather surprisingly, given his background, he shows himself to be all too eager to attack Pétain:

> Sans lui, la collaboration n'eût été l'affaire que d'une poignée d'idéologues ralliés au nazisme et de quelques centaines de vendus prêts à toutes les besognes. Grâce à ses encouragements, d'honnêtes gens, dont beaucoup se résignaient mal à cette solution, se sont laissé entraîner. Je ne suis même pas sûr qu'il ait eu raison de demander l'armistice. Mais je suis convaincu qu'il eut tort de rester à la tête de l'État. Ce n'était pas sauver ce qui pouvait l'être; c'était offrir une caution française aux exigences allemandes. (p.93)

It is soon evident, though, that Jean criticises the Maréchal principally in order to rehabilitate certain members of the Milice, and especially its leader Joseph Darnand, whom he considers to be an almost innocent victim of the repressive system instituted by Vichy. To emphasise this point, he tells of a *milicien* he met in 1944; the man summarised Darnand's position as follows: 'Sans le Maréchal, il y a longtemps qu'il serait au maquis, et moi avec lui. Seulement, il y a le Maréchal, à qui nous faisons confiance et qui sait mieux que nous ce qu'il faut faire pour sauver la France' (p.85).[43] A few pages later, the same acquaintance is allowed to restore the reputations of even more of his erstwhile colleagues:

> Je suis un militaire et, parmi les militaires de la Milice, il y a également de tout. Il y a ceux qui se battraient contre n'importe qui, pourvu qu'ils se battent, et qui, dans le feu de l'action, sont capables du pire. Il y a ceux qui, comme les politiques, croient au fascisme et je suis heureux qu'ils soient rares, car ils sont prêts à toutes les violences pour assurer le triomphe de leur cause. Il y a enfin ceux, les plus nombreux, qui, comme Jo et moi, se sont trop battus contre les Allemands pour les aimer, qui sont entrés à la Milice parce qu'ils croyaient que c'était une reconstitution clandestine de l'armée française, au service du Maréchal, quel que soit l'ennemi, et en souhaitant qu'un jour cet ennemi soit le boche. (p.87)[44]

This subtle defence of 'les plus nombreux' is reinforced when Jean refers to Joubert, another *milicien*. Significantly, Joubert is shown to be an idealist, and is presented in an extremely favourable light. He too believes that 'S'il n'y avait pas le maréchal Pétain, la Milice n'existerait pas' (pp.183–4), and he wants posterity to know that, in the Milice, 'les braves types n'étaient pas obligatoirement dupes des salauds et que, chez nous, il y avait au moins autant de braves types que de salauds, sinon beaucoup plus' (p.192). Jean readily accepts this claim, and elaborates upon it to conclude his argument: 'Dans les hautes sphères de la Milice, on rencontrait de parfaits honnêtes hommes, tels Raybaud ou Vaugelas, et des partisans d'une relative modération, tels Bout de l'An ou Knipping, qui valait mieux que ce que ses camarades survivants – soucieux de se blanchir aux dépens de sa mémoire – ont raconté' (p.267).

Such statements, on the face of it, seem perfectly acceptable by their reasonableness. The short final chapter, though, totally transforms the reader's perception of things. Jean takes over the narration and admits that he is a mythomaniac, torn between the life he has invented for himself and his fear of revealing his true misdeeds. François was just another figment of his imagination, a narrator who acted as a shield for him while he wrote what were, in effect, his memoirs – he could not have written them unless they were presented dishonestly, through someone else's mouth. So what had at first appeared to be a moderate, considered reassessment of the Occupation was really the work of a man who confesses: 'C'est vrai que je ne dis jamais la vérité. Sauf lorsqu'elle dérange. Autrement, je la reconstitue. Et je ne l'aime que dans ses contradictions' (p.294). In this way, the ending throws the rest of the novel into confusion. Is the case for a rehabilitation of the Milice being put because it is based on fact and appeals to Jean as being suitably provocative? Or does Jean believe that the Milice has no case at all, but makes one up for the pleasure of distorting the truth? It is impossible to say. But what can be said is that the ex-*collabo* has obviously accomplished what he set out to do: encompassed by the puzzlement he has created, to such a degree that no one will be able to challenge his actions with any certainty in the future, he has, to all intents and purposes, successfully justified himself.

Self-justification is also at the heart of Paul Werrie's *La Souille* (1970), in which the narrator Yves Ickx is basely trying to avoid punishment for assisting the German war effort. Hiding from his enemies, the Resistants, while the *épuration* rages on around him, he is so obsessed with the question of judgement that he frequently directs his remarks to a prosecutor and judge he has never actually met. Consequently, the book tends to read like an anguished plea for the defence: 'J'ai juré de tout vous dire, il le faut, il faut que je me justifie, que je sois justifié. . . comme une confession publique' (p.263). This pressing need to speak out in public derives from his conviction that he has been treated unjustly. He could rightly have been condemned for any number of things in different circumstances, he admits, but he refuses to accept that what he did do was against the law. To use his own expression: 'Ordure! Capable de tous les crimes – sauf le seul, qui n'est pratiquement plus possible: celui dont on m'accuse, dont vous m'accusez et pour lequel vous m'avez condamné à mort' (pp.273–4). Nevertheless, when he strangles Alice, his perspective alters slightly: 'Justifié, vous voilà justifié. Après coup. A rebours. Par moi' (p.292). This experience totally invigorates him, and the transformation is such that he boldly decides to head for the border. Having sworn that he would never be captured, he now sees escape as a matter of honour.

Les Chiens aveugles (1972) is the sequel to *La Souille*, and commences with Yves about to cross into Spain. Once there, he is interned, along with SS men, French *gendarmes* and other fugitives from justice. Yet despite this degradation, he maintains an unashamed pride in his 'délit d'opinion', and contrition is the last thing on his mind: 'On est les rebuts, nous, les rebuts de l'humanité, des détritus, les rescapés du grand naufrage, ceux qu'on appelle les salauds, ceux qui ont cru, ceux qui n'ont pas su se retourner à temps, qui auraient eu honte de faire machine arrière, de retourner leur veste, comme il y en a eu tant' (p.19). One of his companions, Job, is equally forthright in his analysis of the situation: 'Si nous avions gagné. . . serais un héros. Et maintenant qu'on a perdu, tu vois. . . ne suis plus bon qu'à jeter aux chiens' (p.224). Similar reflections on the relativity of Right and Wrong have, of course, been made by other novelistic *collabos* ever since the Occupation ended. In Roger Nimier's *Les Épées*, for example, François Sanders comments, in his typically perverse style: 'Je ne doutais pas de la victoire des roses. Ils auraient la vérité historique pour eux – nous aurions la vérité des vaincus, tellement plus enivrante' (p.113). But this is not to suggest that Werrie does little more than imitate Nimier. On the contrary. Yves and Job are far more committed to their cause than Sanders, and this is the telling point, for it demonstrates quite strikingly that, after 1969, the collaborator had become an *acceptable* fictional hero, no matter how much of a *salaud* he was shown to be. To discover just how radically attitudes had changed, one has only to consider the fate of Boisdeffre's *Les Fins dernières*. As already noted, this novel caused tremendous shock waves when it initially appeared in the 1950s, yet in 1973 it was republished in paperback, obviously for consumption by a larger public. Without doubt, then, the collaborationists had finally come in from the cold.[45]

This was all the more evident in that the trend in the novel was accompanied by a flood of memoirs from those who, in real life, had unwittingly compromised themselves during the *années noires*. Especially worthy of mention in this context is Lucien Rebatet's *Les Mémoires d'un fasciste . . .* (2 vols, 1976), which incorporates a slightly revised edition of *Les Décombres*, the polemical, anti-Semitic work which was a best-seller when it first came out in 1942. With blatant and thought-provoking effrontery, Rebatet stresses that few people protested at *Les Décombres* prior to the Liberation, and adds that *Je suis partout* was the best-read newspaper of the period, partly because of the weaknesses of the competition, but partly because it catered for popular tastes: 'Sans aucun doute cette foule de lecteurs ne nous achetait pas seulement pour savoir jusqu'à quelles ignominies irait notre bassesse' (II, p.100).[46] In Rebatet's eyes at least, the implications of this state of affairs are clear: 'Un collaborateur extrémiste était loin de vivre en 1942 dans une solitude amère et déshonorée [. . .]. Paris dans sa majorité attendait pour choisir son opinion de voir de quel côté pencherait la balance de la guerre. Si nous nous trouvions à l'épilogue sur le bon plateau, sans aucun doute une belle foule de partisans nous rejoindrait avec empressement' (II, p.64).[47] *Les Mémoires d'un fasciste . . .* are thus indeed what their title proclaims them to be: an unrepentant restatement of the Fascist point of view.

If Rebatet is frequently outrageous and controversial, then Christian de la Mazière is quite the opposite, favouring lucidity and moderation, and using his autobiography, *Le Rêveur casqué* (1972), to denounce all forms of ideological *engagement*. As this self-confessed 'dreamer' evokes his right-wing, anti-communistic background, and reveals that, to be true to his principles, he enrolled in the Waffen SS *after* the Normandy landings,[48] he elicits a certain understanding, and consequently rehabilitates a whole section of French manhood which had previously been scorned. Moreover, to complement the intelligent depiction of an ideologue's adventures, he fundamentally questions the Resistance myth, making a less than appealing analysis of the *épuration*:

> On ne doit pas oublier que la police française avait torturé, même si elle ne l'avait fait qu'accidentellement; et qu'à la Libération, FFI et FTP s'en étaient donné à cœur joie. Les lieux où s'étaient déroulés sévices et exécutions sommaires demeuraient gravés dans tous les esprits, ils s'assemblaient pour constituer une légende qui, dans le domaine de l'horreur, rejoignait parfois celle de la Gestapo. (p.232)

This horrific tale of illegality echoes those told in Jacques Chardonne's *Détachements* (1969).[49] Like La Mazière and Rebatet, Chardonne was imprisoned at the Liberation, so he can hardly be expected to have fond memories of the period. But that said, he makes no attempt to pull his punches and overtly displays his bitterness:

> La Cour martiale, si pressée d'exécuter les coupables qu'il fallait, huit jours après, réhabiliter les morts, est remplacée par une cour civile. On choisit les jurés d'après les preuves qu'ils ont données de leur haine pour cette sorte de prévenus. Plus que la rapine et le meurtre franc, après de rituelles tortures, dont nous eûmes l'échantillon jusque dans les Charentes modérées, ce qui scandalise c'est de voir l'aveuglement populaire promu à la fonction de tribunal. (pp.39–40)

Hand in hand with this condemnation of the *épuration* goes a defence of the Collaboration, and Chardonne is quick to emphasise that things could have worked out so very differently: 'Si les Américains avaient changé d'idée en route, ou les Russes, si Hitler avait écouté ses meilleurs conseillers, si la quantité infinie des circonstances, toutes imprévisibles, qui font une victoire ou une défaite s'étaient combinées autrement, nous serions interrogés par une autre sorte de juges qui choisiraient le bon grain avec la même assurance' (p.23). Rebatet and others, it may be recalled, made comparable comments on the importance of ultimate victory.

Judging by all this evidence, it would now appear that the former *collabos* seek not merely to promote the Collaboration – most markedly by stressing that they were not as isolated from the masses as postwar orthodoxy implies – but furthermore to discredit the Resistance. This is scarcely surprising, for in rare outbursts between 1944 and 1969, other *réprouvés* had employed the same tactic, making the same complaints as Rebatet, La Mazière and Chardonne.[50] The thrust of the argument has therefore changed little over the last twenty years or so. What has changed, of course, is the general public's reaction to collaborationist utterances. It was André Harris who said that 'les collaborateurs ne se sont jamais exprimés, non parce que la France, unanimement résistante, les a bannis de la collectivité, mais parce que, s'ils parlent, on risque de se sentir gêné ou complice. Alors mieux vaut qu'ils se taisent.'[51] The collaborators' vocal re-emergence since 1970 suggests that many French people no longer find them intimidating. Apparently, the national taboo has at long last been lifted.

Three reasons to explain why the *mode rétro* saw the Collaboration in a favourable light can thus be discerned. First, the sons and daughters of actual *collabos* were able to show that their parents were ordinary human beings, not monsters; second, many *gestapistes* and the like were portrayed as victims of Fate who might have joined the other side if fortune had smiled on them; and finally, the Collaboration was permitted to put its own case at length, either in memoirs or through the mouthpiece of a fictional character. These three ploys proved just as great a threat to *la France résistante* as the direct deflation of the Resistance was, and understandably so: they too rendered palatable to the French the dissent which, up until 1969, had effectively been stifled.

It would be a mistake, however, to assume that a true appraisal of the Occupation was offered to the nation from 1970 onwards. This was plainly not so, as the representative works examined above illustrate. Regarding the presentation of freedom fighters and their struggle against the occupant, Boudard and Friang hardly have a good word to say. Heroism, self-sacrifice and idealism are terms which are notably absent from their vocabulary, having been replaced by cowardice, egoism and cynicism. On the basis of their intimations, one could be excused for thinking that every Resistant was either a murderous criminal or an egocentric opportunist, which is indisputably preposterous. Yet the viewpoints of Daninos and Ophüls are only marginally more optimistic. In fact, it is the depiction of the collaborators which, unconventionally, seems to be better geared towards stimulating empathy. Lacombe Lucien is so enigmatic that it is as easy to identify with him as it is to reject him, and Jacques Bonny's portrait of his father and Serval's sketch of Darnand are both so intentionally flattering that they contradict the historians' nominally more objective assessments of the two men.[52] This emphasis on an uninspiring Resistance and an appealing Collaboration certainly undermines the concept of *résistancialisme*, but as a result another partial account of the Occupation emerges, an account which is no less deceptive than the one it attempts to subvert. In the words of the critic Pierre Viansson-Ponté:

> Non, la France des années 1940–1944 n'était pas peuplée uniquement de héros, loin de là. Mais elle n'était pas davantage peuplée que de gestapistes et de dénonciateurs.
>
> Le pendule était allé très loin d'un côté, il revient très loin, trop loin, dans l'autre sens. L'exaltation du patriotisme était mystificatrice. La dérision poussée à ce degré ne l'est pas moins. Il faut se rendre à l'évidence: cette fois, de Gaulle est bien mort.[53]

In short, myth has been replaced by countermyth. Accordingly, if there is to be talk of enlightenment, it must be in the sense that the *conflict* between the old myth and the more recent countermyth has produced a better knowledge of occupied France, for the interpretation of events generally put forward in the 1970s was not, *per se*, any more reliable than its predecessor.[54]

Such is the situation as it appears today. After 1969 the myth of a *France résistante* was attacked from two opposite directions: the Resistance was hauled down from its pedestal whilst the Collaboration was raised from the depths of contempt. And should any lingering doubts about this remain, they can easily be dispelled by consulting *La Collaboration, 1940–1944*, in which historian Jean-Pierre Azéma judges the aims of the *mode rétro* to be:

> En premier lieu, remettre en cause un unanimisme d'essence gaullienne par lequel le chef de la France libre (plus encore que le P.C.F.) réduisait les collaborateurs à une poignée de traîtres ou d'égarés et cherchait à donner aux Français (contrairement aux mea-culpisme délirant de l'année 1940) dans un miroir volontairement déformé une image rétrospective d'eux-mêmes patriotique sinon héroïque. [. . .] Le second objectif de l'offensive rétro est d'ordre thérapeutique: mettre fin à une coupure manichéenne qui ne se justifie ni d'un côté ni de l'autre, en

> développant un révisionnisme par en bas, à ras de terre, quotidien, par lequel le Français – et pas uniquement le 'Français moyen' – pourra se féliciter de n'avoir été – comme tout le monde – ni un traître ni un héros. Il en résultait, subsidiairement, une réévaluation partielle des collaborationnistes présentés moins comme des idéologues irréductibles que comme des jeunots, pas méchants, naïfs, embrigadés en quelque sorte malgré eux (ils auraient pu aussi bien se retrouver 'de l'autre côté') ou comme des aventuriers – comme il en naît dans les périodes difficiles – et si peu nazis. (pp.11–12)

This double thrust, like its inevitable result – countermythification – is not new, for a similar tactic had been employed to the same effect from the Liberation onwards. Yet before 1970 such heresy had never developed into a fashion. The novelty of the *mode rétro* therefore lies not in what it says, but in the fact that it is, precisely, *une mode*. Or to put it another way, the type of contestation which was once scorned and only sporadic has, since 1969, been readily accepted and widely practised. It is the nation's attitude to demythification which has changed, not the nature of demythification itself.[55]

But although the demythifiers of the 1970s plainly build on a heritage of postwar dissent, there are two aspects of their recent cultural past which, as a group, they unfailingly reject: the revolutionary approach to narrative pioneered by the *nouveaux romanciers* and the iconoclastic analytical method of the Structuralists.

The loose-knit New Novel 'movement' emerged in France in the 1950s and derived largely from the activities of four modern-minded writers: Michel Butor, Alain Robbe-Grillet, Nathalie Sarraute and Claude Simon. Each of these authors worked independently of the others, but they quickly came to be linked together as a 'school', mainly because, in their common drive to update novelistic techniques, they all made a radical departure from tradition. Abandoning the well-established obsession with chronology and linearity, they preferred instead the notion of human time, conveyed through a juxtaposition of immediate sense impressions, mental flashbacks to the past, speculative forecasts of the future and imaginative forays into the realms of fantasy. Objects and events were thus no longer presented *objectively* in their novels, through the device of an omniscient, detached narrator, but *subjectively*, as elements of a specific character's consciousness. To illustrate this procedure, Claude Simon's *La Route des Flandres* (1960) and Alain Robbe-Grillet's *Dans le labyrinthe* (1959) are the obvious texts to turn to, for they both have an additional relevance in the present context – they exemplify the *nouveau roman*'s treatment of war.[56]

La Route des Flandres is actually set in peacetime, but looks back extensively to the débâcle of 1940, retracing the steps of a small band of French cavalrymen abroad in the Flanders countryside. 'Trapped' in a maze of hedges, riding round and round in circles, and having lost all temporal awareness, these horsemen eventually come under German fire, and their commanding officer, Captain de Reixach, is killed. This death so preoccupies one of the survivors that, on numerous occasions over the next few years, he endeavours to reconstruct the incident and unearth the background to it. What perplexes him is quite simple: was de Reixach secretly longing to die because his wife was having an affair? It is a question to which, frustratingly, an answer is never found, so the reader is left in a state of some bewilderment, all the more so in that the very form of the novel is geared towards generating uncertainty. The narration is sometimes in the first person, sometimes in the third; traditional punctuation and paragraphing are dispensed with; unusually long parentheses abound, often containing further parentheses; and different sets of memories smoothly but confusingly flow into each other. All in all, it is as if Simon were trying to give his work the same qualities as those which characterise 'le cheminement même du temps, c'est-à-dire invisible immatériel sans commencement ni fin ni repère' (p.30).

Dans le labyrinthe has much in common with *La Route des Flandres*, for it too depicts a period of military disaster, and it too revolves around a central, puzzling enigma: in a labyrinth of uniform, snow-covered streets, a disoriented soldier wanders about seeking to deliver a package, the contents of which he knows nothing about, to a stranger he has arranged to meet, but no longer knows where. He never succeeds in his quest, falling victim to enemy bullets, but a reason for his mission does emerge at the end of the novel, thanks to the doctor who tends his wounds. Not that every piece of the jigsaw finally falls into place, though. Robbe-Grillet's prose, with its circular structure, its changing narrative standpoint and its countless mirror images, ensures that initial interpretations of the text remain tentative. For how much of the time is the infantryman, known to be feverish, hallucinating? How reliable is the information he imparts? Exactly whose experience is being evoked? These grey areas, and others like them, make a second reading of the work essential, but even then comprehension scarcely improves. Indeed, as soon as the opening paragraph is scanned again, all hope of definitive knowledge disappears, dashed on the rock of contradiction:

> Je suis seul ici, maintenant, bien à l'abri. Dehors il pleut, dehors on marche sous la pluie en courbant la tête, s'abritant les yeux d'une main tout en regardant quand même devant soi, à quelques mètres devant soi, quelques mètres d'asphalte mouillé; dehors il fait froid, le vent souffle entre les branches noires dénudées; le vent souffle dans les feuilles, entraînant les rameaux entiers dans un balancement, dans un balancement, balancement, qui projette son ombre sur le crépi blanc des murs. Dehors il y a du soleil, il n'y a pas un arbre, ni un arbuste, pour donner de l'ombre, et l'on marche en plein soleil, s'abritant les yeux d'une main tout en regardant devant soi, à quelques mètres seulement devant soi, quelques mètres d'asphalte poussiéreux où le vent dessine des parallèles, des fourches, des spirales. (p.9)

The title of the book is therefore extremely well chosen, for the soldier is not the only one who is drawn deeper and deeper into an exitless labyrinth – the unsuspecting reader is as well.

As can perhaps now be appreciated, Robbe-Grillet and his colleagues were nothing if not heretics in the France of the 1950s and 1960s. Yet in spite of the inevitable fire directed at them from more traditionally-minded quarters, they were by no means isolated in their stance, since similar heresy was being committed by another group of (in)famous writers – the Structuralists.[57]

Structuralism made its mark on French intellectual life slightly later than the *nouveau roman*, in the 1960s to be precise, but its emergence as a concept can be traced all the way back to the First World War and even further, to the time when Ferdinand de Saussure was still alive. Saussure was a Swiss university professor who specialised in the field of linguistics, and between 1906 and 1911 he gave a series of lectures which were to guarantee him permanent celebrity. These lectures, published posthumously from his students' notes as *Cours de linguistique générale* (1916), totally revolutionised contemporary linguistic thinking, for they embodied the argument that, in essence, languages were composed of arbitrary signs. For example, consider the word *pen*. According to Saussure, this particular linguistic sign, like all others, can be split into two parts: a *signifiant*, that is to say a sound-image or its written equivalent (the three letters *p*, *e* and *n*, *pen*) and a *signifié* (the *concept* of the writing implement called a pen). However, there is no necessary reason why the three letters *p*, *e* and *n* should evoke the concept of a writing implement (French favours *s*, *t*, *y*, *l* and *o*), so the combination is plainly arbitrary, a matter of pure convention. What is more, nor is there any intrinsic link between the compound sign (*pen*) and its referent (the concrete object to which it refers –

the pen on the office table, the pen in the stationary shop, etc.), so here too *pen* is of quite arbitrary status.

This is all very well on the face of it, but such reasoning does, of course, raise one unavoidable question: given that arbitrariness reigns supreme, how can meaning be accounted for? It is a question to which Saussure has a ready reply – the notion of *difference*. *Signifiants*, *signifiés* and signs could indeed be seen to be meaningful, not through any inherent qualities of their own, admittedly, but rather because they *differed* noticeably from their closest relatives. Hence, the sign *pen* can be understood because it differs from *pet*, *peg*, *hen* and *den*; the *signifié* 'pen' can be recognised because it stands apart from 'pencil', 'biro' or 'charcoal'; and so on and so forth, ad infinitum.

Promotion of the ideas of difference and arbitrariness is thus of vital importance to Saussure. Yet implicit in the analysis given above is another, more challenging concern, a concern which now needs to be made explicit and developed – the denial of the accepted relationship between language and reality. Linguistic signs do not derive from, or reflect, the outside world, the argument continues, but on the contrary, *they* give coherence to *it*. In other words, to illustrate the point, the fact that the Earth's surface often shoots upwards does not make English speakers naturally think of hills. Quite the opposite. It is only because the word *hills* exists that actual hills can be thought of, for were this not so, the phenomena in question could not be distinguished from hillocks, barrows, mountains, mounds and the like. Without the linguistic means to categorise and classify it, then, external reality would be totally chaotic and meaningless.

Having laid the foundations of his theory in this manner, placing tremendous emphasis on differentiation and establishing the predominance of the sign over the object it refers to, Saussure spells out in detail how, in his opinion, language study should be approached. It is the linguist's job, he maintains, to concentrate on *langue* (by which he means the language *system* as a whole, contrastive relationships, sign structures and all) and ignore both *parole* (what people say, the type of expression the system generates) and referents. Only if such a focus is adopted can any useful results be achieved, since only in this way are the mechanisms of language accessible. Other approaches simply will not get to the heart of the matter.

Such are the basic tenets of Saussure's thought. Not every aspect of his work has been dealt with – that would take far too long in a survey of this nature – but hopefully enough has been said to explain his posthumous influence, for nobody would today deny that 'it was his idea of the arbitrary and differential nature of the linguistic sign, and therefore of the essential disjunction between language and reality, that became the foundation of the structuralist movement'.[58]

But what exactly *is* the Structuralist movement? In succinct terms, it is a 'movement of thought, in which all forms of social and cultural life are seen to be governed by systems of signs which are either linguistic or analogous to those of language'.[59] Take the realm of literature, for instance. When reading a novel, Structuralists, following Saussure, will seek meaning not in what is *said*, as common sense demands, but rather in the underlying *structure* of the book itself. Defining each section of the narrative in terms of other sections, they will discover significant internal relationships (parallels, inversions, etc.), and hence they will achieve understanding with no reference to anything outside the text at all.[60]

Clearly, such a procedure makes Structuralism just as great a menace to orthodoxy as the *nouveau roman*, so one might have expected the dissidents of the *mode rétro* to take up the subversive techniques which these two movements bequeathed to them. Yet as already indicated, on the whole they did not. It is true that Jardin and Modiano do dispense with conventional chronology, as Part II of this study will show. But these two authors are exceptional in this. For the most part, demythification of *la France résistante* was accomplished by 'telling a story' and by rejecting drastically non-conformist innovations. Thus, even though a novelist like Boudard manifestly takes liberties with formal grammar, his sentences remain coherent (if somewhat colloquial) as they stand, and his plot is easy to grasp. Moreover, the key films in the trend are no less readily comprehensible. *Lacombe Lucien*, which relies on a linear narrative, shows no sign of the experimentation that characterised Malle's early work, and *Le Chagrin et la pitié*, for all the flashbacks which are an unavoidable feature of the genre, is conceived in Ophüls's own words as 'une forme de récit', a 'récit cohérent'.[61] Most remarkably, then, those who sought to demythify saw *content*, and not *form*, as the means to secure their objective. The lead of the Structuralists and the *nouveaux romanciers* was not followed.

One obvious reason why this should be so is not hard to discern: Structuralism and the *nouveau roman* are distinctly ill-suited to a specific attack on *le résistancialisme*, because the subversion they represent is too wide-ranging. As demonstrated above, the New Novelists stoutly challenge normal assumptions about the outside world (rarely portraying it independently of its perception by an individual consciousness) as indeed do the Structuralists (who argue that language *constructs* reality instead of merely reflecting it), and it may well appear, at first sight, that such a stance is scarcely dissimilar from the fundamental belief of the *mode rétro*, namely that the act of recounting events effectively *creates* them as a sort of myth. But this is most definitely not the case. The demythifiers of the 1970s are far from being subjectivists, and the last thing on their mind is to bring the existence of the universe into question or reject the traditional notion of meaning. They have no such radical aims. They accept that words like *resistance* and *collaboration* are meaningful in their own right, and they do not deny that there is some sort of objective, non-linguistic reality behind the Gaullist myth. Seen in this context, therefore, their ignoring of both the Structuralists and the *nouveaux romanciers* is perfectly understandable.

There is, of course, another possible reason for this neglect – the composition of the target audience. It almost goes without saying that, in order for a national, collective myth to be satisfactorily combated, a new version of what happened has to be presented in such a way that it too may appeal to the entire nation. But the use of structuralist and new-novelistic techniques will not permit this, for those members of the community who are not prepared, or unable, to make the immense intellectual effort required of them will be alienated by such an approach. The same cannot be said though if demythification takes the form of telling a simple tale in simple fashion, since committed demythifiers can then be sure of reaching everybody they want to. This being the case, it comes as no surprise that the contributors to the *mode rétro* act as they do, for the stories they compose could not be simpler or more instantly accessible – with scarcely even a sideways glance at Saussure, Robbe-Grillet or Simon, they just say the opposite of what the myth-makers have said before them.[62]

This explains why irony tends to be an essential feature of their works. As has been seen, the texts of Boudard, Friang and Daninos are all heavily dependent on this device, and Ophüls could be speaking for most debunkers of *la France résistante* when he says of *Le Chagrin et la pitié*: 'Sans l'usage systématique de l'ironie, et d'une complicité avec le spectateur au niveau de l'ironie, ce genre de récit serait tout à fait impossible.'[63] Furthermore, those who invoke Fate to upgrade the Collaboration seem to adopt a similar stance, especially if the critic Mona Ozouf is to be believed: 'Le seul héros de ces films et de ces livres, c'est le hasard, maître ironique de l'existence humaine.'[64] Such recourse to irony is, to say the least, hardly unexpected, since Curtis and Vailland (to name but two) had already used this strategy to exactly the same end in the immediate postwar period.[65]

This latter point is important, for it serves to underline, once again, that the dissident trend of the 1970s most certainly built on precedents, and that these precedents were provided not by the Structuralists or the *nouveaux romanciers,* but by the early *anti-résistancialistes.* They too brought *l'armée de l'ombre* crashing down from its pedestal, they too found mitigating circumstances for the *collabos,* and they too used countermythification as the brunt of their attack. In fact the only thing they conspicuously failed to do was to make their dissension popular. It was consequently in this area, and in this area alone, that their successors had room to innovate. And innovate they most certainly did. The *mode rétro* arrived.

Notes

1. The scenario of *Le Chagrin et la pitié* has been published along with explanatory statements by the director in Marcel Ophüls, *Le Chagrin et la pitié.*
2. Pierre Loubière and Gilbert Salachas, 'Libre cours: Marcel Ophüls', p.31.
3. Marcel Ophüls, 'Regardez donc dans vos greniers', p.10. Another version of this article, only slightly different, can be found in Ophüls, *Le Chagrin et la pitié* (pp.15–22).
4. These points are suggested by the Graves brothers and by d'Astier de la Vigerie. See *Le Chagrin et la pitié*, pp.140, 143–4.
5. Loubière and Salachas, 'Libre cours: Marcel Ophüls', p.24.
6. Loubière and Salachas, 'Libre cours: André Harris', p.38.
7. Danièle Heymann, 'Français, vous saurez', p.19. This article also provides a brief but useful sketch of the film's controversial career.
8. Cf. Philippe Ganier-Raymond, *Une certaine France: l'antisémitisme, 1940–44*: 'Un écolier des années soixante pouvait croire en toute bonne foi que, pendant quatre ans, la France [. . .] était peuplée de trente millions de héros. Chiffre dont il convenait de retirer une poignée de canailles appelées miliciens, et de quelques tristes sires s'adonnant au marché noir' (pp.15–16). Further dissatisfaction with the *manuels d'histoire* is voiced by Marie Gatard (*La Guerre, mon père*, p.27) and, of course, by André Harris (see p.43 above).
9. Cf. Michel Tournier, *Le Vent paraclet* (1977): 'En vérité la Résistance

n'est devenue un phénomène d'ampleur nationale qu'après le départ des Allemands. Pendant l'occupation elle ne fut le fait que d'une infime minorité de héros' (p.77). As a useful *point de repère*, it is worth noting here that in *Vichy France: Old Guard and New Order, 1940–1944*, historian Robert Paxton puts the figure for active resistance at 2 per cent of the adult population (p.295).

10. Popular singers of the 1970s, generally of the postwar generation, helped to disseminate the points made by their writer colleagues. For example, Michel Sardou's two songs 'Les Ricains' and 'Monsieur le Président de France' acknowledge the tremendous role played by the Americans in liberating France, whilst Renaud's 'L'Hexagone' asserts that few people actively resisted the Germans.
11. Cf. Frédérique Moret, *Journal d'une mauvaise Française*: 'La Résistance est devenue la grenouille qui veut égaler le bœuf. Comment croire sérieusement que, sans eux, les Américains n'auraient jamais pu vaincre?' (p.237).
12. 'Regardez donc dans vos greniers', p.10 (*Le Chagrin et la pitié*, p.21). It is perhaps worth adding here that even Daninos's statement at the end of his first point (namely that economic collaborators got off more lightly than those who engaged in cultural collaboration) had been foreshadowed on numerous occasions. See e.g. Pierre de Boisdeffre, *Les Fins dernières*, p.41; Jean Dutourd, *Le Demi-solde*, p.102; or Maast, 'Morceaux choisis: épurés', p.1696.
13. To facilitate the giving of references, these three titles will hereafter be abbreviated to *B*, *CPB* and *CJ* respectively. For reasons of propriety, *Bleubite* was first published as *Les Matadors* (Plon, 1966).
14. This 'invasion' of the Resistance by former *collabos* is repeated time and time again in the novels of the *mode rétro*. See e.g. Solange Fasquelle, *Les Falaises d'Ischia*, p.259, or José Giovanni, *Mon ami le traître*, p.51.
15. Cf. Fasquelle, *Les Falaises d'Ischia*: 'La colère populaire [. . .] atteignit son paroxysme lors de quelques exécutions hâtives qui tinrent plus d'actes de barbarie que de l'exercice de la justice' (p.97). See also p.71.
16. For other post-1969 presentations of wrongful *tontes*, see Guy Croussy, *La Tondue*, pp.11–43 or Denis Lalanne, *Le Devoir de Français*, p.172.
17. Cf. *Le Chagrin et la pitié*, in which Madame Solange recounts how the FFI subjected her to the torture of *la baignoire* at the Liberation (pp.183–5).
18. Cf. Giovanni's *Mon ami le traître*, where the courts of justice are compared to revolutionary tribunals: 'Pas de jury. Un juge flanqué de deux assesseurs et un avocat général. Un public vengeur. Les cuisiniers de la LVF prenaient vingt ans' (pp.186–7). To confirm that the above picture of an unlawful Liberation has some foundation in historical fact, see, passim, Robert Aron, *Histoire de l'épuration* or Philippe Bourdrel, *L'Épuration sauvage, 1944–1945*.

19. Cf. *Le Corbillard de Jules*, pp.239–40.
20. Cf. Michel Robida, *Le Déjeuner de Trieste*, p.141 and 'Le Retour de Bibendum' in Gilles Perrault, *Les Sanglots longs* (pp.54–5). Cf. also Erik Orsenna's *La Vie comme à Lausanne*, in which a politician is advised by his biographer: 'Surtout, soignez votre Résistance. Sans Résistance, une carrière politique a toujours quelque chose d'incomplet, une allure d'imposture' (p.193). That a good war record is indeed a useful political asset in France is illustrated by the 1981 presidential election campaign. For details, see Henry Rousso, *Le Syndrome de Vichy, 1944–198 . . .*, pp.194–7.
21. Cit. in Gerhard Heller, *Un Allemand à Paris*, p.110.
22. Cf. *Le Corbillard de Jules*: 'Deux ans plus tôt, l'idée me traverse. . . Gaston, il aurait raccompagné de la sorte le Maréchal ou Laval. . . et pourquoi pas le Reichführer si l'occase s'était offerte' (p.251). Cf. also Alain Buhler, *Enfer et ses fils*, p.217 and Fasquelle, *Les Falaises d'Ischia*, p.260.
23. Cf. *Le Chagrin et la pitié*, pp.146–8.
24. Cf. Roger Frison-Roche, *Les Montagnards de la nuit*, pp.54–5, 206–7.
25. But NB Jacques Delperrié de Bayac's point: 'Il convient de garder à l'esprit que tous les maquis n'avaient pas la même orientation politique. Il est encore plus nécessaire de ne pas exagérer ces différences. Contre les Allemands et leurs alliés, la Résistance était une' (*Histoire de la milice, 1918–1945*, p.384n.).
26. Cf. *Bleubite*, p.128.
27. See José Giovanni's allusion to the Maréchal in *Mon ami le traître*: 'Le peuple qui l'avait acclamé était toujours là. Le même acclama de Gaulle (à moins que la population n'ait doublé en six mois). [. . .] Avec le peuple il ne faut être là qu'aux bons moments, avoir de la chance au jeu [. . .] et craindre la petitesse de sa mémoire quant aux circonstances atténuantes' (pp.189–90). Cf. Robida, *Le Déjeuner de Trieste*, pp.136–7, 235. A useful perspective is given by historian Jean-Pierre Azéma in *De Munich à la Libération, 1938–1944*: 'Rien ne prouve – comme on l'affirme généralement – que ce furent bien les mêmes qui se déplacèrent pour acclamer à Paris Philippe Pétain en avril et Charles de Gaulle en août: il subsistait un public vichyssois' (p.323).
28. Cf. Ophüls, *Le Chagrin et la pitié*, pp.51, 76–7, 149–50, 153, and Jean-Luc Maxence, *L'Ombre d'un père*, p.182. See also the second of Daninos's five points on p.45 above.
29. Cf. Brigitte Friang, *Comme un verger avant l'hiver*, p.269. Cf. also, in the non-fictional domain, François Nourissier, 'Le Cadavre dans le placard', p.87.
30. Although the Gaullist view of the Occupation is the one most consistently disparaged, it should permanently be borne in mind that demythification also affected the Communists, for as has been demonstrated, the PCF promoted a vision of the period which overlapped considerably with that of de Gaulle.

31. As noted earlier, the question raised here and elsewhere in this chapter – why did the French accept demythification after 1969? – is one which will be fully discussed in chapter 3.
32. See also Jean-Luc Maxence, *L'Ombre d'un père*. The father in question here is the right-wing journalist Jean-Pierre Maxence.
33. Cf. Maxence, *L'Ombre d'un père*. Speaking of his father, Jean-Luc opines: 'Incontestablement, tu étais vichyssois mais non pro-allemand. Tu as entretenu dans la rédaction de tes articles un réel esprit de résistance à l'Occupant. [. . .] Jamais, tu n'as éludé l'occasion de rendre un service illégal, fût-il dangereux, à quelqu'un' (p.217). Hence: 'Je suis convaincu, avec le recul des années, que tu fus injustement condamné et qu'il me serait possible à l'heure actuelle de te faire réhabiliter à titre posthume' (p.20).
34. There is a possible reference here to Bertrand Blier's film, *Hitler, connais pas* (1963).
35. This explanation of Bonny's collaboration is repeated in Pierre Serval's *Une boule de neige en enfer*, pp.56–7. For another real-life example of 'unintentional' collaboration, see Delperrié de Bayac, *Histoire de la milice*, p.179.
36. Former *gestapistes* often evoked the force of destiny in their defence. See Philippe Aziz, *Tu trahiras sans vergogne*, pp.36, 67. The technique of letting a condemned father make his own defence is echoed in Maxence's *L'Ombre d'un père*.
37. Cf. André Chamson, *La Reconquête*, p.60; Jacques Laurent, *Histoire égoïste*, pp.216–17; Paul Noirot, *La Mémoire ouverte*, p.60; Serval, *Une boule de neige*, p.192, and Pascal Sevran, *Vichy-Dancing*, p.161.
38. For other examples of siblings taking opposing sides, see Michèle Saint-Lô, *Les Inséparables*, Adèle Fernandez, *Le Fruit sans douceur* and Régine Deforges, *La Bicyclette bleue*. Such family disintegration is, of course, a stunning metaphor for France's own schism during the war.
39. The scenario of *Lacombe Lucien* has been published under the joint names of Louis Malle and Patrick Modiano. There is thus an immediate and important link to Modiano's fiction, which will be discussed in Part II.
40. Michel Delain, 'Louis Malle: dernier zigzag', p.48.
41. Jean-Jacques Olivier, 'L'Engagement de Louis Malle', p.V [p.15]. Cf. Alphonse Boudard: 'Mes ennemis, je les gaffouille sérieux. Je voudrais qu'ils aient des vraies sales gueules. . . [. . .] des tronches de monstres. . . [. . .]! Je m'efforce mais ça ne passe pas. Leur chef il est quelconque. . . hors de son uniforme bleu, on le prendrait pour n'importe qui. . . un contremaître, un employé de banque' (*CPB*, pp.217–18).
42. This concern with chance did not materialise out of the blue at the Occupation, of course; it has been associated with periods of conflict for centuries, and can be traced back at least as far as the 1600s. See e.g.

Pierre Corneille, *Sertorius*, in *Théâtre complet de Pierre Corneille*, edited by P. Lièvre and R. Caillois: 'Lorsque deux factions divisent un empire, / Chacun suit au hasard la meilleure ou la pire, / Suivant l'occasion ou la nécessité / Qui l'emporte vers l'un ou vers l'autre côté' (II, pp.730–1).

43. In his *Mémoires de guerre*, de Gaulle also recognises that Darnand was the victim of a system, and uses this fact to help establish his own legitimacy. 'A cet homme de main et de risque', he writes, 'la collaboration était apparue comme une passionante aventure qui [. . .] justifiait toutes les audaces et tous les moyens. Il en eût, à l'occasion, couru d'autres en sens opposé. [. . .] Rien, mieux que la conduite de ce grand dévoyé de l'action, ne démontrait la forfaiture d'un régime qui avait détourné de la patrie des hommes faits pour la servir' (III, p.251). Cf. Henri Frenay, *La Nuit finira*, p.496.
44. Cf. *milicien* Jean Bassompierre's last words, quoted in Marcel Hasquenoph, *La Gestapo en France*: 'Dans les forces de la Libération et de la Résistance comme à la LVF et à la Milice, on retrouve la gamme des mêmes tempéraments, des mêmes caractères: depuis le chevalier sans peur et sans reproche jusqu'à l'aventurier sans scrupule' (p.200). Cf. also Roger Nimier, *Les Épées*: 'Il y avait du bon et du mauvais dans la Milice' (p.101).
45. See also Robert Poulet, *La Conjecture*.
46. Historian Pierre-Marie Dioudonnat confirms the success and popularity of *Je suis partout* – see *'Je suis partout', 1930–1944*, p.346.
47. Cf. Céline, *Rigodon*: 'Hitler gagnant, il s'en est fallu d'un poil, vous verriez je vous le dis l'heure actuelle qu'ils auraient tous été pour lui. . . à qui qu'aurait pendu le plus de juifs, qui qu'aurait été le plus nazi' (p.316).
48. At about the same time Rebatet joined the Milice, only to resign the next day. See Rebatet, *Les Mémoires d'un fasciste* . . ., II, p.165.
49. Written in 1945, this work was not widely published until after the author's death in 1968 (at his own request), obviously because of the heretical nature of the content. Fifty copies did appear in 1962, however.
50. See e.g. Céline's version of the *épuration* in *D'un château l'autre*: 'Des milliers ce jour-là, s'être fait lyncher. . . ce jour-là même! . . . reconnus LVF ou autres . . . ci! . . . là! . . . en province . . . et Paris . . .' (p.88).
51. Loubière and Salachas, 'Libre cours: André Harris', p.38.
52. See e.g. *Tu trahiras sans vergogne*, in which Philippe Aziz exposes the so-called 'premier flic de France' by quoting Commissaire Clos: 'Bonny ne fut jamais, comme le prétend la légende, un grand policier. L'apostrophe du ministre Chéron n'est qu'une phrase maladroite. Bonny a toujours eu une activité marginale, [. . .] un côté peu rassurant, équivoque, à la limite du policier marron' (p.81). Cf. Pascal Ory,

Les Collaborateurs, 1940–1945, p.262. For a reaffirmation – albeit an implicit one – of Darnand's guilt, Pétain's initial endorsement of the Milice notwithstanding, see Delperrié de Bayac, *Histoire de la milice*, p.640.

53. 'Au fil de la semaine: *Lacombe Lucien* ou l'ambiguïté', p.7. Cf. Mona Ozouf, 'Sans chagrin et sans pitié': 'Ainsi s'achève le conte bleu où, grâce à de Gaulle, les Français s'entendaient dire qu'ils avaient été collectivement héroïques. Il s'est mué en son contraire exact, également trompeur [. . .]. Ce n'est donc pas encore le temps de l'objectivité' (p.55).
54. Cf. François Nourissier, 'Le Cadavre dans le placard': 'Bien entendu le risque est grand [. . .] de montrer une nation lâche et veule dans sa majorité, après avoir abusé des clichés d'une France blessée, digne et courageuse. Entre l'excès d'honneur et l'indignité perce pourtant la vérité' (p.86).
55. The youth of many of the demythifiers, and the detachment from the *années noires* which it represents, are, of course, new developments. Nevertheless, the works of the 'innocent' writers still manifest a dependence on the past in their *content*. See also note 31 above.
56. A more theoretical, if somewhat unreliable insight into the New Novel at this time (the late 1950s and the early 1960s) is given by Robbe-Grillet's polemical essays, which have been published under the title of *Pour un nouveau roman*. See also, for a sense of perspective, the same author's *Le Miroir qui revient*.
57. The details which follow owe much to Terry Eagleton's *Literary Theory: An Introduction* and to *Modern Literary Theory: A Comparative Introduction*, edited by Ann Jefferson and David Robey. These two works provide excellent introductory studies of Structuralism, as also do *Structuralism: A Reader*, edited by Michael Lane, *Structuralism and since: From Lévi-Strauss to Derrida*, edited by John Sturrock, and Jonathan Culler's more demanding *Structuralist Poetics*.
58. David Robey, 'Modern Linguistics and the Language of Literature', in *Modern Literary Theory: A Comparative Introduction*, edited by Ann Jefferson and David Robey, p.51.
59. Ibid., p.46.
60. For a first-hand – and more diverse – demonstration of structuralism at work, see Roland Barthes, *Mythologies*. As is likewise the case with Claude Lévi-Strauss's *Mythologiques*, the very title of this text indicates just how applicable the structuralist method is to myths of all kinds.
61. *Le Chagrin et la pitié*, pp.211 and 264 respectively.
62. Further to support this general argument, it is interesting to note that when Robbe-Grillet himself turns his hand to demythifying the Occupation, he does not do so in one of his 'new' novels, but rather in the more traditional, largely autobiographical *Le Miroir qui revient*, making such 'objective' statements as: 'Dès la libération de Paris, papa avait

considéré avec dégoût la sarabande grotesque des F.F.I. de la onzième heure, et la veulerie du bon peuple qui se sentait subitement gaulliste et guerrier' (p.130).

63. *Le Chagrin et la pitié*, p.263.
64. 'Sans chagrin et sans pitié', p.54.
65. Another writer who springs to mind here is inevitably Paul Guimard, author of *L'Ironie du sort*.

–3–

Why a *Mode Rétro*?

> Ces nouveaux narcisses, cinéastes, metteurs en scène, créateurs en quête de mythologies et de transgressions. Alors, que cherchent-ils? Pourquoi remuent-ils si complaisamment les cendres mal refroidies des échecs de leurs aînés? Pour justifier les leurs? Pour invoquer un passé souvent mythifié par le courant écologique? Pour inventer des frissons nouveaux? Cela n'explique pas tout.
>
> Martin Even

> Qui vient réveiller de pareils souvenirs. . . quel besoin? Je me demande.
>
> Alphonse Boudard

> Il serait peut-être intéressant de savoir pourquoi les enfants de cette guerre ont mis un tel temps à écrire leurs souvenirs et pourquoi ils le font aujourd'hui.
>
> Marie Gatard

As may perhaps now be apparent, up until about 1970, written depictions of the Occupation left much to be desired in France. Novelists had not, admittedly, ignored the period in its entirety, but on the whole they had turned to it only as a source of *situations fortes*, with the result that their narratives – little more than heroic adventure stories for the most part – reinforced, rather than undermined, the 'official' myth. However, with the end of the 1960s came clear rumblings that certain French writers were not happy with this neglect. Armand Lanoux, for example, observed in his preface to André Pierrard's *On l'appelait Tamerlan*:

> Nos littératures n'ont pas encore, paralysie, pudeur, interdits collectifs, créé les chroniques stendhaliennes ou balzaciennes de la résistance. [. . .] je souhaite que se développe une littérature de la résistance libérée de ses interdits, dominant son sujet au lieu d'être dominée par ses conformismes

> [. . .], une littérature qui nous rende enfin la pulpe des événements qui ont marqué le monde de 1940 à 1944 d'une telle façon que le monde ne s'en est pas encore remis, une littérature de la palpitante vérité des hommes. (pp.14–17)[1]

When explanations of the *mode rétro* are sought, this wish to create a new literary vision of the *années noires* will obviously be seen to have had a part to play. But only a relatively minor part, for as chapter 1 has shown, views similar to Lanoux's had been expressed before without spawning anything like a comparable fashion for dissent. This being the case, the true explanations of the trend must lie elsewhere. But where? Why *did* retrospection suddenly come into vogue after 1969? Exactly *what* turned discussion of the Occupation into an enduring national pastime? It is the aim of the present chapter to answer these and other such questions.

One reason for the emergence of a *remise en cause* is instantly apparent to even the most short-sighted of observers – by the start of the 1970s, there had been a perceptible downswing in the popularity of Charles de Gaulle. Symptomatic of this were the events of May 1968, when protesting students and workers brought the country to a standstill and almost forced the general to relinquish the presidency. He did not do so as things transpired; indeed, he actually came out of the *événements* in a stronger position than when he went in. But his authority was no longer inviolate. Less than a year later, in April 1969, a national referendum went against him and he had no option this time but to resign. His subsequent death, on 9 November 1970, simply confirmed what most people already knew: the Gaullist era had finally come to an end.

This political and physical demise of de Gaulle was, without doubt, the essential catalyst for what was to become the *mode rétro*, for the general's passing signified more than the disappearance of a great statesman; it represented, above all, the departure of the man who had embodied and institutionalised *la France résistante*.[2] With this once-daunting obstacle to a re-evaluation of the *années noires* removed, demythification could at last begin in earnest, all the more so in that the new President – Gaullist Georges Pompidou – was himself 'volontiers agacé par la geste de la Résistance et de surcroît soucieux de réconcilier pour des affaires plus sérieuses les honnêtes gens'.[3] When Pompidou in turn died (in 1974), to be replaced by the more liberal, non-Gaullist Valéry Giscard d'Estaing, the movement away from past orthodoxies was most manifestly sealed and completed.

It was thus, initially at least, the political changes in France from 1969 onwards which fostered the widespread reappraisal of the German occupation, and if just one example is sought to show how these changes affected the French writers of the period, that example must surely be provided by Jacques Laurent's *Histoire égoïste*, which is both a catalogue of the author's brushes with authority when criticising de Gaulle prior to 1970, and actual proof that things could be said in 1976 which would not have been acceptable ten years earlier.

If the cultural atmosphere had become more liberal in Pompidolian and Giscardian France, though, this was not merely due to the downfall of 'l'homme du 18 juin'; the late 1960s and early 1970s was also the time when the postwar generation was reaching maturity and joining forces with those who had lived through the war without really experiencing it. Having successfully, albeit forcibly, obtained a *remise en cause* of their future through their rebellion in May 1968, these *jeunes loups* then began to conduct a pointed re-examination of their past.[4] The result was every bit as dramatic as the *événements* had been, largely because, for the first time ever, the *années noires* could now be approached free of prejudice. As Pierre Billard says: 'En 1943, Nourissier, Jardin, Chaix, Joffo, Malle, Drach, Ophüls, Harris, Sédouy ont entre 1 an et 17 ans. Ils ont été engendrés par l'époque sans en partager les compromissions. Assez proches des faits pour raconter, assez lointains pour rassurer, ils ont un regard innocent.'[5]

More specifically, this 'regard innocent' derived from the fact that, no matter what the year of their birth, the various members of this generation had one, vital characteristic in common: they knew next to nothing, in essence, about life in France under Pétain. Those born after the war received no information because of their parents' silence.[6] Those who were children at the time were not mature enough to understand what was going on, as the case of André Harris suggests: 'Je n'étais pas adulte, donc je n'ai pas pu ressentir tous les problèmes relatifs à l'engagement vis-à-vis de la collaboration, la résistance ou l'attentisme.'[7] And finally, many of those who were adolescents, and who might have been able to grasp the situation, were prevented from doing so because of 'la fréquente démission de ceux, parents, aînés, éducateurs qui auraient pu exercer une certaine pédagogie [. . .] de la clairvoyance.'[8] Such basic ignorance, allied – it should not be forgotten – to the distortions imparted by the postwar myth-makers, meant that the younger section of French society grew up feeling alienated from the period in which it had its roots. France had, as it were, produced a generation of orphans. And it was the thirst for knowledge of these orphans, their determination to discover their true heritage, which was to spark off and nourish the *mode rétro*.

This is best exemplified, not unnaturally, by those writers whose orphanage was actual, or at least as close to actual as to make no difference. The most interesting of these – Pascal Jardin, Marie Chaix and Evelyne Le Garrec – will be discussed in Part II, but for present purposes, the lesser-known Jacques Bonny and Marie Gatard will serve equally well.[9]

As previously noted in chapter 2, Jacques Bonny is the author of *Mon père, l'inspecteur Bonny*, an investigation into the life of his infamous, *gestapiste* father Pierre, who was executed in 1944. *Investigation*, rather than, say, *memoir*, is certainly the correct word to use here, because even before the execution took place, Jacques suffered acutely from paternal absence and the ignorance it entailed: Bonny senior, it is readily revealed, spent a great deal of his time at work and never spoke about what he did there when he came home, so the only man the family knew was the warm, loving and tender person who earned the daily bread.[10] Little wonder, then, that the mature writer-son should admit: 'Ce père avec qui j'avais passé toute mon enfance et ma jeunesse, cet homme que j'aimais et que j'admirais, restait une énigme' (p.16). And little wonder either that, precisely because Pierre is as enigmatic as this, and because Jacques loved and admired him so, the book should ultimately be viewed as a *search*, 'la quête d'un fils à la recherche de la vérité sur son père' (p.17).[11]

The motivating force behind this quest, already implicit in the two quotations given above, is not all that difficult to discern, for Bonny will elsewhere say quite openly: 'Quoi qu'il ait fait, quoi qu'on m'ait dit, je n'y puis rien: je l'ai aimé; il m'a élevé; c'était mon père' (p.15). In other words, the son patently needs to justify his filial affection, both to himself and to others; he needs to be able to respect 'cet être connu de moi que certains avaient voulu m'apprendre à renier, et qui n'en était pas moins mon père' (p.16). That this is indeed so is further evidenced by the way he approaches his investigation, or rather by the way his standpoint alters as his work progresses. At first, he is to be found asserting: 'Je me sentais [. . .] la force de juger mon propre père. De le juger à mon tour, sans plus d'indulgence que les hommes. Mais avec moins de hâte, peut-être' (p.17). Yet less than fifty pages later, he has undeniably – and radically – changed his tune: 'Je n'avais pas l'intention de juger mon père', he now confides, 'd'autres s'en sont chargés à ma place' (p.59).[12] This blatant contradiction is not as inexplicable as it appears at first glance, since by coming to ignore the ethical consequences of Pierre's acts, Jacques can facilitate what is, deep down, his principal task – an exculpation of the love he feels for a despised *gestapiste*.

This should not be taken to imply, by any manner of means, that Bonny is merely penning a sort of *belle histoire d'amour*. Nothing could be further from the truth. What he is actually doing, or trying to do, is re-establish the heritage he lacks – the heritage which the war stripped from him – and thereby ensure that he will never again be forced to concede: 'De vieux papiers [. . .], plus une somme de souvenirs d'enfants, voilà tout ce qui me restait pour savoir vraiment, peut-être, de qui j'étais le fils' (p.16).[13] And he is doing something more besides. He is investigating, as he acknowledges, 'pour essayer de voir clair en mon père, et en moi-même' (p.182). In the final analysis, therefore, his search for an inheritance represents the search for an identity – his own identity.

It will no doubt seem to some, at this stage, that Bonny's predicament is perfectly understandable, a simple consequence of his father's wartime activities and the terminal judgement to which they gave rise. A reading of Marie Gatard's *La Guerre, mon père* (1978), however, suggests that there may be a good deal more to the matter than this.

Unlike Jacques Bonny, Marie Gatard did not have to suffer the stigma caused by paternal collaboration, for her father was a member of the Resistance and, as part of the special services section, a relatively important one at that. Yet in spite of this fundamental contrast, which tends to distance her from the son of the ex-*gestapiste*, there is one, vital feature of her background which she plainly shares with her fellow author: important her father may have been within the underground movement, but he was not untouchable – betrayed and arrested in 1943, during the big Gestapo offensive which was to net Jean Moulin, he was tried, convicted and eventually executed. So at the age of about eight, Gatard too became a war orphan.

The effect of this on her was devastating, more devastating than might have been expected, because her whole world, and not just a sizeable segment of it, suddenly turned into a void, leaving her entirely alone to come to terms with her loss: 'Si je ne pouvais m'appuyer ni sur un père, ni sur une mère, de peur de casser la mienne, ni sur quelqu'un à l'extérieur de crainte de la blesser dans ses prérogatives maternelles, je devais chercher protection en moi-même' (p.99). At the best of times this is a hard enough thing to do, but during the Liberation it was virtually impossible. The trouble was not that the parent she loved was dead, buried and gone forever, but rather that he was not allowed to rest in peace. And neither was she:

> Je sentais qu'était tissée progressivement autour de moi, une trame d'imagerie d'Épinal par une société trop intéressée pour être tout à fait honnête à mon égard, un canevas dans lequel il allait falloir me débattre de crainte d'être brodée vivante dans le rôle de l'orphelin satisfait de l'être, au pied d'un père défiguré. (p.129)

The point raised here is a major one, so major that Gatard continues along these lines at length, delving ever more deeply into her subject:

> Pour moi, [la guerre] était terminée, mais je savais que pour d'autres enfants tout commençait: celui de la tondue, celui du collaborateur, celui de l'Allemand. Comment aurais-je eu de la haine pour ces enfants-là soudain devenus mes frères? Je ne dirai jamais que nos pères et nos mères eurent quoi que ce soit de commun, mais nous, les enfants, frères nous le fûmes et qu'elles s'étouffent d'indignation, les dames d'âge! Nous le fûmes à cause de la torture, à cause des menottes aux poignets, à cause d'une société d'adultes qui tuait à la suite d'impulsions individuelles ou, qui pis est, plus incompréhensible encore pour un enfant, d'une préméditation institutionnalisée. Ami orphelin, mon frère, ami sidéré, m'entends-tu?
>
> Encore une fois, il n'est pas question de comparer nos pères. L'intensité d'un amour ne se mesure pas à la qualité de l'objet aimé, il est parfaitement concevable d'aimer autant un héros qu'un bandit de grand chemin. Ainsi peut-il exister pour les enfants de condamnés à mort une sorte de tronc commun, du moins dans le cas où ils aiment leurs parents: on prend l'objet de leur amour, leur protection face au monde, en le maltraitant on le manipule comme un objet puis, tout vif, en état physiologique de survivre, on le tue. Après vient le reste, la différenciation. A l'enfant du héros on dit 'tu dois être fier, tu dois chérir', à l'autre, 'c'est la honte, tu n'a plus le droit d'aimer un tel individu'. Le premier n'a plus, s'il avait quelque haine pour son géniteur (un héros peut être détesté pour toute autre raison que son héroïsme et même pour celui-ci) qu'à la cacher soigneusement s'il veut respirer en paix; le second n'a plus qu'à taire, s'il y a lieu, son amour coupable. Le devoir d'amour est sûrement moins inconfortable que le devoir de haine. Que peut faire, en effet, l'enfant du 'méprisable'? Ou il obtempère au prix d'un broyage qui en fait un être écrasé pour la vie, ou il lutte en secret pour la survie de son amour et s'acharne à ressembler à l'objet aimé, ou encore il se venge d'une société qui a condamné en lui un innocent, on sait où mènent ces dernières solutions. (pp.138–40)

As this long elucidation unfolds, it becomes more and more transparent that, far from being limited in its impact, the postwar mythification hit children on both sides of the political divide, and hit them equally hard. Gatard's basic predicament and subsequent riposte accordingly come to resemble those of Jacques Bonny. She too is plagued by a father who is permanently absent (absent because he is dead, obviously, but absent as well because the myth has transformed him and thereby alienated him from her), and she too takes up the pen to consolidate a *search*, a search for the parental legacy she should have had, but of which, through no fault of her own, she has been deprived ('J'ai pu retrouver dans ce qui était écrit, auprès des survivants, ce que j'ignorais en ce temps', she admits on p.18). This, then, is the beauty of her work in the present context: starting with a focus diametrically opposed to that of most of the other orphan-writers – the Resistance, instead of the Collaboration – she arrives at exactly the same point, demonstrating, in explicit fashion, that one of *le résistancialisme*'s most tragic side-effects was a disinheriting process, a disinheriting process more widespread and more acute than anyone could have imagined.

The corollary of this would plainly seem to be that, in a sense, the state of real-life orphanage is a total irrelevance, for if the myth is really as strong as is being suggested, an inheritance can be lost forever without a parent actually dying or disappearing.[14] Is this indeed an acceptable inference to make? It would certainly appear to be so, for when Gatard and her *amis orphelins* are removed from the spotlight, and attention transferred to the young fiction writers of the *mode rétro*, the theme of a missing heritage is still found to be a predominant one.

Take, for example, Pascal Sevran.[15] Born in 1945 and inveterately obsessed with nostalgia, Sevran has written three novels in which a lost heritage features prominently: *Le Passé supplémentaire* (1979), *Vichy-Dancing* (1980) and *Un garçon de France* (1982). All three of these works are extremely similar in content and approach, but *Vichy-Dancing* stands out as the one text to concentrate on because, as its title indicates, this is the text where the Occupation is most tangibly to the fore, the text which, moreover, best shows the links between the *années noires* and the notion of a legacy.

The legacy in question is the one bequeathed to the fatherless narrator, François, by Vera Valmont, his music-hall-star mother. Or to be more precise, it is the one she does *not* pass on to him, for throughout the various stages of her career she is regularly, if not permanently absent. At first, during her heyday in the late 1930s and up until 1944, she is unable to give him the love he craves through sheer pressure of work:

> Avenue du Suffren, je ne l'avais pas vue beaucoup. Quand, par hasard, elle n'était pas en voyage, elle rentrait tard et je dormais.
>
> Lorsque je la réclamais, les bonnes me répondaient qu'elle travaillait. (p.28)

Then later, after the Liberation, there is a different problem. Out of favour – and *tondue* – for having sung on Radio-Paris under the Germans, Vera is now able to spend more time at home, but still remains aloof through her silence, refusing to talk to François and neglecting even to explain why she has stopped singing all of a sudden.[16] So the unfortunate son is no closer to having a proper mother than he was before.

Understandably, he considers this situation to be intolerable, and endeavours to do something about it. One remedy he dabbles with is the indulgence in short-lived love affairs. Another is the adoption of a man (a German soldier he sees on an old photograph) to stand in for the father he never knew.[17] But neither of these two ploys give him the meaningful contact he seeks. Because of this, there soon remains only one course of action with any likelihood at all of giving him satisfaction – a quest to reconstruct his mother's past. As he observes:

> Les journaux d'autrefois racontent des tas d'histoires sur sa vie. Je les ai lus depuis. Mais je n'ai jamais osé lui demander d'explications. Je craignais qu'elle ne se fâche. Elle ne savait pas que je fouillais l'appartement dès qu'elle sortait, dans l'espoir de trouver des coupures de presse où son nom était imprimé. Récemment, je suis allé m'inscrire à la Bibliothèque nationale, pour consulter tranquillement des publications vieilles de cinquante ans. Un peu de moi se cache là, entre leurs pages jaunies. (p.42)

The final sentence confirms what could, perhaps, have been guessed at the start, namely that, by trying to find out about the Vera he does not know, and by listening – but only on record – to 'la voix d'où je suis né' (p.133), François is hoping to do more than simply rediscover a lost parent – he is aiming, above all, to bolster his own identity.

When this vital point is placed alongside the others made apropos of *Vichy-Dancing*, the thematic accord between Sevran, Bonny and Gatard can no longer be in doubt. Nor can there be any doubt that, behind the works of these three authors, the driving force is the postwar legacy of the *années noires* and the troublesome imperfections it comprises, all of which would seem to substantiate earlier claims and establish the notion of collective orphanage as an immensely relevant one. However, any argument about the *mode rétro* as a whole based solely on the contribution made to it by a group of writers will, of necessity, be insufficient, no matter how representative the writers may be. For this reason, it will be useful, in conclusion, to switch genres within the trend and see how the makers of that seminal film, *Le Chagrin et la pitié*, compare to their author colleagues in this respect.

The results which such a comparison yields immediately stand out as being significant, particularly where André Harris is concerned, because 'Harris, lui, eut son père fusillé par les Allemands, car travaillant pour l'Intelligence Service, ce qui fait qu'il ne fut pas homologué par les organisations professionnelles et commémoratives de résistance car il travaillait pour l'étranger'.[18] Thus, like Jacques Bonny and Marie Gatard, Harris too lost his father in traumatic circumstances, once during the war, when the man was physically executed, and then again later, when the *résistancialistes* held sway and deliberately ignored his sacrifice. Against this sombre background, it comes as no surprise to learn that, over the years, the *cinéaste* son has unceasingly been drawn to the Occupation by forces beyond his control. 'S'il est vrai que je ne l'ai pas vécue', he notes of the period, 'je ne l'ai tout de même pas découverte en faisant *Le Chagrin et la Pitié*. Et je m'en suis toujours senti le produit.'[19] The closing remark says it all – like so many others of his age, Harris is obsessed by Vichy France first and foremost because his roots lie severed there.

The position of Marcel Ophüls is slightly different in detail, but undoubtedly similar in essence. Born in Frankfurt in 1927, Ophüls moved to Paris with his family in 1933 to avoid Hitler's purge of the Jews, only to have in turn to emigrate to the USA in 1941. By the time he returned to France ten years later, the damage had been done – a gap had developed in his knowledge of his adopted country, and this gap had quickly been filled by a myth, as André Harris was well aware: 'Il avait [. . .] de l'occupation en France une espèce de vision très déformée par la production "imaginée" par Hollywood.'[20] This distorted vision was to be the stock from which *Le Chagrin et la pitié* grew, so whatever else Ophüls may have been trying to achieve through his film, one of his prime aims in making it was, plainly, to unearth and appropriate his true historical inheritance. After all, did he not describe his crew as 'hommes qui sont eux-mêmes, sinon les témoins ou les acteurs, du moins les enfants et les héritiers de l'époque qu'il s'agissait de décrire', and then add, tellingly, 'Comme nous tous'?[21]

'Comme nous tous'. There could hardly be a better phrase with which to conclude than this one, whose resonance stretches out far beyond the confines of Ophüls's production team to encompass the 'innocent' generation *en masse*. For as has now been shown, whether the medium exploited be semi-biography, fiction or the cinema, the young contributors to the *mode rétro* form an unshakeably united front, with each and every one of them dogged by the same obsession as the makers of *Le Chagrin et la pitié*: the legacy bequeathed by the Occupation, the legacy which, ironically, deprives them of a legacy. In other words, to take up the term used earlier, France had, well and truly, produced a generation of orphans – a generation of orphans in search of a heritage.

This is all very well, but Ophüls and his colleagues were not the only ones to engage in retrospection after the death of de Gaulle; the war veterans and the over-forty-fives in general also had their stories to tell, and once the *résistancialiste* dam had been breached, come forward and tell them they did. But why? Why did this older section of French society suddenly renounce its twenty-five-year silence? Superficially, the answer to this question is simple, if twofold – in order to assist the *jeunes loups* on the one hand, or in order to disparage them on the other. By definition, though, superficial explanations do not get right down into the heart of the matter; so to find out what the basic stimuli *really* were here, it will be necessary to dig a bit deeper. And an ideal starting point for the new excavations is *Et pourquoi pas la patrie?* (1974), an essay by Henri Spade.

Spade (b. 1921) is an *ancien combattant* staunchly opposed to the post-1969 revisionism, and to describe his work as polemical is almost to make a grave understatement. Barely has the book begun than *Le Chagrin et la pitié* is unmercifully assailed, and when the net is then cast wider, to haul in other *bêtes noires*, the caustic tone loses none of its intensity:

> Des gosses de Vichy et de Singmaringen [*sic*] racontent leur enfance. C'est doux, l'enfance, c'est feutré, c'est tendre. On ne se préoccupe pas de ce que fait son père, on ne juge pas, on ne sait pas. On aime. On est enfant pour ça. Personne ne vous le reprochera jamais. Ce serait plutôt le

> contraire: il ferait horreur, le fils qui se voudrait le bourreau de son père condamné. Le petit Jardin de l'hôtel du Parc, la Marie du lac de Constance méritent le respect. Nous, nous méritions peut-être le silence. Celui qu'a su garder la fille de Pierre Laval, par exemple. (p.14)[22]

This reference to silence should not be mistaken and viewed as a subtle call to limit free speech, for Spade is proposing no such thing. What he is trying to suggest is that, rather than offer a partial account of the Occupation, an account which neglects the Resistance and gives pride of place to the *collabos*, his younger compatriots would do better to bite their lips and say nothing.[23] That they have not done this, of course, is precisely what drives him to speak out and confront them head on.

The way in which this head-on challenge is actually effected proves to be an all-too-familiar one, comprising two distinct lines of attack. The first of these involves swimming against the tide and recalling acts of wartime courage:

> Si la vérité était celle qu'on veut bien nous dépeindre, tous les Juifs, tous les francs-maçons, tous les communistes auraient été arrêtés, tous les réseaux démantelés, tous les résistants dénoncés, tous les aviateurs alliés abattus eussent été livrés à l'occupant. Il y a, heureusement, des survivants. Je ne sais pas s'ils sont plus ou moins nombreux que les disparus. Mais ils ne sont pas tous rescapés des camps de la mort. Ils sont aussi sortis des fermes, des maisons, des soupentes où on les cachait, ils ont pu déchirer les faux papiers que les mairies leur avaient délivrés. (p.23)[24]

Furthermore, while it may be true that such valiant deeds were anything but widespread, this is not accepted to be important because 'le nombre ne fait d'ailleurs rien à l'affaire: si 90% des Français avaient été les lâches qu'on nous peint aujourd'hui, les autres 10% auraient suffi à faire pencher le fléau de la balance du bon côté: la peur, la veulerie, le reniement ne pèsent pas autant qu'un moment de courage' (p.59).

Be that as it may, Spade is not content to let his extolment of the Resistance simply speak for itself, so the second phase of his tactical master plan requires the collaborators' influence to be minimised. And to begin at the beginning, this means pointing out that, contrary to the prevailing belief, when the Germans entered Paris they were met not by enthusiastic crowds of future traitors, but by closed shutters and deserted streets.[25] Similarly, in the longer term, the situation is deemed to have been that 'le pays, dans sa masse, ne collaborait pas avec l'occupant' (p.25), with even the most blatantly defeatist readily exempted from censure: 'Quant à ceux qui ont accepté et subi, je ne crois pas qu'on puisse leur reprocher de n'avoir pas su, pas osé, pas trouvé la bonne occasion de se défiler, pris qu'ils étaient dans le carcan de ce temps-là. La bonne coupure n'était pas facile à trouver. La Résistance ne recrutait pas au coin des rues' (p.27).[26]

The end result of all this is a depiction of the *années noires* which, like the two-pronged approach from which it arises, can hardly be said to be new. Consider, for instance, the passage in which Spade draws his argument together, and where the sense of *déjà vu* is at its most overpowering:

> Un assez petit nombre de résistants – c'est vrai pour le début – l'a emporté, dans le cœur de la nation, sur un plus petit nombre encore de collaborateurs; il a attiré à lui, petit à petit, l'immense majorité d'un peuple qui, fondamentalement, ne demandait qu'à faire ce choix, une fois perdues les illusions que la confiance dans le passé d'un homme avait pu entretenir un moment. (pp.106–7)[27]

There can be no mistaking such telltale signs: the small 'elite' of early Resistants at one extreme; the minute group of collaborators at the other; and the misled, but well-intentioned mass of French people in the middle – it could well be de Gaulle himself painting this picture. Indeed, the only thing missing here which is present in the Gaullist formulation of events is a mention of the general's own role in the proceedings, and this is supplied (albeit implicitly) when Spade highlights the political nature of the *remise en cause*:

> Ils sont clairs, les buts de cette campagne [. . .]. En particulier, il s'agit, on l'a vu, pour tenter d'abattre un homme puis d'effacer son souvenir, de nier son œuvre en essayant de démontrer non qu'il ne l'avait pas accomplie, mais qu'il n'avait même pas eu la possibilité de l'accomplir, puisque le peuple était au moins indifférent à ses efforts. (p.83)

The weight of the evidence thus appears to be damning, and deserving of just one verdict – Spade must be found guilty, guilty of resurrecting the Gaullist myth.

But is this really a fair judgement to make? Closer examination of *Et pourquoi pas la patrie?* shows that, to say the least, there are mitigating circumstances to ponder, for if Spade's prime concern were truly to mythify, he would surely have stuck to type and presented de Gaulle as exceptional, if not unique. Yet he does not do this, as the following extract indicates:

> Oui, nous voulions la restaurer, la patrie. Si ce n'avait été de Gaulle, un autre sans doute nous y aurait encouragés. Je ne sais pas si l'honneur a été en partie inventé. Je sais seulement que nous, nous étions entièrement là. Assez nombreux pour que la patrie renaquît [. . .]. Car, tout seul, de Gaulle n'aurait rien pu prouver. (pp.15–16)[28]

And as if this were not enough to confuse the issue, the waters soon become even muddier:

> Entendons-nous bien. Il ne s'agit pas de passer la réalité à la dorure. Des faiblesses, il y en a eu. Des lâches, des collabos, il y en a eu. Et quelques traîtres parmi nous aussi. Et du marché noir, et des trafiquants qui s'enrichissaient de la faim des pauvres. Et de la LVF, et des Waffen SS à écusson tricolore sur la manche [. . .].
>
> Mais je dis que ma patrie fut sauvée de ce déshonneur par tous ceux qui souffrirent et moururent [. . .].
>
> Les faibles, les lâches, les collabos, je crois que ces gens-là [the demythifiers] n'ont pas le droit d'en parler.
>
> Car c'est à nous qu'ils appartiennent. Nous les avons conquis avec le reste. Et recouverts de notre manteau. (pp.54–5)[29]

It is clear from this that, no matter how strong the initial urge to do so may be, Spade cannot be dismissed as an anachronism. He is not an out-and-out mythifier, attacking the *remise en cause* on purely negative grounds, that is to say in order to turn the clock back and regain the *résistancialiste* paradise lost in 1969. On the contrary, his motivation is totally positive: he is seeking to protect the two concepts which he holds most dear and which, for him, are irrevocably *real – la patrie* and the redemption of those who erred. This being the case, a whole new aspect of the *mode rétro* emerges from the shadows, for what Spade is actually saying is that, despite the fashionable talk of there being a Gaullist 'myth', de Gaulle was not the only *résistant* to have 'une certaine idée de la France'.

That there is perfectly just cause for this claim is further attested by the works of other war veterans, and in particular by two texts from the pen of André Chamson. The first of these is the opening section of *Suite guerrière* (1975): 'Écrit en 1940'. Composed (naturally) in 1940, and originally published as part of the *Suite* in 1944, this short, intimate piece contains such noteworthy comments as:

> Il suffit que chacun de nous, pour aussi humble qu'il soit, sauve la part de grandeur qu'il a reçue en partage pour que cette grandeur soit sauvée tout entière. [. . .] Personne ne peut aliéner ce que la France a gagné pour l'homme, pendant les siècles, mais un seul d'entre nous, s'il reste fidèle et fraternel, pourra le sauver pour tous les autres. (pp.29–30)

The second testimony is offered by *La Reconquête* (1975), which Chamson himself categorises as 'le livre d'une Reconquête qui ne fut pas seulement la reprise d'un territoire, mais la reconquête d'un héritage immatériel, notre véritable patrie, au-delà de ce que nous appelions naguère: la patrie' (p.9).

The concordance of these statements with those made by Spade is astonishing, and it is on this basis, and by making an informed generalisation, that the position of the *anciens combattants* can provisionally be defined. The soldiers of the 'Old Guard', it is now possible to affirm, fought in the knowledge that their very resistance guaranteed France's purity. What happened in their mother country was, in a sense, irrelevant to them, for their *patrie* was a mental concept, and they were convinced that, should their struggle prove successful, they would automatically redeem the crimes of their non-*résistant* compatriots.[30] This was what gave value to their commitment, and if they have since become so sensitive about the matter, it is because of the sheer magnitude of what is at stake for them – their prized and precious 'héritage immatériel', as Chamson calls it.

So, like the young generation, the war veterans are preoccupied with their heritage. But the potential loss of this legacy is not the only reason why they deprecate the *remise en cause*. There is an additional motive behind their riposte, a motive which pertains to their youth, and which is best exemplified – once again – by the author of *Et pourquoi pas la patrie?*: 'Ma jeunesse ne regarde que moi', he insists. 'A condition, encore une fois, qu'on la laisse tranquille. Ce que j'en ai prêté aux personnages de romans n'avaient rien de rose ni de claironnant, et j'en ressens encore l'amertume' (p.118).

Consultation of Spade's novels, *Le Temps des cerises* (1968) and *La Renaissante* (1969), confirms the assertions made in this statement, for the two works are strongly autobiographical in flavour and Bernier, the character with whom the novelist largely identifies, reflects all the bitterness and disappointment to which his creator refers. To give merely the most evident illustration of this, *Le Temps des cerises* finds him involved in 'la guerre avec ses parfums de jeunesse morte' (pp.267–8), which ensures that 'il n'allait rien retrouver de son adolescence' (p.271), and in *La Renaissante* the war may well have given way to the Liberation but not a lot has changed, either in respect of 'l'enfance, si lointaine et si proche' (p.25), or with regard to the battalion, which is still represented by 'ces quelques poignées d'hommes, vivants et disparus à jamais unis dans la même mort de leur jeunesse' (p.30). Such repetition cannot be intended to pass unnoticed, so the significance of these four phrases is manifest – Spade was, and remains, deeply and excruciatingly scarred by the untimely loss of his youth.

This state of affairs, as intimated above, is one which holds true for virtually every member of the war generation,[31] and the extreme touchiness about the *années noires* to which it gives rise is entirely understandable in the circumstances. At the best of times anybody's pre-adult days are sacred, but when the innocence which normally accompanies them is prematurely destroyed, as it was for those who lived through the Occupation, natural nostalgia is fuelled by a sense of what might have been and the feeling of sacredness is intensified. To some extent, therefore, Guy Dumur is correct to say of the *mode rétro* that 'au fond, les gens qui protestent sont ceux qui ne veulent pas qu'on transforme en passé historique l'époque de leur jeunesse'.[32]

Yet for all the decisiveness of such a pronouncement, this by no means represents the end of the matter. It is merely the juncture at which the wheel comes full circle, for in addition to being of interest in its own right, the trauma of a lost youth further accounts for the most basic of all the Old Guard's various *prises de position* – the refusal to make any comment whatsoever about life in wartime France. And, as always, it is in *Et pourquoi pas la patrie?* that the point is best articulated. Witness the passage below, which focuses on Bernard Blier and his son, Bertrand:

> On s'étonna de l'indifférence de cette jeunesse. On découvrit qu'elle n'était au courant de rien. Sans doute parce qu'on ne lui avait rien raconté. Ni à la maison, ni à l'école. Pas si vantards que ça, les anciens de 39–45. Pas tellement installés à Épinal, autour de leurs presses à images.
>
> Et surtout désireux d'oublier qu'ils avaient été malheureux, humiliés, affamés, effrayés souvent, pourchassés, arrêtés, déportés parfois. Vous en connaissez beaucoup, des gens qui passent leur journée à se repaître de leurs cauchemars de la nuit? Moi pas.

> Ce qu'il voulait, comme ses confrères, papa Blier, c'est que son fils ne connût jamais ce qu'il avait vécu. Il a cherché à faire à son Bertrand l'enfance ou la jeunesse heureuse qu'à lui on avait volée. (p.12)

With this key piece of the jigsaw firmly fixed into place, the overall, composite picture begins to take on a more definite shape. Having fought the Germans to protect and secure their heritage, the *anciens combattants*, or at least a sizeable proportion of them, rapidly came to believe that victory had legitimised their vision of the Occupation and that, consequently, no one was better qualified to talk about the period than they were. Indeed, if they should make up their minds to say nothing on the subject, then nobody, they were convinced, would have the right to stand up and speak out for them. And hold their tongues was precisely what they did, never thinking for one moment that this would have an adverse effect on their sons and daughters. Quite the opposite in fact. Because they had had to sacrifice their own youth to The Cause, they were determined that their children should have the carefree adolescence of which they themselves had been deprived, and the best way to achieve this, they decided, was not to mention the horror-packed *années noires* at all.[33]

As has already been seen, this was their great mistake, for the silence to which they were committed served not to cocoon the young generation, as intended, but rather to traumatise it by cutting it off from its roots. Furthermore, when the 'orphans' they had thus produced then embarked on a *remise en cause*, they suddenly found that their own inheritance had come under threat and needed to be defended as a result. In other words, what they had created through their deliberate muteness was, ironically, not so much a *conflit des générations* as a *conflit des héritages*, a *conflit des héritages* in which the assertion of their particular heritage simultaneously negated that of their offspring and vice versa. And it was this selfsame, insoluble conflict which, for well over a decade, was to nourish the *mode rétro* and drive it relentlessly onwards.

However, as noted at the outset, not every old campaigner was inclined to condemn Ophüls and his colleagues. On the contrary, many war veterans shared the *jeunes loups*' belief that not enough had been said about the Occupation, and so they began to take up their pens and ensure that – at long last – the legacy they held was made widely available. Of course, when Spade and the Old Guard defended their past in public, they too were endeavouring to make a bequest.[34] But the value of this bequest was diminished by its overt resemblance to the Gaullist myth – it was a bequest made, almost uniquely, to satisfy the parents. This was certainly not the case for those writers mentioned above, for their prime concern was the well-being of their children, as Roger Ikor's *Pour une fois, écoute mon enfant . . .* (1975) indicates:

> Maintenant, ma génération est en train de pénétrer doucement dans la retraite, quand ce n'est pas dans la mort. Et elle s'aperçoit que rien n'a été exprimé de ce qui fait sa substance.
>
> Cela signifie qu'il me faut parler, coûte que coûte, avant qu'il soit trop tard. Non pas seulement parce que chaque génération humaine a le droit, et le devoir, de lancer au passage son message propre, mais parce que, si elle ne le fait pas, une déchirure s'ouvre dans le tissu de l'humanité, et c'est vous, vous la génération d'après, qui en souffrez. J'ose affirmer que d'une certaine manière le présent désarroi des esprits est dû à l'étouffement dont notre génération a été victime. Effet au moins indirect, mais quelquefois en ligne toute droite. (p.10)[35]

Unlike Spade, then, Ikor shows great concern about the predicament of his successors, and this new sense of *rapprochement* between the two generations provides a fitting note on which to conclude the present section because, as may be apparent by this stage, no matter how much the *jeunes loups* and the *anciens combattants* disagree about the need for demythification, on the purely fundamental level they are irrevocably united – united by their common obsession with a heritage.

The notion of inheritance is thus an essential one as far as the *mode rétro* is concerned, for not only does it account for the young orphans' interest in the *années noires* (they set off to discover the legacy they lack), it also explains why their elders join with them in retrospection (either to reassert the 'héritage immatériel' they fought for during the Occupation, or to make public the bequest they had for so long kept private). But this is by no means the full extent of the concept's importance; there are other areas in which its presence can be detected as well, areas which it will now be useful to elaborate.

One such is the widespread belief, held by 'innocent' demythifiers and experienced war veterans alike, that the past can supply insights into the present and the future. This conviction has already been seen to underpin Ikor's work, and it is no coincidence either that Chamson confessed in *La Reconquête*: 'Comme beaucoup, j'ai voulu prévoir l'avenir en me retournant vers le passé' (p.206). As with most aspects of the post-1969 trend, though, it is the younger generation, rather than the old campaigners, who represent the most fascinating subjects to study, for the very good reason that, being less sensitive about Vichy France than their parents are, they are able to draw negative parallels across the decades, as Pierre Billard points out:

> Ces témoins-là croient reconnaître dans la France des années soixante-dix certains stigmates des années quarante: l'asservissement aux préoccupations matérielles (hier déclenché par l'extrême pénurie, aujourd'hui par une relative abondance), la domination des nouveaux riches (les B.O.F. de jadis devenus les promoteurs de maintenant), le refus de s'intéresser aux conflits de l'époque, la peur de l'engagement.[36]

What is more, again because of their total detachment from the early 1940s, they can go on to exploit these parallels and use a wartime décor to examine problems of their own day.

The best illustration of this is, arguably, their handling of the burning issue of Fascism, with Louis Malle's *Lacombe Lucien* offering a perfect case in point. Originally to be entitled *Le Milicien*, this film was inspired by events in modern-day Mexico, where the government confronted protesting students with a sort of Militia made up of poor boys recruited from the slums. Fascinated by such a phenomenon, yet unable – obviously – to gain approval for on-site filming from the Mexican authorities, Malle was forced to depart from his initial plan, switching both geographical and historical settings, but losing none of his immediacy in the process: 'Avec son amoralité candide et son appétit de vivre en ignorant toute idéologie, le Lacombe Lucien de 1944 est un jeune homme d'aujourd'hui', he took pains to stress in an interview.[37] And to make sure that this fact was not lost on his audience, an audience probably unaware of the film's origins and background, a thought-provoking caption was used to inform them that 'ceux qui ne se souviennent pas du passé sont condamnés à le revivre'.

Interestingly enough, exactly the same phrase could also be applied to Michel Rachline's *Le Bonheur nazi* (1972), and with even more pertinence if anything, for the didactic, anti-Fascist slant here is far more pronounced than it was in *Lacombe Lucien*, as the author's *avertissement* testifies: 'Je voudrais crier que les séductions du fascisme sont réelles; attention! Derrière le masque, le vrai visage attend sa proie' (p.13).[38] The hidden truth to which Rachline refers is a simple one – 'le fascisme, c'est la mort' (p.343) – but the method he adopts to convey this is anything but straightforward, for his narrator, Frédéric Marelle, is a controversial, unrepentant Nazi whose outpourings constitute an apologia for National Socialism.[39] 'Hitler a gagné la guerre', he proudly asserts (p.166), amidst gruesome descriptions of how, thirty-odd years ago he experimented on prisoners in the death camps, 'le nazisme a gagné puisque partout encore on tue, on égorge, on arrête, on détient' (p.275).[40] Claims such as these can hardly be said to be reassuring, let alone elevating, but then again they are not meant to be. They are, primarily, designed to enlighten, and one of the first to acknowledge this is Marelle himself when, at his unsettling best, he observes: 'c'est votre avenir que vous allez découvrir dans mon passé' (p.24). This revelation could not be more explicit, and its significance is clear – like Malle and, indeed, others too numerous to count, Rachline believes that the lessons of the war remain vitally relevant today.[41]

So, as *Lacombe Lucien* and *Le Bonheur nazi* attest, the young dissidents of the *mode rétro* regularly seek guidelines for the present in the troubled and insalubrious waters of the past. But why? Why should they choose, or need, to do this? Considering what was said earlier in the chapter, one possible answer to this question is not difficult to unearth – the guidelines they crave are simply part of the wider inheritance they are trying to obtain for themselves. Yet to imply that their motives are exclusively selfish would be both erroneous and unfair, for their work is evidently infused with a second emotional charge, a charge embodied by Rachline's dedication of his novel to his children – the determination to lay down modes of action for those who follow. In other words, ironic as it may seem, and even though they are diametrically at odds as far as their own, individual heritages are concerned, the *jeunes loups* and the *anciens combattants* can once again be judged to form an unholy – and no doubt unwitting – alliance, an alliance born of their common drive to leave the next generation a fitting legacy.

It is not, however, merely as a source of instructive lessons that the *années noires* have an avowed relevance in modern-day France. The Occupation was a time of such horror and atrocity that, for many French people, the nightmare lingers on, colouring their every thought and action. Not surprisingly, perhaps, these poor unfortunates have a different reason for participating in the *mode rétro* – the need to purge themselves of the ghosts which haunt them.

This is especially true of those who experienced the war at first hand, and who had never previously been able to publicise their feelings. On the side of the *collabos*, Christian de la Mazière is typical of many, saying nothing for years on end and then all of a sudden appearing in *Le Chagrin et la pitié* and penning his memoirs, *Le Rêveur casqué*. 'Je laissais s'éloigner ma jeunesse, avec les imaginations généreuses qui l'avaient soulevée', he writes, looking back over his life, 'jusqu'à ce film, un jour, et à ce livre que voici, où je ne la ressuscite que pour, définitivement, la rendre au passé' (p.15). Across the old political divide, the picture is scarcely any different. Alphonse Boudard describes his novel, *Le Corbillard de Jules* as 'une manière d'accommoder les restes de la guerre trente ans après' (*CJ*, p.12); the narrator of André Pierrard's *On l'appelait Tamerlan* spotlights, in his own words, 'le moment le plus pénible de cette nuit dont je me délivre' (p.79); and countless other ex-*résistant* authors present similar admissions of self-purging.

But this is not to say that the war veterans are alone in trying to exorcise the *années noires*. Members of the young generation also have their crosses to bear, and, like their elders, they too seek to lighten their load by putting pen to paper.

To the forefront in this respect are the sons and daughters of infamous collaborators, those who, from their earliest days, have been stigmatised through no fault of their own. Jacques Bonny – once again – exemplifies the stance of this group of writers, confessing in *Mon père, l'inspecteur Bonny*: 'Je m'appelle Bonny. Il y a près de trente ans que ces deux syllabes hantent ma vie, jour et nuit' (p.15), and then divulging shortly afterwards that, in reality, his book is 'une autre forme d'expiation' (p.18).

No less in need of *expiation*, though for slightly different reasons, are a number of other 'innocent' authors who, while not having had the sins of their (collaborationist) fathers visited upon them, nevertheless still feel the weight of the war years pressing down on their shoulders. The key figure among this collection of novelists (for novelists is what they are, seeking therapy in fiction rather than in the semi-biographical searches of Bonny et al.) is Patrick Modiano, who will be studied in detail in Part II. For present purposes, however, a sufficient flavour of the procedure involved can be gained by consulting *Nice, pour mémoire* (1980), the first novel of Dominique Garnier (b. 1954).[42]

Garnier's text focuses on the character of Noémi Fogelman, or to be more specific, on her extraordinary holiday in Nice, which provides her with anything but a sense of relaxation. The reason for this is simple. During the *années noires*, her mother, Sarah, had waited for her own mother to join her in the resort, but sadly she had never turned up, having been deported before she could flee the occupied zone. This endless wait and the debilitating anxiety which accompanied it have tormented Sarah ever since and, amazingly, been passed on to her daughter, with the result that Noémi has become 'ce fruit douteux, déjà pourri par la peur' (p.95). Such a transmission of anguish from parent to child is, in itself, highly peculiar, but not half as peculiar as the most important feature of the book: after Noémi has seen the flat in which her mother stayed during the war, she begins to recall and relive the past as if it were she, and not Sarah, who had been abandoned in Nice all those years ago. 'Depuis un mois je parcours la ville', she discloses. 'Les rues me parlent. Les maisons, la mer, le soleil, les odeurs, [. . .] tout me rappelle que quelque chose s'est passé. Mais quoi? Moi, Noémi Fogelman, sans souvenirs, je crois, je ne suis pas. Ce sont . . . [. . .] Ce sont les souvenirs d'une autre' (pp.91–2). Obviously, as long as the city can exert its influence upon her in this way, constantly imposing its presence and triggering her 'memories' uncontrollably, she will find it impossible to restore peace to her mind and escape her mental entrapment. Luckily though, from her point of view, help is near at hand, for throughout the novel the slipping of the temporal plane has been reflected by geographical slippage in the form of earth tremors, and by the time the closing pages arrive an all-consuming and, for her, liberating earthquake seems to be on the point of resolving matters:

> Depuis la veille, le calme de la ville presque entièrement désertée avait pris un caractère sacré. La mort n'était plus loin. Mort joyeuse, spectaculaire, dont les effets attendus et tant décrits ne cesseraient cependant pas de surprendre. Engloutissement d'un espace et d'un temps usés, d'où ne renaîtrait plus aucune parole. (p.134)

This purifying earthquake (which will no doubt commence as soon as the novel has ended, the radio time checks in the text acting as a form of countdown) may already have convinced some that, at least in part, Garnier is using her fiction to wipe her own, personal slate clean. But that this is indeed the case is much better demonstrated by a critic who has all the relevant background information at his fingertips:

> Que cherche Noémi? De quels détails de sa grand-mère maternelle, immigrée arrivée à Paris en 1936, se souvient la jeune romancière Dominique Garnier? L'errance dans Nice ne lui apprendra rien, bien sûr. Mais il lui fallait fixer cette errance, la marquer de quelques petites pierres sur une tombe juive absente. Comme ça, pour rien, pour mémoire. Car

> cette mort juive là [*sic*], sa douloureuse caractéristique est d'être elle-même encore errante, encore vouée au dehors, expulsée de la terre même. [. . .].
>
> Dominique Garnier, née de mère juive, n'en finit pas d'être à l'écoute de ce côté-là de sa mémoire. L'écoute attentive d'un silence.[43]

With these contextual details now firmly established, the exorcistic nature of *Nice, pour mémoire* can no longer be called into question. But before moving on from Garnier's novel, there is another aspect of the text which it will be extremely useful to dwell upon: the wider ramifications of the theme of memory.

As has been noted, Noémi's problem derives from her bizarre possession of her mother's powers of recall, and this transference of the recollective faculty can, to a large extent, be seen to typify the stance of the young generation as a whole. There are two main reasons for this, the first of which is the more obvious: whenever the 'innocent' writers re-create or relive the Occupation, they too, like Noémi, do so by assimilating the memories of their elders, their sole source of information. This is, of course, why virtually everything the *jeunes loups* say has already been said somewhere else before (a fact which in turn illustrates that a certain inheritance is being taken up), and why Henri Spade, the representative of the Old Guard *par excellence*, quickly found himself moved to complain: 'Aimer ou non de Gaulle, cela regarde qui aime et qui n'aime pas. Mais je ne veux pas que chacun, pour sa bataille, vienne chercher des pierres dans mon jardin. Mes pierres sont à moi: ce sont mes souvenirs.'[44] But extrapolating to show that the *mode rétro* centres on just one set of recollections (a set of recollections which, coveted by young and old alike, binds the two generations together while at the same time engendering their discord) accounts for only part of the interest inherent in Garnier's use of memory. Also worthy of elaboration is the whole process whereby Sarah's past is 'implanted' into Noémi.

To bring out the full significance of this phenomenon, it will be necessary – briefly – to recall the conditions under which *Nice, pour mémoire* was produced. These can be summarised as follows: absence and silence created a break in the author's family chain, ensured that her heritage was problematically incomplete, and thereby left her looking for a way to combat the void. Fiction writing, we now know, was to provide her with the answer to her predicament, but only if she adopted a specific type of formal approach: her novel must allow her to re-enact the role played previously by her mother. It is in this context, then, that the theme of remembrance emerges in all its glory, for what Garnier ultimately achieves by the usurping of her parent's memories is the penning of a powerfully therapeutic, personal *myth*. And as mentioned above, this too is typical of many other young authors of her generation.

Pascal Sevran provides an excellent demonstration of the point, for in each of his first three novels (referred to earlier), an orphaned narrator can also be found reliving the past vicariously. 'Que ne suis-je né plus tôt? Ma jeunesse était en décalage; la mémoire des autres m'aidait un peu à la supporter', Laurent remarks in *Un garçon de France* (p. 133), a statement which could be used to sum up any of the three works in the series. Yet, if anything, an even better indication of the author's concern is given in the epigraphs he decides to employ. 'Ma vie ne ressemble pas à ma vie,' he lets Emmanuel Berl tell us in *Vichy-Dancing*. 'Elle ne lui a jamais ressemblé. Mais ce décalage entre moi et moi, je le supportais assez bien, je le supporte de plus en plus mal.' In the previous novel, the words of Raymond Radiguet were rather more explicit: 'C'est un travers trop humain de ne croire qu'à la sincérité de celui qui s'accuse, or, le roman exigeant un relief qui se trouve rarement dans la vie, il est naturel que ce soit justement une fausse autobiographie qui semble la plus vraie.' It would therefore seem that what Sevran is doing in his fiction is appropriating other people's memories in order to give himself, to use the revealing title of his first work, a 'passé supplémentaire', a 'passé supplémentaire' which will be more emotionally appealing to him than the life he has actually lived.[45] And this procedure, this fabrication of 'une fausse autobiographie', is most manifestly mythopoeic.

A similar analysis can be made with respect to authors like Jacques Bonny and Marie Gatard. Admittedly, these orphan-writers do not take their predecessors' recollections to be their own, but they still depend entirely on the testimonies of their elders to secure their literary objectives, cobbling together their fathers' lives from paternal documents, written histories, hearsay, anecdotes and whatever other records happen to be available. Evidently, such piecemeal, often unreliable source material can but produce a work which is less than objective, and Gatard herself acknowledges this very early on in *La Guerre, mon père*:

> Il ne s'agit pas de souvenirs rigoureusement calqués sur une réalité objective, ni même subjective – les souvenirs à l'état brut n'existent pas – mais de ce qui en tient lieu dans les biographies mêmes les plus sincères, c'est-à-dire d'images, de paroles, de sentiments, d'un univers sans cesse remaniés par les stratifications ultérieures. (p. 15)

This focus on an 'histoire qui n'est pas dans l'Histoire' (p.18) has a consequence which it is impossible now not to recognise: the orphan's search must, once again, ultimately take the form of a personal myth.[46]

Comparing this conclusion to those reached above in respect of Sevran's and Garnier's works, the extent of the *jeunes loups'* predicament quickly becomes apparent. Cut off from their roots by the silence of their parents, these 'innocents' are so disturbed by the legacy they have received that, virtually *en masse*, they feel obliged to try and secure alternative, more acceptable heritages for themselves. Yet they are not content simply to *seek out* these better inheritances, as may have been implied earlier in the chapter – they actually endeavour to *concoct* them by a process of personal mythification. This, then, is why, when viewed from the outside, the position of the *jeunes loups* is so intensely and continuously fascinating. And this is of course also why, to a large degree, the *mode rétro* can be seen to embody a *countermyth*.

So far, the spotlight has been turned almost entirely on the question of heritage, and rightly so, for this notion is without doubt the most fundamental, underlying cause of retrospection in post-Gaullist France. Yet it is by no means the only driving force visible behind the trend. Other factors too are involved, and although their influence may be relatively minor in comparison, it will still be of interest to record their presence here.

François Nourissier's article, 'Le Cadavre dans le placard', is an ideal text with which to begin in this respect, because it offers no fewer than three further explanations of the movement towards demythification. The first of these has to do with the postwar military position, crystallised in the fact that 'les échecs successifs essuyés par l'armée française, au Vietnam, en Algérie, ont détruit le tabou militaire. Il est désormais permis d'évoquer l'écroulement de 1940 sans que la mythologie guerrière culpabilise le raisonnement' (p.87). This initial observation is then quickly followed by a second, which relates, for the most part, to more recent wars, wars which did not even directly concern the French. 'On peut penser', the author continues, 'que le mouvement philosémite, si sensible depuis le rapatriement des Français du Maghreb, les guerres des Six Jours et du Kippour – amitié nourrie malencontreusement, peut-être, de racisme anti-arabe – on peut penser que ce mouvement aide et pousse à dire la vérité sur les persécutions anti-juives' (p.87). Finally, the third extra determinant of the *remise en cause*, it is suggested, is the variable amount of time writers need to digest the effects of a political crisis. In the case of the *années noires*, Nourissier believes, a period of almost thirty years was the lapse which was required.[47]

It is one thing, though, to seize on these three points as being relevant, and quite another to decipher what the exact level of their relevance is. So instead of saying any more on the matter, it will perhaps be easier to move on and identify a number of additional forces at work behind the scenes, forces which, without now indicating why the *mode rétro* actually came about, nevertheless ensured that, once it was established, it remained in the public eye for well over a decade, and did not simply fizzle out after six months or a year.

The vital point here is, unquestionably, the controversial nature of the phenomenon itself, for this meant that the trend rapidly took on a self-generating character, with almost every contribution immediately provoking a riposte, an endorsement, a clarification, or some other similar sort of reaction. This 'knock-on' effect has already been seen to underpin Henri Spade's *Et pourquoi pas la patrie?*, but a far better demonstration of the procedure can be found in the works of Philippe Ganier-Raymond.[48]

Born in 1934, and a man with more than one string to his literary bow, Ganier-Raymond came to the fore in France as one of the new, young generation of historians, who, like their novel-writing counterparts, were determined not to view the Occupation through rose-tinted spectacles.[49] *Une certaine France: l'antisémitisme, 1940–44* (1975), was the text which earned him his reputation, and from very early on in this anthology-cum-survey his stance as an author is clear: his objective is to attack the right. But this does not mean that he can be ranked alongside other left-wingers like Marcel Ophüls or André Harris. On the contrary, he takes great pains to decry the *mode rétro* and all it stands for, because, in his eyes, the sole beneficiaries of the trend are his hated political opponents. The analysis which leads him to this conclusion is, in essence, an uncomplicated one. Looking back to the Collaboration and its postwar consequences, he recognises that

> il fallait que la droite s'en sorte. A la longue l'héroïsme emprunté ou bien la minimisation de la résistance ne suffisait pas. C'était bien simple: il fallait que l'opinion de droite redevînt ce qu'elle était avant la guerre. Une simple opinion, justement. Aussi respectable a priori que la croyance dans le culte adventiste, ou le positivisme.[. . .] La mode, parce qu'elle est la mode, ne peut être boueuse. C'était gagné. Le fascisme, le racisme reprenaient droit de cité par les chemins de la nostalgie! (pp.17–18)

His reason for delving into anti-Semitism, then, is to try to counteract this *mode*, to illustrate – like Henri Spade before him – that the works of Ophüls, Malle and their colleagues are merely the thin end of a very menacing wedge. 'Je suis [. . .] persuadé', he remarks, 'qu'au fil des années, ces livres, ces films, si confortables pour les âmes, prendront valeur de documents irréfutables. Si seulement ce livre-ci pouvait servir de postface utile à cette littérature . . .' (p.19).

As a declaration of intent, this statement could scarcely be any more conclusive. But in spite of this, there is, in the present context, something else which needs to be said about *Une certaine France* – quite apart from its stated aim of countering other works, it sent out shock waves of its own which, in turn, caused a reaction further on down the line. The pages dealing with Céline had to be cut, and, to say the least, the reference to 'les communistes, les vrais résistants' (p.15) did not exactly make Gaullists want to start dancing in the aisles. Furthermore, while it was all very well to denounce *Le Chagrin et la pitié* for its 'objectivité bien dirigée' (p.18),[50] Ganier-Raymond's political *engagement* left him wide open to identical accusations.

The inherent provocativeness of this *prise de position* can, arguably, be even better demonstrated by turning to another of the author's controversial projects: the interview he conducted with an unrepentant Darquier de Pellepoix, the former head of Vichy's Commissariat aux Questions Juives.[51] Using, ironically, precisely the same technique as his *bête noire*, Ophüls, that is to say allowing the interviewee to talk and then juxtaposing his words with historical documents which contradict them, Ganier-Raymond once more gives would-be detractors plenty of ammunition with which to attack him – partly, again, because his outlook as interviewer and journalist is anything but neutral, but mainly because the mere publication of Darquier's views can, at the end of the day, patently be interpreted as a victory for the right. Many of his readers were indeed quick to recognise this: condemnation followed condemnation, cries of pain followed cries of pain, and the whole debate about the Occupation was regenerated anew.[52]

With time, of course, this permanent sparking of discussion created an atmosphere which was much more liberal, much more conducive to a re-evaluation of the *années noires*, and this too helped the *mode rétro* to prosper. Louis Malle, for one, certainly took this factor into account before he made *Lacombe Lucien*, even though, as things transpired, he sadly misread the situation. 'I wouldn't have dared to make the film 10 years ago', he confessed, 'because I would not then have been capable of walking on this sort of tightrope. And in a sense I was astonished at the fuss everybody made because the Ophüls film, *Le Chagrin et la Pitié*, had prepared the ground by forcing Frenchmen to question themselves on this matter.'[53] A year later, Alphonse Boudard was to couch the same concern in far more explicit language. Writing the *avertissement* to *Bleubite*, which was just his earlier novel, *Les Matadors*, republished under a different title, he disclosed:

> En 1966, on les a trouvés, mes *Matadors*, excessifs . . . que mon personnage de capitaine FFI ancien de la Gestapo était assez peu vraisemblable . . . qu'il outrageait une Cause sacrée.
>
> Pourtant, là encore, je m'aperçois que le temps a travaillé pour moi. Peu à peu des choses se dévoilent, des livres se publient, quelques témoins s'approchent de la barre. (*B*, p.13)

The moment certainly was more propitious, and perhaps not only because the old taboos had started to crumble away. The world oil crisis had just begun to bite by this time, and the harsh economic climate which it fostered marked the final termination of *les trente glorieuses*, the period of non-stop growth which de Gaulle had ushered in after the Liberation, and the best years of which he had then presided over as Head of the Fifth Republic. In other words, by 1975, developments in the economic domain were sending out exactly the same message to the nation as those in the political domain: the Gaullist era had, at long last, most definitely come to an end.

Throughout this chapter a whole host of factors have been seen to have helped produce the *mode rétro* in France. Some of them, like the amount of time taken for personal experience to be translated into novel form, the desire to fill a perceived literary void, the peaking of pro-Jewish feelings, and the succession of postwar military defeats, were clearly only relatively minor as far as the impact they had was concerned. Others, such as the belief that the past holds valuable lessons for the present, the intention to paint a truer picture of events, the overpowering need for exorcism, the existence of a freer atmosphere, and the 'knock-on' or chain-reaction effect, were unquestionably much more instrumental and resonant, yet without being in any way *fundamental*, for that honour belonged to the fact that, in François Nourissier's phraseology, 'Le Père est mort, on fait l'inventaire de l'héritage'.[54] De Gaulle's death most certainly was a key development, and so too was the notion of inheritance, although it should perhaps be re-emphasised here that the general was a paternal figure solely for the members of his own generation. For younger French people, he was simply the man who had falsified the national heritage – the very opposite of a benign father who, without forethought or calculation, passes on the family heirlooms so as to preserve his children's roots. In short, he was a creator of orphans.[55] And once he had departed, it was these selfsame orphans who, setting off to secure a more acceptable bequest for themselves, provided the stimulus which would rapidly make retrospection the order of the day.

But just how unique is this cultural orphanage? And exactly how significant are the *années noires* to its occurrence? To answer these questions it will be necessary now to introduce a sense of perspective, and this will be done in two stages. Firstly, by seeing how the theme of parentlessness is depicted in evocations of the 'dark years' published between 1945 and 1969. And secondly, by going back even further and seeking the same leitmotif in works written before 1940. In this way, it should become clear whether the recent trend is merely the latest manifestation of a perennial concern, whether it is a long-standing consequence of the Occupation, or whether it is something totally different, something never really seen before – a seed sown in the early 1940s, but not having borne its bitter fruit until thirty-odd years later.

To open stage one of this contextualisation, there is no better author to consider than Corinne Luchaire, for like Jacques Bonny and his colleagues, she too is a war orphan (her father Jean having been executed for his journalistic collaboration with the Germans), and she too responds to her bereavement by writing a book. What is more, the work in question, her memoirs, *Ma drôle de vie* (1949), can in many ways be judged to have set the pattern for the 1970s texts, since a large number of the points it makes echo out articulately across the decades. By far the most striking of these is the portrait of the father-figure, who is deemed to have been badly mistreated by the postwar myth-makers: 'Qui connaissait Jean Luchaire?' Corinne asks rhetorically, pre-empting Jacques Bonny by a good twenty-five years, 'On ne connaissait que sa légende savamment orchestrée' (p.238). And just as such mythification will touch a chord in later writers, so does the reaction to it have a foreshadowing effect. This is because the orphaned daughter is determined to 'remettre les choses au point', and in order to do so sets herself a target which is not all that unfamiliar: 'Dire des choses qu'un autre mieux que moi et plus habile que moi aurait sans doute, s'il était demeuré vivant, quand les passions se seraient calmées, écrit un jour à ma place' (p.9). The two-pronged offensive which results (rehabilitation of the *collabos*, criticism of the Resistance) is one which has been seen countless times before, and this, when added to the avowed doubling up of parent and child, can mean but one thing: *Ma drôle de vie*, like so many of its successors, is a work of countermythification.

Yet if Corinne Luchaire can be said, at least in those respects outlined above, to have beaten many young Turks of the *mode rétro* off the mark, then so can a number of postwar fiction writers be observed to join her.

Michel del Castillo is one such additional *avant-coureur*, for the eponymous hero of his novel *Tanguy* (1957) is, yet again, an orphan, though not because his parents are dead, rather because, as his adventures begin, they are separated and the family unit has irrevocably broken down. 'S'il souffrait', we are told, 'c'était justement de ne pas être comme les autres garçons; de ne pas avoir comme eux un foyer avec un père et une mère qui s'entendent, ou feignent de s'entendre' (p.23). And as if this were not bad enough, once the Second World War commences his position becomes even more unbearable: he is arrested before he can cross the border into Spain, and is thereby prevented from joining his mother, who, up until then, had provided him with at least a modicum of the normal parental presence. The consequence of this enforced isolation is not long in coming. The only constants in his life become his rootlessness (emphasised by his perpetual movement from one camp or institution to another) and his hope of eventually overcoming his sorry plight, as his conversation with Père Pardo illustrates:

> 'C'est dur de se passer du mythe des parents, lui dit un jour le Père, car c'est l'illusion la plus fortement ancrée dans le cœur des enfants. Ici, vois-tu, il m'arrive souvent de voir des enfants abandonnés par leur mère ou dédaignés par leur père, s'accrocher avec un désespoir farouche à ce mythe du père et surtout de la mère.'
>
> 'Oui. Mais à quoi d'autre peut s'accrocher un enfant?'
>
> 'A très peu de chose, bien sûr.' (p.205)

In an attempt to improve this situation, Tanguy embarks on a search for his father, his ultimate goal being, predictably, 'de retrouver une identité' (p.211). But he is not immediately successful. It is only after many years of trying that he actually meets the man, and then he quickly rejects him for being too snobbish.

Furthermore, when he meets up with his mother again more than a decade after their traumatic separation, he finds that he cannot tolerate her simplified, communistic view of the world either. The effect of these two developments on him is decisive: he finally has to accept that his childhood is over.

Although del Castillo's novel would, by itself, appear to show that the key theme of orphanage surfaced long before the *mode rétro* came about, the definitive edition of Romain Gary's *Éducation européenne* (1961) brings further grist to the demonstrative mill. This is because its central character is the parentless Janek, a young boy who, still hoping to find his missing father, joins the Resistance and quickly convinces himself that 'le mystérieux partisan Nadejda ne devait être autre que son père' (p.42). Unfortunately for him, this is not the case, and he is forced to recognise his mistake when his comrades divulge a long-held secret to him:

> Pour nous redonner du courage et pour désorienter l'ennemi, nous avons inventé le Partisan Nadejda – un chef immortel, invincible, qu'aucune main ennemie ne pouvait saisir et que rien ne pouvait arrêter. C'était un mythe que nous inventions ainsi, comme on chante dans la nuit pour se donner du courage, mais le jour vint rapidement où il acquit soudain une existence réelle et physique, et où il devint réellement présent parmi nous. (p.302)

After hearing these words, Janek comes to realise that his childhood has ended, and that, henceforth, despite his tender years, he will have to face the world as 'un homme instruit' (p.306).

Placing this summary of *Éducation européenne* alongside those made above of *Tanguy* and *Ma drôle de vie*, the evidence of the three works combined elicits just one possible conclusion: the themes of orphanage, the search for a father and the 'adoption' of surrogate families were already visible in texts published between 1945 and 1969.[56] So, does this mean that the *mode rétro* is not particularly significant? Not at all. In spite of the undeniable thematic concord across the decades, there are many areas in which fundamental differences can be noted.

Take Corinne Luchaire's memoirs for instance. What is different here, when the practice of Bonny and his *confrères* is borne in mind, is the notable lack of a *quest*, for the author's subject matter is not her absent father's life, but rather, as her title immediately suggests, her own. And there is a very good reason for this – Corinne has no need to go off in search of Jean because, writing at the age of twenty-seven, just a few years after his execution, she obviously got to know him extremely well before he died. Moreover, having been an adult during the Occupation and the *épuration*, she was able to see that the mythifiers had had a hand in proceedings and had 'stolen' him from her as well. This was far from being the case for her young successors, who suffered both from a dearth of paternal contact and from being caught up in a myth without actually realising it.[57]

Tanguy and *Éducation européenne* can similarly be seen to come from a slightly different mould to the post-1969 texts, for their focal points are greatly extended in comparison. Del Castillo's story stretches from the 1930s to the 1950s and meanders through France, Germany and Spain, while Gary's, although more localised, comes no closer to the French borders than eastern Europe. In other words, attention is being centred on the Second World War in general and not on the Occupation of France in particular. And this is not the only difference visible in the two novels. The theme of a premature loss of youth, it can be argued, has more in common with Henri Spade's generation than with those whose 'regard innocent' survived the war intact, so the link with the later orphan-writers can be said to break down here as well.

On the basis of these all-too-brief analyses, the uniqueness of the *mode rétro* in the postwar context can now confidently be asserted, for what characterises the trend, it may be recalled, is the association of parental absence and the quest for a legacy with the problematic historical setting of the *années noires*, and this is a conjunction which, as has just been shown, does not occur all that frequently in texts published prior to 1970. The implication is, therefore, that there was indeed something peculiar to the 'dark years', something which could produce a generation of orphans three decades on. But what? To try and answer this question, it will prove useful to go back to the period 1918–39, for this will allow the theme of rootlessness to be examined independently of Vichy France's influence.

Turning, then, to the *entre-deux-guerres*, there are two writers who instantly spring to mind as being well worthy of consideration: Maurice Sachs and Drieu la Rochelle, both of whom inspired numerous young novelists of the *remise en cause*.

Of the two, Sachs is perhaps the more interesting, as his autobiographical *Le Sabbat* (1946) suggests. Written in 1939, but not published until after the war, this work quickly establishes its author as yet another orphan who has been driven to take up the pen. 'Mon père disparut de ma vie en n'y laissant aucune trace. Je ne l'ai jamais revu', he confesses (p.26), adding shortly afterwards that his part-Jewish extraction served to compound this painful rootlessness: 'Je ne me croyais même pas le droit de *lever la tête* avec *le peuple d'Israël*, et je savais que je n'étais même pas fidèlement de ce peuple-là. Je n'étais de nulle part' (p.41). This predicament is a familiar one, and so too is the reaction it provokes. Jacques Bizet is admitted to be 'un semblant de père' (p.66), while the delle Donnes are clothed in the mantle of a surrogate family (p.114). And that is not all. Precisely because Sachs has no moral guidelines of his own, he seeks to provide 'un petit mémoire moral' (p.107) to help others. 'Je ne veux essayer d'analyser ici mes sentiments particuliers', he remarks, 'que parce que quelques jeunes gens éprouvent des difficultés semblables, ont du mal à s'en débrouiller, plus encore à se tracer une ligne de conduite' (p.238). This is not to say, however, that *Le Sabbat* is totally altruistic in intent. Nothing could be further from the truth, for what Sachs is also doing throughout his text is endeavouring to exorcise his troubled past, as an early declaration confirms: 'Puisse ce livre achever de me délivrer du premier moi et lorsque je l'aurai terminé, puissé-je m'écrier: Voici une vie close à jamais. Elle est vécue, confessée, expiée' (p.23).

Looking back over all these themes, the only leitmotif which, by its absence, differentiates *Le Sabbat* from post-1969 works is the vital one of the Occupation. But even here a form of correspondence can be found, because Sachs's generation was another generation afflicted by war:

> Génération heurtée, secouée à laquelle personne n'avait eu le temps de bâtir un squelette moral, qui s'était élevée à peu près seule, pendant la guerre, et dont l'adolescence allait se vivre dans un monde en pleine euphorie.
>
> Mais participer à l'euphorie, sans soupçonner qu'il y a griserie collective, à la joie sans avoir sciemment pris part à la peine, c'est se préparer les plus fortes désillusions. (pp.101–2)

The legacy which the First World War bequeathed to Sachs was thus strangely reminiscent of the one passed on by the Second.

This apparent ability of war to leave a problematic heritage could well prove to be essential, and deserves to be kept in mind as the spotlight is now moved to Drieu la Rochelle's *État civil* (1921).

The thing which is immediately striking about these *souvenirs de jeunesse* is that, like Sachs's, they too are clearly the work of an orphan: 'Je voyais rarement mon père', the author readily admits (p.38). But this abandonment is not the only cause of his problem. He also feels himself to be the 'petit-fils d'une défaite' (p.161) – he was born in 1893 – and this is much more disconcerting for him:

> France, mon adolescence t'a aimée douloureusement. Mes parents, vous n'aviez pas su vous taire. Une ombre malfaisante couvrait le pays où j'étais né. Toute parole tombait lourdement sur mon cœur. Ils n'ont pas su se taire: il se répandait autour de moi des mots qui contaminent.
>
> Mais moi, je veillais sur notre vie. Et des rages me prenaient de m'arracher à tout ce que, dès longtemps, sans me tromper, j'avais bien vu marqué d'un signe de destruction.
>
> [. . .] D'autres qui l'avaient déjà acceptée, j'avais reçu une faible image de ma patrie. L'âme, l'esprit étaient atteints. Je souffrais d'un malaise que je sentais partout. J'étais malade, et c'était le mal de tout un peuple. (p.161)

So, like the *jeunes loups* in post-Gaullist France, Drieu considers himself to be plagued by his nation's recent history. And it matters not in the slightest that his elders' constant garrulousness, and not now their silence, is at the heart of his torment, for the ultimate effect of the inheritance is still the same: a need for exorcism. As he says: 'J'écris ceci pour me débarrasser de moi, ou d'un que j'ai été, particulièrement pendant une certaine guerre dont l'événement coïncida avec mon entrée dans la vie. [. . .] je trace ces pages pour fixer hors de moi tout ce dont je veux me séparer' (pp.177–8).

With this figurative waving of a goodbye by Drieu, the present contextualisation is brought to a rather appropriate end.[58] All that it remains to do now is draw the relevant conclusions, and these would appear to be two in number. First, it is blatantly clear that, as regards its driving force, the *mode rétro* can hardly be said to be unique, for orphanage, cultural or otherwise, is in many ways a 'classic' problem and can be unearthed in a whole variety of postwar situations. Yet that said, it is nonetheless true that never before has this perennial occurrence developed into such an all-pervasive, emotionally necessary *fashion* as the one which grew up after 1969, and this leads on to the second conclusion – there must, in the final analysis, have been something special about the *années noires* for this extraordinary state of affairs to arise. The singularity of these 'dark years' is not hard to discern. During the early 1940s, France was, for the very first time in modern history, totally and humiliatingly *occupied*. As a result *la patrie* broke up, the nation became acrimoniously divided against itself and, to make matters worse, this already explosive cocktail was then laced with a full – and unprecedented – measure of myth-making by both Vichy and the Resistance alike. The Liberation and the *épuration*, when they duly arrived, did nothing to defuse this volatile concoction. Quite the opposite. National factionalism became so entrenched that, surreptitiously, much of the wartime mythification was continued and intensified in order to try and cure France of her ills. The *résistancialisme* which ensued was something that had never been observed before, something which, given its nature, could not fail to have widespread repercussions, and which, unerringly, most certainly did. This, then, is why the *années noires* are so special. And this, in turn, is what makes the *mode rétro* unique.

Notes

1. Roger Rabiniaux, drawing up Vichy's balance sheet in *Les Bonheurs de la guerre*, supports Lanoux's observations: 'Resteraient enfin à écrire les romans de cette époque: les *Lucien Leuwen*, les *Illusions perdues*, les *Chabert* et les *Chouans*, d'un temps qui semble effrayer encore beaucoup d'écrivains. Alors, seulement il sera possible de juger ce régime et cette époque dont les cendres sont si brûlantes que chacun n'y touche qu'avec une extrême prudence' (p.447).
2. Cf. François Nourissier, 'Le Cadavre dans le placard': 'Il semble que ce soit la mort du général de Gaulle qui ait abattu le grand obstacle, dressé par lui, entre la nation et le juste reflet qu'elle voudrait mériter d'elle-même' (p.87). Cf. also Bertrand Poirot-Delpech, '1978, Année des "collabos"': 'La mort de de Gaulle, en 1970, a sans doute enhardi les iconoclastes' (p.11).
3. Jean-Pierre Azéma, *La Collaboration, 1940–1944*, p.11. See also Henry Rousso, *Le Syndrome de Vichy, 1944–198 . . .*, pp.129–30.
4. This link between the *mode rétro* and May 1968 is acknowledged by Marcel Ophüls, at least if *Le Chagrin et la pitié* is deemed to be the start of the trend. See Marcel Ophüls, *Le Chagrin et la pitié*, pp.221–2.
5. 'L'Occupation: pourquoi tout le monde en parle', p.88. Cf. Stanley Hoffmann, 'Dans le miroir: *Le Chagrin et la pitié*', p.108.
6. For numerous examples of such silence, see Ophüls, *Le Chagrin et la pitié*, pp.31, 136–7, 240. See also Jean Dutourd, *Le Demi-solde*, pp.23–4, and Paul Guimard, quoted in Pierre Billard, 'L'Occupation: pourquoi tout le monde en parle' (p.85).
7. Pierre Loubière and Gilbert Salachas, 'Libre cours: André Harris', p.37.

8. François Nourissier, 'Les Français étaient-ils des veaux en 40?', p.24.
9. Although, strictly speaking, Bonny is somewhat on the margin with regard to his age during the war – he was born in 1924 – he nevertheless remains *typical*, especially as he waited until 1975 to write his book. A less marginal, but otherwise comparable case is offered by Jean-Luc Maxence, as notes below will indicate.
10. Cf. Abel Danos, another member of the Bonny-Laffont gang, of whom Philippe Aziz writes in *Tu trahiras sans vergogne*: 'Chose inattendue: ce tueur, ce technicien du crime, avait une femme et deux enfants qu'il adorait. Il aimait beaucoup la vie de famille. C'était un mari très gentil et un père affectueux' (p.63).
11. Cf. Jean-Luc Maxence, *L'Ombre d'un père*. Son of an extreme right-wing journalist convicted to twenty years' hard labour during the *épuration*, and an orphan at the age of ten, Maxence too is driven to try and find out what his absent father was really like – using the *tu* form of address to increase the child-parent contact, he recognises: 'J'ai voulu savoir, tout savoir. [. . .] En quelque sorte, j'ai joué les flics avec ton fantôme des années 1941–1946' (p.215).
12. Cf. Maxence: 'De toute façon, je me garde de te juger, mon père' (*L'Ombre d'un père*, p.171).
13. Cf. Maxence's reference to 'cette silhouette évanouie Dieu sait où et à qui je dois d'être ici' (ibid., p.16).
14. Cf. François Nourissier's remark in *Un petit bourgeois*: 'Le silence autour d'un père vivant risque en effet de ressembler singulièrement au silence autour d'un père mort' (p.25).
15. The most notable case in point is Patrick Modiano, but discussion of this author's work will be deferred until chapter 5, where full justice can be done to it. In the meantime, for additional illustration, see: Jacques Lanzmann, *Tous les chemins mènent à soi*; Dominique Garnier, *Nice, pour mémoire*; Solange Fasquelle, *Les Falaises d'Ischia*; Guy Lagorce, *La Raison des fous*; Guy Croussy, *La Tondue*; and Gilles Perrault, 'Les Sanglots longs', in *Les Sanglots longs*.
16. 'On parlait encore beaucoup de la guerre à la T.S.F. Elle n'en parlait jamais', François notes (p.39). Cf. Perrault, *Les Sanglots longs*: 'Pour qu'elle restât si paisible en sa compagnie, il fallait que son père ne lui eût rien dit du passé, tout comme sa mère à lui s'était tue pendant vingt et un ans' (p.178). On the more general level of Vera's disgrace, a link can be made with Émile Ajar's *L'Angoisse du roi Salomon*, which also features a fallen star – Cora Lamenaire. Cora, like Vera, was popular for her *chansons réalistes*, and if Sevran can say of his heroine, 'S'il n'y avait pas eu la guerre et tous les ennuis qui vont toujours avec la guerre, Vera Valmont n'aurait pas été obligée de renoncer au music-hall' (p.30), so too can Ajar say of his: 'S'il n'y avait pas eu la guerre et l'occupation, elle aurait été une gloire nationale, comme Piaf' (p.52). Cora's demise is more spectacular than Vera's, however: whereas the

once great Miss Valmont has to alter dresses to earn a living, her erstwhile colleague, in true Ajar style, is forced to become a toilet attendant.

17. François's family background mirrors the one depicted in *Le Passé supplémentaire*, where the narrator's parents – *Le Soldat inconnu* and Evita Peron – form another soldier–singer couple. *Un garçon de France* departs from this format, but only marginally, the parents of the central character being a man killed in a shooting accident and, it is assumed, an actress of exotic, Spanish stock.
18. Gérard Langlois, 'Entretien: *Le Chagrin et la pitié* de Marcel Ophüls, véritable histoire de la France occupée', p.11.
19. Loubière and Salachas, 'Libre cours: André Harris', p.37. Cf. his earlier comment during Ophüls's interview: 'Si nous sommes les produits de l'Occupation, nous le sommes bien plus de la Libération. C'est là que toutes les mythologies auxquelles nous nous sommes attaqués dans *Le Chagrin et la pitié* se sont mises à vivre' (Loubière and Salachas, 'Libre cours: Marcel Ophüls', p.33).
20. Loubière and Salachas, 'Libre cours: André Harris', p.37.
21. Marcel Ophüls, 'Regardez donc dans vos greniers', p.9. (Page 16 of *Le Chagrin et la pitié* gives a slightly different version.)
22. Pascal Jardin and Marie Chaix, the two writers alluded to here will not be discussed until Part II. Nevertheless, the strength of Spade's feelings can still be gauged by applying his remarks to Jacques Bonny, whom they suit equally well. With respect to the closing comment, it should be noted that Laval's daughter (Josée de Chambrun) did in fact contribute to *La Vie de la France sous l'Occupation, 1940–1944*. Moreover, if she has indeed said little apart from this, her husband, René de Chambrun, has regularly defended her father for her, as his appearance in *Le Chagrin et la pitié* illustrates. For examples of his written defences, see *Pierre Laval devant l'histoire* or 'Pierre Laval et les Israélites', p.8. (See also 'Réponses à M. de Chambrun: Pierre Laval et les Israélites', p.6.)
23. Cf. Luce Giard, 'La Honte': 'Je ne demande pas qu'on interdise de parole les fils aimants [. . .]. Je demande un peu de décence, un peu de retenue dans la louange. Je demande surtout qu'on ne soit pas dupe: par ce biais, c'est aussi la *rentrée en grâce* de tout le passé qui s'insinue d'un air de rien' (p.74).
24. Cf. André Frossard, 'Occupation: le temps de mes 20 ans'. Frossard asserts that during the war he actually met 'des héros comme on en trouve dans les livres, ou plutôt comme on en trouvait avant que les romanciers ne prennent le parti de nous entretenir de personnages blafards dont le sort nous laisse indifférents' (p.89).
25. Spade fails to add, however, that such a welcome may *not* have been a tacit protest – many Parisians had fled, and many of those who stayed did not know what treatment to expect from the Germans, and so kept a low profile. Cf. Henri Amouroux's *La Vie des Français sous l'Occupa-*

tion: 'Les renseignements sur l'attitude de la population le 14 juin et les jours suivants varient [. . .]. Stupeur, honte, terreur, détresse patriotique, haine, curiosité, soulagement, indécence, tout est vrai' (p.21).

26. Michel Robida, in *Le Déjeuner de Trieste*, does not agree: 'En vérité, ceux qui n'entendirent pas parler de la Résistance n'étaient pas faits pour elle. Une prudence instinctive les retenait qui leur faisait arrêter jusqu'aux conversations s'ils les estimaient dangereuses' (p.140). For additional illustration of Robida's view, see M. Leiris in Ophüls's *Le Chagrin et la pitié* (p.136) and Elsa Triolet's 'Alexis Slavsky' in Elsa Triolet, *Le Premier Accroc coûte deux cents francs*.
27. Cf. Marcel Haedrich, *Le Maréchal et la dactylo*: 'Tout ce qui se faisait visait un même but, la libération. Comment faire comprendre aux jeunes producteurs d'un film (effrayant) comme *Le Chagrin et la Pitié* que la France résistait naturellement, selon la loi d'Archimède: l'eau déplacée supporte le bateau en cherchant des failles pour s'introduire dans son poids, afin de l'entraîner au fond' (p.168).
28. Cf. Germaine Tillon's epithet for the general: 'l'homme qui était du même avis que nous' (cit. in Henry Rousso, 'Où en est l'histoire de la Résistance', in *Études sur la France de 1939 à nos jours*, p.116).
29. With regard to the closing remarks, cf. p.60: 'Défense de juger, d'expliquer, de pardonner à notre place.' For other (implicit) manifestations of this belief, see André Frossard, 'Occupation: le temps de mes 20 ans', p.89 and André Chamson, *Suite guerrière*, p.13. (Further reference to Chamson's text will be made shortly.) Marcel Ophüls's 'Regardez donc dans vos greniers' shows that the young demythifiers were well aware of the existence of this interdiction (p.10; *Le Chagrin et la pitié*, p.21).
30. The notion of national redemption by the few can also be found in Brigitte Friang's *Regarde-toi qui meurs*: 'Nous avions conscience de faire partie de l'élite qui sauvait l'honneur de la France. [. . .] Nous étions les Justes' (p.188). For further references to an idealised *patrie*, see Jean Guéhenno's views on 'la France qu'on n'envahit pas' in his *Journal des années noires* (pp.18–19, 24) and cf. Max-Pol Fouchet's preface to Pierre Durand's *Vivre debout: la Résistance*. No less eloquent than Guéhenno and Fouchet in this respect are reviews from the 1940s such as *Confluences*, *Fontaine* and *Messages* – see the bibliography for details of selected articles.
31. For other literary reflections of this widespread loss of youth, see: Georges Bordonove, *La Toccata*, p.191; Jean-Louis Bory, *Mon village à l'heure allemande*, p.248; Robida, *Le Déjeuner de Trieste*, pp.108–9; Jean Sanitas, *Un jour et une nuit*, p.102; and finally Marie-Reine Sorel, *Les Roses de sel*, p.115.
32. '*La Polka*, de Patrick Modiano', p.72.
33. This lack of foresight is supremely typified by the words of René Chateau. Participating in Jamet's *Rendez-vous manqué de 1944*, he

confidently announced: 'Ce passé, en effet, date de vingt ans. C'est un passé pour nous, les vieux ou demi-vieux. Mais, par bonheur, les jeunes, par exemple ceux qui ont entre quinze et vingt-cinq ans, n'ont eu dans ce passé aucune part, et ils n'ont point, en général, l'intention de rien en emprunter pour construire leur avenir' (p.190). Nothing could have been further from the truth.

34. See e.g. *Et pourquoi pas la patrie?*: 'Peut-on [. . .] laisser faire et déformer aux yeux de nos enfants une vérité que, par pudeur ou par lassitude, nous leur avons cachée?' (p.21).
35. Michel Audiard similarly confesses to writing for the postwar generation. See *La Nuit, le jour et toutes les autres nuits*, p.102. Note also François Nourissier's observation in 'Le Cadavre dans le placard': 'Ceux qui parlent aujourd'hui le font au nom des cadets, qui n'ont pas ou pas vraiment vécu l'époque' (p.86).
36. 'L 'Occupation: pourquoi tout le monde en parle', p.89.
37. Michel Capdenac, 'Révolte dévoyée, film fourvoyé', p.267.
38. A similar justification was given for the republishing of Rebatet's *Les Décombres* – see the *avertissement* attached to *Les Mémoires d'un fasciste*. . . .
39. Cf. 'Rapport au Reichführer-SS' in Perrault's *Les Sanglots longs*.
40. The belief that Hitler and Nazism live on is a major theme of the *mode rétro*. For further examples see Marc Blancpain, *La Grande Nation*, p.252; Pierre Bourgeade, *Deutsches Requiem*, pp.91–3; and Alain Buhler, *Enfer et ses fils*, p.85. As with most aspects of the trend, however, this view is not new, as Ian Higgins's *Anthology of Second World War French Poetry* (pp.158, 227) and Vercors's *La Bataille du silence* (p.338) demonstrate.
41. Although, as indicated, it is impossible to mention every writers who shares this view, a rough outline of the breadth and variety of the trend can quickly be sketched. In *La Tondue*, Guy Croussy examines the abiding problem of reconciling innocence and punishment; Gilles Perrault's 'Le Retour de Bibendum' (in *Les Sanglots longs*) likens the Gestapo to French paratroopers in Algeria, American soldiers in Vietnam and the Israelis in the occuped territories; André Halimi justifies his work, *La Délation sous l'Occupation*, by noting that 'la délation accompagne notre quotidien' (p.9); and Pierre Bourgeade's *Le Camp* and Philippe Ganier-Raymond's *Les Chanteurs de cordes* both deal with the persistently thorny subject of concentration camps, the latter of these texts also broaching the timeless question of racism.
42. A host of other 'innocent' novelists also depict an exorcism of the *années noires* in their works, and although they do not all have the same pressingly personal therapeutic intentions as Garnier or Modiano, their persistent recourse to this theme still says much about their concerns and obsessions in general. See e.g. Perrault, 'Les Sanglots longs' (in *Les Sanglots longs*) or Solange Fasquelle, *Les Falaises d'Ischia*.
43. Henri Raczymow, 'L'Écoute d'un silence', p.19.

44. *Et pourquoi pas la patrie?*, p.15. This simply confirms the principle laid down by Evelyne Le Garrec in *La Rive allemande de ma mémoire*: 'Le déclenchement d'une seule mémoire met en route un mécanisme dans lequel d'autres seront pris malgré eux. On ne sait pas ce qu'il en résultera pour eux, le mal que ça peut leur faire' (p.91). Le Garrec's work will be studied in detail in Part II.
45. A fictional echo of this practice – and its relationship to the notion of a lost heritage – can be found in Guy Lagorce's *La Raison des fous*: 'Jusqu'à cet instant il tenait ces affaires de 1944 pour un vague folklore [. . .]. Il comprenait peu à peu [. . .] que la génération qui précédait la sienne avait été marquée à jamais [. . .] par ces jours-là, dont les vieux ne parlaient plus [. . .]; il comprenait en même temps pourquoi il avait [. . .] tenté de s'inventer un passé sur mesure' (pp.199–200).
46. See also Maxence's *L'Ombre d'un père*, in which the phrase 'mon père, mon mythe secret' is actually used (p.13).
47. While it is true that the fruit of Nourissier's own wartime experiences, *Allemande*, did indeed take about three decades to ripen into literary form, not everyone would accept this point to be a valid one. See e.g. Armand Lanoux's preface to Pierrard's *On l'appelait Tamerlan*, written as the *mode rétro* was about to take off: 'La résistance est, sur [le] plan de sa transposition littéraire, beaucoup moins bien servie que la guerre d'Indochine, par exemple, qui l'a suivie pourtant, ce qui prouve bien que le 'retard fonctionnel' dû à la lente digestion par l'écrivain de sa propre existence, n'est pas l'explication du phénomène' (p.14).
48. See also Micheline Bood's *Les Années doubles*, which was published because 'les quelques témoignages retenus dans le film *Le Chagrin et la Pitié* semblaient donner à entendre que la jeunesse des lycées, notamment, avait été parfaitement indifférente à l'Occupation et à tout ce qui en résultait à l'époque – quand rien n'est plus faux' (p.10).
49. Other prominent members of this group include Philippe Aziz, Jean-Pierre Azéma (both born just before the outbreak of the Second World War) and Pascal Ory (b. 1948).
50. There is a certain resonance here with Boudard's *avertissement* to *Bleubite*: 'L'époque où il se situe, aujourd'hui plus de la moitié de mes contemporains ne la connaît que par ouï-dire, par les racontars, les films de montage toujours montés en vue de prouver ceci cela' (*B*, p.13).
51. 'Un entretien avec Darquier de Pellepoix'. See also *Les Chanteurs de corde*, Ganier-Raymond's virulent, polemical novel.
52. For confirmation of this, see André Halimi, *La Délation sous l'Occupation*, pp.30–1, Luce Giard, 'La Honte', p.78n., or Rousso, *Le Syndrome de Vichy*, pp.157–8. Darquier's views on Auschwitz give a good idea of what caused passions to become roused: 'Les Juifs sont toujours prêts à tout pour qu'on parle d'eux, pour se rendre intéressants, pour se faire plaindre. Je vais vous dire, moi, ce qui s'est exactement passé à

Auschwitz. On a gazé. Oui, c'est vrai. Mais on a gazé les poux' (p.173).

53. Derek Malcolm, 'Turning fascist', p.10.
54. 'Le Cadavre dans le placard', p.87.
55. According to Tom Bower, writing in *Blind Eye to Murder*, German youth finds itself in exactly the same position as its French counterpart: 'The postwar generation [. . .] could not be allowed to ask the collective question: "What did you do in the war, Daddy?" It was not just that the question was embarrassing to individual parents; it would also open to undesirable debate the values and assumptions of the Establishment which stood *in loco parentis* to a new and fragile nation' (p.405). There is evidently scope here for a fascinating comparative study to be made.
56. See also: Armand Lanoux, *Le Commandant Watrin*, p.314 and *Quand la mer se retire*, p.240; François Nourissier, *Bleu comme la nuit*, p.189; and Sylvain Reiner, *Après la guerre*, p.299.
57. While it is true that Jacques Bonny is almost as old as Corinne Luchaire, he is, and always has been, emotionally linked to the *jeunes loups*, not having read his father's *carnets* until the 1970s. (See also note 9 above.)
58. For a taste of what could be discovered if even earlier precedents of the post-1969 trend were sought out, see Stendhal's *Le Rouge et le noir*, in which Julien Sorel also feels he belongs to an *après-guerre* generation, his allegiance to a rejected and hated leader leader (Napoleon) placing him in a similar position to the *collabos*' children. Moreover, he too seems drawn towards substitute father-figures (the surgeon-major, Chélan, Pirard and the Marquis de la Mole) and arguably even a surrogate mother (Mme de Rênal).

PART II

First among Orphans

Pour nous, adultes, ces années ne sont pas drôles, mais pour les jeunes c'est encore plus dur. Ils seront une génération marquée.

Marilène Clément

Nous sommes tous frappés d'amnésie. Enfin eux, la génération des pères. Nous, les fils, les filles, nous essayons de vivre comme si nous étions une génération spontanée, engendrée par personne, issue de nulle histoire [. . .]. A présent le silence, ce silence . . .

Dominique Garnier

Chercher à comprendre, n'est-ce pas [. . .] l'intention première, et profonde, de ceux qui aujourd'hui témoignent, même si, parfois, [. . .] ils témoignent à travers les souvenirs des autres?

Pierre Billard

–4–

Pascal Jardin, Marie Chaix and Evelyne Le Garrec

C'était un enfant de la guerre: il l'avait vécue trop jeune pour en garder des souvenirs conscients, mais il avait cette aptitude à la contemplation, qui caractérisait les bébés de l'Occupation.

Alain Buhler

S'il y avait un héritage à refuser, c'était bien celui de la vengeance. Les Français de 1970 sauraient-ils le faire? Et surtout les enfants des nazis pourraient-ils ne pas rêver de revanche?

Henri Spade

Mon père, c'est le Soldat Inconnu.

Gilles Perrault

In Part I of this survey, through the example of Jacques Bonny, the contribution made to the *mode rétro* by 'orphans' of wartime collaborators was, on more than one occasion, shown to be highly significant. Given the general, broad-based nature of the preceding chapters, however, the full importance of this contribution was, of necessity, not expressed in all its glory, for the most interesting writers involved – Pascal Jardin, Marie Chaix and Evelyne Le Garrec – were hardly given a mention at all. With the constraints imposed by a wide focus no longer operative, and with qualitative considerations now well to the fore, there is, henceforth, scope to remedy this apparent neglect. And this, precisely, is what the pages which follow will endeavour to do.

In terms both of chronological precedence and influence exerted, it is logical to turn the spotlight first of all onto Pascal Jardin (1934–80), son of Pierre Laval's *directeur de cabinet*, Jean Jardin, and author of four much-acclaimed works which are of undoubted interest in the current context: *La Guerre à neuf ans* (1971), *Guerre après guerre*

(1973), *Le Nain Jaune* (1978) and *La Bête à bon Dieu* (1980).[1] Taken together, these texts constitute a series of brilliant 'snapshots' of Jardin's life, from his early, prewar experience, through his Vichy childhood to his subsequent adolescence and adulthood, but this is not to say that his writing is totally self-centred. Far from it. With the publication of each successive volume, it has become ever more apparent that his real subject is not so much himself as the man in whose shadow he was obliged to grow up – his one-time *collabo* father Jean.

This obsession with his parent is not all that unexpected in the circumstances, for although Jean, unlike, say, Pierre Bonny, was not executed (or even imprisoned) for his collaboration – he and his family were safely settled in Switzerland – Pascal was still emotionally deprived by the time the war ended. 'J'attends mon père avec impatience', he observes, reliving an incident from 1939. 'Je l'adore mais je ne le vois presque jamais' (*GNA*, p.30). Three years later, in 1942, the situation had patently gone from bad to worse: 'Ma mère est préoccupée par elle-même. [. . .] Et mon père: je ne le vois jamais. Il est nuit et jour à Vichy. [. . .] Je suis donc, dans mes débuts à Vichy, moralement privé de parents. Privé d'amour aussi' (*GNA*, p.76). Indeed, so endemic was this parental, and particularly paternal absence to become that, shortly before his death in 1980, Jardin would claim to have had no more than ten private chats with his father throughout his whole life (*BBD*, p.127). Little wonder, then, that his books should be punctuated with comments such as 'Qui est réellement mon père? Quelles ont été ses activités et quelles sont-elles encore? [. . .] Je ne connais que des bribes, que la surface' (*GNA*, p.129). And little wonder either that he should add, in what could virtually be the same breath: 'Ce que je cherche quand je parle à des gens qui l'ont vraiment connu, c'est à découvrir une part de lui-même que moi je ne connais pas' (*NJ*, p.129). Like so many other contributors to the *mode rétro*, therefore, Pascal Jardin must be considered to be an orphan – an orphan in search of a father.

This quest, this 'travail de recherche que je fais sur mon père', as Jardin himself calls it (*NJ*, p.128), centres, almost inevitably, on the unwholesome period of the *années noires*. Yet for all the apparent predictability of this focus, the depiction of the dark years which results is anything but straightforward and orthodox. Take, for example, the portrayal of Pierre Laval. Throughout *La Guerre à neuf ans* Pétain's prime minister is seen not as a despicable *salaud*, as *le résistancialisme* demands, but rather as a man involved in a game of political poker, and whose conduct deserves no more damning a comment from the author than: 'Je renonce à me faire une opinion précise sur Pierre Laval' (*GNA*, p.168). Similarly, when the key building in Vichy, l'Hôtel du Parc, is mentioned, traditional interpretations are once again most manifestly subverted:

> Si la collaboration qui se faisait là était indispensable à la survie économique de la France, elle se révéla pourtant, après coup, intolérable au regard de l'histoire. Pourtant, dans un pays occupé, noyauté par la fantastique infrastructure militaire et policière du Troisième Reich, collaborer, c'était la raison. Résister, c'était l'espérance. De toute manière, Vichy a perdu. En politique, 'c'est plus qu'un crime, c'est une faute'. (*GNA*, p.87)[2]

As if this rehabilitation of Vichy were not bad enough for supporters of *la France résistante*, Jardin mixes into it, for good measure, a deliberate deflation of the myth-based Resistance. 'Ceux qui sont pour de Gaulle sont partout peu nombreux' (*GNA*, p.80), he discovers as late as mid-1942, and although *l'armée de l'ombre* goes on to increase in size by the end of the Occupation – possibly because 'les collaborateurs devenus gaullistes à la Libération ou juste avant, ou juste après, furent légion' (*BBD*, p.160) – the Resistants are not shown to gain in prestige as a consequence. Quite the opposite in fact, as the reference to the *épuration* demonstrates:

> Avec la liberté, l'épuration commence, et la paix va faire en six mois autant de morts français qu'en fit la guerre en quatre ans: juridictions d'exception, exécutions sommaires, chocs en retour du froid, de la peur, de la haine, de la Gestapo, de la Milice, création d'un nouveau délit, l'indignité nationale, vengeance pour le frère tué en Allemagne, pour le père déporté, pour la sœur violée, règlement de comptes amoureux sous couvert politique, truanderie sous couvert policier, appropriation de fermes, de maisons, de terres et de commerces, par la torture et l'assassinat. Dans les campagnes, plus de dix mille personnes jetées dans des puits en moins d'un an, chambres civiques, hautes cours, camps de concentration de Poitiers, l'un à Biard, l'autre à Jonzac, créés hier par Daladier pour les communistes, à Bordeaux, camp de Mérignac Beau Désert, en Auvergne, Tronçais et Montussant, près de Bergerac, c'est Mauzac . . . (*GAG*, p.197)

And so on and so forth, the ellipsis seems to imply.

Comparing this view of the *années noires* to the one put forward by the *résistancialistes*, the discrepancy between the two versions could hardly be more striking, and this fundamental incompatibility is not lost on Jardin. In a passage in which he articulates his father's assessment of the situation in April 1944 (and in which, at the same time, he takes care to point out that Jean was by no means isolated in holding the opinions he did), he provides a telling insight into why the discordance should have arisen:

> Il a le sentiment, comme beaucoup de gens l'ont eu, que, quel que soit le côté où l'on se tourne, il n'y a plus d'espoir. Il croit qu'en armant la Russie, l'Amérique et les Anglais qui n'ont plus le choix vont installer le régime de Moscou à Paris. Il croit que l'Angleterre, devenue folle sous les V2, et qui répond en bombardant la ville de Dresde au phosphore, n'engendrera que la mort.
>
> Cette analyse qui s'est révélée miraculeusement fausse était fréquente à l'époque. La légende gaullienne au sens le plus large du terme a ensuite tout fait pour la détruire. Elle y a presque parfaitement réussi, pour deux raisons fondamentales. La première, c'est qu'elle proposait aux Français de laver leur mauvaise conscience. La seconde, la plus importante, non prévue au départ, c'est qu'après, non seulement le Général deviendrait l'unique artisan de notre rédemption nationale, mais que, de plus, son génie politique et littéraire tardif le ferait entrer dans la légende et dans la mort par la porte des géants. (*NJ*, pp.170–1)

The conclusion to be drawn from these words is, it would appear, perfectly clear: well aware that a 'légende gaullienne' has as it were banished his father (and others like him) from history, Jardin takes it upon himself to try and right the balance, engaging in blatant heresy, and thereby seeking to undermine the legend's noxious effects. In brief, and to make the use of terminology consistent, he willingly adopts the role of demythifier.

This being the case, there is an obvious, and understandable temptation to dub Jardin a political writer, but to arrive at this judgement would be to overlook the author's own stated position on the matter, for in his very first work he explicitly declared: 'Mon récit est Apolitique, avec un A privatif majuscule. J'ai toujours essayé de comprendre et, comme je n'ai jamais réussi, je continue. Tout petit, dès mon arrivée à Vichy, dès le mois de mai 1942, j'ai essayé de savoir non pas ce que pensaient les gens [. . .] mais bien plutôt ce qui se passait' (*GNA*, p.79). In other words, Jardin's overriding concern is not to be politically iconoclastic, but rather, more simply, to try and make sense of his confusing past. And there is good reason why he should have set himself this particular objective – believing that 'l'avenir reconstruit le passé'

(*BBD*, p.185), he is able, by engaging in retrospection, to secure a number of useful guidelines for himself, and hence acquire the positive, reassuring heritage that he lacks.

This selfsame need to obtain a better heritage was, of course, already implicit in his decision to search for his father, and it is precisely in this filial pursuit of a parent that, ultimately, the true significance of the quest for a legacy can be discerned, for as Jardin himself noted towards the end of his venture:

> J'ai déjà consacré trois livres à mon père, *La Guerre à neuf ans*, *Guerre après guerre*, *Le Nain Jaune*. *La Bête à bon Dieu* constitue le quatrième et dernier volet.
>
> Ces livres, je n'ai pas pu faire autrement que de les écrire. C'est une nécessité sans cesse renouvelée qui me poussait à reprendre la plume, pour témoigner de ce qu'il fut, et pour tenter de découvrir, à travers lui, qui donc je suis moi-même. (*BBD*, p.188)

Jardin's search for a father and a heritage is, then, in the final analysis, simply part of another, more fundamental search which he feels obliged to undertake – the search for his lost identity.

In the context of this quest for self through the pursuit of the parent, it comes as no surprise to find that Pascal constantly claims to be a mirror-image of Jean. 'On peut discuter avec tout le monde', he observes in *La Guerre à neuf ans*, 'sauf avec les chromosomes. Aujourd'hui, à trente-six ans, je ne suis plus, à proprement parler, le fils de mon père mais plutôt une sorte de second lui-même' (p.125).[3] Indeed, after Jean's death in 1976, the doubling of father and son becomes even more striking because, as Pascal readily confesses: 'J'ai dû abandonner ma peau de fils, et devenir pour les miens un peu de ce qu'il était' (*BBD*, pp.187–8).

This enforced change of status is reflected in the content of *Le Nain Jaune*, and *La Bête à bon Dieu*, for as the titles of these two works suggest (they both derive from nicknames applied to Jean), Jardin's focus perceptibly shifts from his own past life to that of his newly deceased parent. And that is not all. His aims as a writer appear to have developed somewhat as well:

> Je me garde mon père, Jean Jardin, tel qu'en la beauté folle de ses vingt ans. Je le mets de côté. Je le fais imprimer avec l'espérance, aussi hasardeuse que la bouteille à la mer, qu'un jour peut-être, dans la vieille bibliothèque d'une vieille maison où passerait ma descendance, ou bien de leurs amis, il se trouvera un jeune homme pour redécouvrir ce livre,

> en souffler la poussière et, par-delà le temps, redevenir le Nain Jaune. (*BBD*, pp.190–1).

So, Jardin is writing not so much now for himself as for his children – 'à leur usage', as he stresses elsewhere (*BBD*, p.11) – and his motives for taking this course of action are all too plain to see. Having suffered from a problematic heritage himself, he is clearly determined not to make the same mistake as his father, and so deliberately – and dutifully – records his bequest to his successors in print.

Such readiness on Pascal's part to ignore Jean's example here may, in the light of what was said above, seem puzzlingly contradictory, but this is not so. Doubles they may have been in many respects, but certainly not in all, for as the son openly admits, one of his basic reactions to his parent was to 'refuser en bloc ses croyances religieuses, politiques et morales' (*GNA*, p.126), and from a very early age he could be found challenging his father's self-proclaimed predominance. 'Pour mon père, il n'y avait qu'un Jardin: lui', he recalls in *Le Nain Jaune*.

> Très vite, dès l'âge de dix ans, pour tenter d'exister, je décidai qu'il y en aurait au moins un second: moi.
>
> Il me détestait de vouloir prendre sa place. Il m'aimait follement d'être un autre lui-même. (pp.124–5)

As has already been seen, Pascal's feelings towards Jean were similarly ambivalent, and this is why, deep down, there is no real inconsistency in the claim that father and son are identical. In spite of their numerous 'guerres immenses, jusqu'à en venir aux mains' (*NJ*, p.12), their mutual flitting between love and hatred for each other does, at the end of the day, seem to justify the assertion that 'nous étions bien le même' (*NJ*, p.12).[4]

Not altogether unpredictably, perhaps, this extraordinary love-hate relationship informs almost every page of Jardin's literary quest, endowing each of his four texts with a quality which no attentive reader can fail to recognise – that of an urgent, compulsive filial exorcism.[5] 'Ai-je voulu mettre mon père à la retraite de sa propre existence en écrivant *La Guerre à neuf ans*?' the author muses to himself in *Guerre après guerre*. 'Et lui, a-t-il vu dans la publication de ce livre une volonté d'indépendance, le goût de m'exorciser de sa présence et de son autorité considérables?' (p.120). Yet it is not just from Jean's domineering character that Pascal feels the need to escape. No less oppressive for him is the war-based legacy that his father has handed down:

> J'étais le fils d'un 'collabo'. En définitive, aurais-je voulu oublier Pierre Laval que je ne l'aurais pas pu. Pendant les dix ou douze années qui ont suivi la fin de la guerre, on m'a rappelé qui j'étais. Il ne m'était pas plus aisé d'ignorer mon enfance qu'il n'était facile à un Juif d'oublier pendant la guerre qu'il était un Juif. (*GNA*, pp.165–6)

This external pressure to see his father in purely negative terms was, quite palpably, extremely disturbing for him, and understandably so because, unlike his personality clashes with Jean, which, ultimately, served to underline the similarities between the two men, the obligation to be ashamed of his parent totally conflicted with his feelings of filial love.

It is precisely to reaffirm this 'forbidden' love, and consequently to praise his father, that Jardin now collects his thoughts and puts pen to paper. 'Papa, je t'aime, tu sais', he intimately confides in his final text (*BBD*, p.182), and a few pages later the worshipful, enshrining nature of his writing is made even more explicit – as far as Jean is concerned, we are informed,

> *La Guerre à neuf ans* était comme les obscures chapelles des premiers chrétiens.
>
> J'ai voulu *La Bête à bon Dieu* comme une arche gothique, d'une architecture qui ne serait plus tournée que vers les fenêtres, toujours plus de lumière, toujours plus haut les voûtes, comme pour capter le ciel. (*BBD*, p.189)

In the heat of such passionate adoration, the traditional, uncomplimentary portrait of Jean Jardin 'the *collabo*' goes up in smoke, to be replaced by the more amenable representations of Jean Jardin 'the man' and Jean Jardin 'the parent', for as Pascal himself is the first to point out:

> Le Nain Jaune demeure pour moi une des sources premières de ce qui a fait ma vie. Mais c'est en lui, en lui seul que réside cette richesse. Il eût été voleur que c'eût été pareil, et le fait qu'il ait conduit telle entrevue avec Laval en 1942 [. . .] ne change rien à l'affaire. (*NJ*, p.130–1)

Most manifestly, then, Pascal is determined to love his father no matter what.

This overtly emotional approach to his writing suggests that Jardin is far from being an impartial author, and that this is indeed the case is confirmed by countless other aspects of his work. Not least among these is the dearth of concrete information that plagues his quest for Jean. 'Je manque d'information', he sadly concedes,

> et les éléments que je possède sont ceux d'un puzzle dont il manque des pièces et qui ne sera jamais fini.
>
> Les seules personnes qui auraient pu vraiment me dire, cerner, peindre, rassembler, reconstruire avec moi [. . .] sont mort[e]s.
>
> Quand je consulte les autres, [. . .] je me heurte au mutisme. (*NJ*, pp.121–2)

Such a blatant lack of first-hand documentation, or rather, to take up a phrase used earlier, such overwhelming silence from the older generation, is, admittedly, compensated in part by Jean's personal 'archives' and by the availability of historical research into Vichy (the debt to Robert Aron's *Histoire de Vichy* in particular is acknowledged – *GNA*, p.80), but even these sources remain somewhat fragmentary and irritatingly incomplete. So Jardin's reliance on his own recollections is more or less total, as he himself indicates in his contention that 'J'écris un livre de souvenirs' (*GNA*, p.148). And it is here, with this very statement, that the subjective nature of his work becomes clear, for not only are his memories, like anyone else's, partial almost by definition, they also relate to a period which, as has already been seen, he was far too young to understand properly in the first place: 'Et moi, là-dedans!' he exclaims, looking back to the war. 'Je ne fais rien, trop petit sous la toise pour entrer dans l'histoire. Je ne suis qu'un enfant, donc un spectateur qui n'a même pas payé sa place' (*GAG*, p.194). He is, therefore, not so much remembering historical events from the Second World War as actively (re-)creating them from whatever materials come to hand.

Further evidence of Jardin's unobjective approach can be found in his readiness – virtually unique amongst writers of the *mode rétro* – to do away with traditional chronology. Each of his four texts jump backwards and forwards in time throughout, and although this flitting between past and present serves, on the one hand, simply to evoke the recollective status of his literary quest – 'au diable la chronologie', he observes at one point, 'je refuse la mémoire de l'historien. Ce n'est pas ainsi que je me souviens, c'est le désordre où je me trouve' (*NJ*, p.27) – on the other hand it does something that is much more significant and telling: it translates one of the author's most fundamental objectives into formal practice. For as he has confided in interview:

> Ce qui me préoccupe, c'est d'arriver à mettre en quelque sorte le temps à plat, et de voir quels sont les points forts qui ont jalonné mon existence. Il me semble qu'ils sont reliés les uns aux autres par des liens invisibles et puissants. Les liens d'hier, d'aujourd'hui et de demain sont pour moi de la même époque. L'ordre intérieur que je cherche n'a pas d'ordre chronologique. Il procède de l'attention, de l'espérance et non de la raison.[6]

'L'ordre intérieur que je cherche', 'Il procède de l'attention, de l'espérance et non de la raison' – these are plainly not the words of a man concerned with objective truth; they are, rather, those of a writer whose aims are well and truly *subjective*.

Should any lingering doubts about this remain, they can quickly be dispelled by reference to another of Jardin's helpful revelations. 'Je suis menteur, comme tous ceux qui écrivent', he readily avows, and then adds in explanation:

> Par menteur, je veux dire que je tente de modifier l'éclairage du réel pour faire dire à la vie, non pas ce qu'elle m'a toujours dit, mais plutôt ce que j'aurais voulu et aimé entendre. [. . .] ma vision des choses, des faits et des gens est complètement subjective [. . .]. La vérité dramatique a pour moi plus d'importance que la vérité tout court.[7]

Indeed, so rigidly does he adhere to this standpoint that Emmanuel Berl, in his preface to *La Guerre à neuf ans*, will be forced to observe: 'J'ai vu beaucoup des choses qu'il raconte. Et je ne les reconnais pas' (*GNA*, p.11). And Berl is by no means the last, nor the least, to recognise that liberties have been taken with historical fact.[8]

Such an intentionally partial approach to the act of writing can, on reflection, signify but one thing: Jardin is fabricating a personal myth of the past for himself. Yet that said, it would be wrong to suggest that he is purely and simply a *mythifier*, for to employ this term would be to ignore both his demythification of the *années noires* and his heretical, near-hagiographical depiction of his father. Bearing this unorthodox tinge to his myth-creation in mind, then, it quickly becomes apparent that there is a much more specific and appropriate epithet to bestow upon Jardin, one which better captures the complexities of his mythopoeia: that of inveterate *countermythifier*.

Having arrived at this conclusion, it is now easy to see why Jardin so infuriated *anciens combattants* like Henri Spade (see pp.88–9 above) – his blatant countermythification nullified, or at least seriously threatened, almost everything the Resistance stood for. And that was only the half of it. No less vital a part of the problem was the *success* which his pursuit of 'Le Nain Jaune' achieved, for this success acted as a powerful stimulus to other war 'orphans', and encouraged them, most visibly, to embark on similar searches for their own missing fathers. In other words, Jardin rapidly became a trendsetter within his literary genre; once he began to publish, the floodgates palpably opened up behind him.

The first author to capitalise on Jardin's trail-blazing was Marie Chaix (b. 1942), whose much-lauded, prize-winning work, *Les Lauriers du lac de Constance* (1974), also gave pride of place to a father who collaborated during the Occupation: Albert B., one of Jacques Doriot's most important *cadres* in the Parti Populaire Français (PPF), and whom it takes no great detective to identify as Albert Beugras.[9]

Given this ultimate transparency of the paternal identity, it might be thought that Chaix's refusal to name her parent fully is somewhat pointless, but this is not so. On the contrary, it is extremely appropriate in the circumstances, since throughout the book, one of Albert's fundamental characteristics is, precisely, to be shrouded in a certain mystery, thanks to his almost permanent absence from his family. In the late 1930s, for instance, well before his writer-daughter was born, his devotion to the PPF had already given a clear indication of what was to come – his elder children had been obliged to suffer

> une enfance maternelle, féminine, traversée par des éclairs: sillages éphémères et lumineux tracés par le père lorsque, par hasard, il arpente la maison. Fulminant, auréolé du mystère de ses occupations secrètes.
>
> Ce père que l'on voit toujours s'en aller et jamais revenir, [. . .] ce père aimé d'amour devient le héros d'une vie quotidienne dont il s'absente de plus en plus. (p.13)

When Marie finally comes into the world, about five years later, little progress has been made: having been away for most of his wife's pregnancy, Albert is not present at the birth, and does not attend the christening either. And it is not simply the fact that he works in one place while his family lives in another that is the source of the trouble, for this geographical separation is overcome in 1943, but without any improvement to the overall situation – his wife and children may well have moved from France's third city to join him in the capital, but 'Il n'est pas plus présent à Paris qu'à Lyon' (p.75), and this will continue to be the case for the rest of the Occupation.

As the Liberation approaches and the war draws to its close, things, if anything, get even worse. Albert flees eastwards with his collaborationist colleagues, leaving behind him – as usual – 'une famille en morceaux' (p.96), and when he finally returns it is as a prisoner, and not as a man with freedom of movement. His subsequent trials and convictions see him sentenced to hard labour for life, and his absence accordingly takes on a more interminable, more absolute form. Not that Marie suddenly begins to miss him, however – she had never seen him often enough beforehand for that. But the lack of a father still has an undoubtedly adverse effect on her, if only because, as she will realise in retrospect: 'D'autres jouent au papa et à la maman. Moi, je n'ai jamais su' (p.178).

It is not, in fact, until Albert is released from prison (in the early 1950s) that Marie becomes aware of any emotional difficulties arising from her position. Confronted by a man who is more of a stranger than a parent, her immediate reaction is one of detestation. Nevertheless, over the next nine years, years during which, for the first time ever, they are together for long periods, the ice starts to melt. But not totally. Albert's health soon deteriorates, culminating in his death in 1963, and when meaningful contact between the two of them does actually take place, some quite significant gaps are left irritatingly unfilled: 'Un mot était banni de notre vocabulaire', the author recalls, as if speaking to her father himself,

> 'politique', ainsi que toute question pouvant te ramener dix ans en arrière. Je voyais ton passé glorieux arrêté à Mers el-Kébir, tu n'allais pas plus loin quand tu racontais ton Levant. Après, un grand vide. Car tu sautais vaillamment aux anecdotes de prison. [. . .]
>
> Tu ne voulais rien nous dire et nous n'avons pas insisté. (p.185)

This refusal on Albert's part to talk about the Occupation, coupled with his previous absences (for one reason or another), convincingly demonstrates that Marie Chaix is in exactly the same boat as

Pascal Jardin – she too is a war orphan, if not strictly by definition, then most certainly in practice.

Against this background of emotional deprivation, Chaix's aim in writing her book becomes abundantly clear – again like Jardin before her, she is endeavouring to track down her 'missing' father, attempting to find a more acceptable heritage than 'l'héritage d'incompréhensions' (p.167) that she inherited in reality.[10] And not surprisingly, the focus of this search is the 'black hole' of the Occupation, the period about which Albert says nothing, and yet the period which holds the key to the legacy she seeks. For as she knows only too well, and acknowledges in another confession to her deceased father: 'Les lauriers de ta guerre je les ai ramassés' (p.185).

Pick up his *lauriers* she most definitely did, because no matter how vague his bequest to her on the general level, the one thing he did pass down was a surname blackened by shame and infamy. 'Nous portions un nom que la presse venait de citer abondamment', she observes, looking back to the postwar *épuration*, 'et en attendant que le temps passe et alimente les esprits exacerbés de l'après-guerre avec d'autres procès, d'autres traîtres, il fallait que l'on nous cache un peu et nous oublie' (p.167). Albert, of course, had never intended that this should happen, and had devised his defence at his first trial accordingly: 'Il m'importe avant tout de faire la preuve que ma conscience n'a rien à se reprocher', he is said to have determined, 'et que – quoi qu'il arrive – mes enfants pourront toujours porter fièrement mon nom. Le reste ne compte plus' (p.151).[11] But the best-laid plans of mice and men. . . , as the saying goes, and Albert is the perfect case in point, for he had badly underestimated the extent of his predicament. Instead of waiting for his trial to try and clear his name, he would have done better to have listened to Doriot who, on 9 August 1944, had explicitly warned him: 'Le crime de ta famille, ce sera de porter ton nom!' (p.87). These words were to prove unerringly prophetic, and the implication they embody is clear – it is obviously not just to create a sense of mystery that Chaix omits the surname Beugras from *Les Lauriers du lac de Constance*; she plainly wants to evoke the burden it represents for her as well.

Just how heavy and painful this burden actually is for her to bear she confides to her readers in no uncertain terms at all. 'Je suis un enfant de la collaboration, du maréchal, de Doriot, de la Wehrmacht et de l'antisémitisme', we learn. 'Je suis née à droite, avec la LVF et *Le Cri du Peuple*. Mon père y écrit. [. . .] On y tient, dès 40, des propos antisémites' (p.44). And that is not all. To compound the trauma of this distressing political heritage there is also the sense of guilt she feels at having been a privileged child, at not having had to suffer – again because of her birthright – the hardships to which countless other young children of her age most harrowingly fell prey: 'Je suis née en 1942. D'autres, enfants de la rafle, Vel' d'Hiv, wagons, Auschwitz. Moi, non. Moi, enfant rosé, aimé, allaité, bercé. Enfant épargné. 1942' (p.48).

This evocation of 1942, the year thousands of Paris-based Jews were arrested and deported, is more significant than it may appear to be at first glance, for contained within it is a revealing insight into what, for many, will be the most fascinating area of Chaix's narrative, namely the fact that, as the author readily admits, she was not born until half way through the *années noires*, and so cannot – by implication – have any personal recollection of the events she so confidently describes. In other words, her text is entirely dependent on the memories of others – on those of her mother and Juliette, the maid, obviously, but above all on those of Albert, who, although absent and uncommunicative for a great deal of the time, nevertheless consigned his most intimate of thoughts and opinions to his diary.

Jardin too, it may be recalled, was obliged to use such second-hand raw material to re-enact the past, with the result that his writing became somewhat less than objective.[12] And in Chaix's case the effect is exactly the same, as her reference to the family flat in Paris demonstrates: 'Cet appartement dont je n'avais que des souvenirs vagues, je le reconstituai plus tard en collant les bouts de récits fantastiques que j'entendais à son sujet' (p.91). The procedure invoked here, which relies far more on pure fantasy than on documentation, is one which most manifestly applies to the book as a whole, except, of course, to those pages which quote directly from Albert's *journal*. But the paternal *confidences* are not rendered any more reliable for that. On the contrary, they are as problematic as everything else in the text. Take, for example, the self-portrait they present to the reader. The Albert Beugras depicted is totally committed to the PPF, admittedly, but he is not thereby earmarked for collaboration from the start. Not in the slightest: 'Sans Mers el-Kébir, je ne serais pas rentré en France en 40, j'aurais rejoint les troupes gaullistes' (p.27).[13] Furthermore, hand in hand with this claim to be an 'unfortunate' *résistant manqué* goes that of being no more than a simple idealist: 'Je me suis toujours opposé', we are informed,

> à tout ce qui constituait une activité louche et déshonorante, menée à l'abri de notre drapeau au bénéfice matériel de quelques-uns. [. . .] J'ai voulu consacrer toute ma foi, toutes mes forces à un idéal, ô combien chimérique, je le vois aujourd'hui. C'est là que réside mon erreur capitale. (pp.149–50)

Clearly, the picture which Albert paints of himself is by no means an impartial one.

Be that as it may, responsibility for the subjective tinge to *Les Lauriers du lac de Constance* must, in the final analysis, be put down entirely to Chaix herself, and this is all the more transparent in that, quite palpably, the lack of objectivity in her work does not stem solely from her reliance on fragmentary, second-hand source materials, but also from how she chooses to present these snippets of information. To give just one obvious illustration of this: not for her a fixed, unchanging narrative voice. From first person to third person, and from the author to her mother and father, the perspective jumps around with no apparent consistency whatsoever. Yet along the way one particular viewpoint stands out in this refreshing and skilful technique – that characterised by the use of the intimate *tu*. Such a plainly emotive device, which creates a sympathetic bonding between Chaix, her two parents (to each of whom this pronoun is applied) and the vast majority of her readers, is hardly the stylistic trait of a dispassionate biographer; it is, rather, more the trademark of a writer of fiction.

What all this amounts to, when all else is said and done, is that Chaix, like Jardin before her, has fabricated a personal myth for herself, a myth which, despite her constant critical irony, allows her father to be seen in a much better light than is traditionally the case, for at the end of the day, no matter what else is disputed, one significant fact remains – Albert's repertoire has been vitally expanded; to the orthodox role of PPF militant have been added those, far more heretical, of doomed idealist and much-loved family man. Chaix has, in short, formulated a *countermyth*.

It is easy to deduce why she should need to do this. From as far back as she can remember, that is to say from the time when, in the midst of the post-Liberation *résistancialisme*, she had to 'ouvrir les yeux sur un monde à l'envers' (p.105) and 'réapprendre l'histoire de France' (p.105), she has been painfully aware that Albert has been cast as one of the blackest of villains, a man who, a priori, was deserving only of scorn. This was all very well as long as he was in prison, and a virtual stranger, but, as noted earlier, once he was released tremendous difficulties arose: part of her still wanted to hate him, but more and more she was coming to love him. Something, then, most manifestly had to give, and give it duly did – slowly but surely, her hatred subsided, overwhelmed by her more natural filial affection. 'Cela prit du temps mais je ne t'en veux plus', she now admits (p.185), and then appends, shortly afterwards: 'Tu m'as quittée le jour de mes vingt et un ans, j'allais t'aimer. [. . .] Je n'ai pas tout compris mais je commence à te connaître. Adieu monsieur. Tu peux dormir tranquille' (p.187).[14] With these telling words, the root cause of her countermythification emerges for all to see – what she is plainly trying to do in her work is exorcise the past, and thereby standardise her relationship with her father. For if successful, she will do more than secure emotional peace for herself; she will, at long last, come to terms with her inherited identity.

Adding these conclusions now to those made earlier in the section, the extent to which Chaix has followed in Jardin's footsteps, both with regard to her basic predicament and in her reaction to it, no longer remains a subject for doubt – the correlation between the two writers is almost perfect. And if this, in itself, already suggests that something important is taking place, then future developments will transform this impression into a certitude, because Chaix was by no means the last to make the same journey as Jardin. Numerous others were to appear in her wake as well.

Of these subsequent fellow travellers, Jacques Bonny, Jean-Luc Maxence and, indeed, Marie Gatard have all been discussed previously, either in Part I above or in a number of comparative footnotes. The final member of the group, however, Evelyne Le Garrec, most definitely has not, so it is on her, and more particularly on her book, *La Rive allemande de ma mémoire* (1980), that the remaining pages of this chapter will focus.

To begin by saying that Le Garrec is in a position which is all too familiar is almost to make a grave understatement. Daughter of a provincial *chef de section* in the PPF, and hence 'l'héritière d'une trahison' (p.26), she too, like Chaix and Jardin, is most visibly and emphatically an orphan – an orphan, though, not now in the sense that she suffered from paternal absences while she was growing up (quite the opposite: 'Notre vie familiale était normale, avec un père présent en dehors de ses heures de travail et, peut-être, de sorties pour des réunions' – p.132), but rather in the much more serious sense that, in 1943, when she was only nine, her father was shot dead by the Resistance for collaborating. So the void in her life is irrevocably total, as she herself knows only too well: 'Que mon père ait appartenu au parti populaire français, [. . .] c'est [. . .] à peu près la seule chose que je savais de lui en commençant ce récit' (p.103). And needless to say, or so it seems, this oft-seen void, in turn, has a consequence which is not all that unfamiliar either – the Le Garrec we encounter is a writer who has embarked on a personal quest, 'une fille à la recherche de l'image perdue de son père' (p.122).

But this search is not an easy one for her to conduct, for she has precious little to go on, even less, in fact, than the already ill-informed author of *Les Lauriers du lac de Constance*:

> Mon père, un parmi des milliers, n'écrivait pas, ou, s'il le faisait, ses textes n'étaient pas publiés et ne sont même pas restés dans les archives familiales. Rien de comparable, par exemple, avec le personnage des romans de Marie Chaix, personnalité éminente du PPF qui a légué à sa fille des carnets qui ont permis à celle-ci de lire son histoire à livre ouvert, sinon de la comprendre facilement. Mon père n'a rien laissé. (pp.119–20)

Given this dearth of first-hand raw material, she has no option but to try and make do with whatever other sources of information are available to her, and these, it rapidly emerges, are no more than two in number: historical *documents* from the Bibliothèque Nationale and the recollections of a mother who, by choice, has said nothing about her husband for the last thirty-five years.

To be restricted to two such uncertain lines of enquiry is, quite evidently, highly unsatisfactory, and it is not long before the inherent limitations of the procedure predictably rise to the surface. For example, reading up on her father's death in a contemporary newspaper, the author is absolutely amazed by what she discovers there: 'Quel est cet étranger dont il est question dans les nécrologies? Je comprends, comme jamais je ne l'avais fait, à quel point on peut, dans un article, donner d'un homme une image totalement fausse sans pourtant déformer la vérité des faits' (p.141). And what she learns from her mother is hardly any more trustworthy or objective, because as she realises: 'Ma mère, c'est encore moi, un prolongement de moi. Tandis que je la questionnais, je savais que sa mémoire ne me renverrait que ce que la mienne suggérait' (p.119). Thus, the picture of her father which she constructs is of necessity both partial and unreliable. It is, in reality, not so much a faithful portrait that she produces as a blatant *myth* – a myth cobbled together out of the all-too-rare scraps of knowledge that happen to be at hand.

Clear confirmation of this, should any further illustration be required, is given by the form of *La Rive allemande de ma mémoire*. Extracts from PPF newspapers, interview transcripts, the *procès-verbal* of the murder, signposted hypotheses and passages of pointed self-analysis – all of these are incorporated into the text *tels quels*, with no rewriting to ensure uniformity of presentation at all. And as if that were not enough, it is an unstable narrative voice which helps bind these diverse *documents* together, a narrative voice which just as easily accommodates the third-person *elle*, that 'fiction d'un personnage faussement romanesque' (p.18), as the less distant, more autobiographical first-person *je*. Most palpably, then, Le Garrec's work is, in purely formal terms, the most honest and modern of all those so far considered; not only does it make no attempt to hide its fragmentary origins, it also reveals – albeit by implication – its debt to a process of mythopoeia.

All of this, once again, inevitably gives rise to a strong sense of *déjà vu*. But this is not to say that the links between Le Garrec and her predecessors are total. Nothing could be further from the truth, for there is one vital aspect of *La Rive allemande de ma mémoire* which, in the present context, is undoubtedly unique: the love-hate relationship between parent and child, previously omnipresent, has now been replaced by one of pure hatred. Why should this be? Why should the author search for a man she knows she detests? There are, quite patently, a variety of possible answers to these questions.

The first of these can be summed up in one seven-letter word: Germany. Knowing that German blood runs in her veins (thanks to her maternal grandparents), and knowing also that Germany is France's hereditary enemy, Le Garrec feels that she, like her mother, has within her a Germanic 'tare', a 'tare' which, nevertheless, her father was well qualified to remove: 'Mon père [. . .], authentiquement français, aurait pu nous sauver de la malédiction originelle' (p.19). But of course he did not. In fact he did the exact opposite: 'Mon père, par son choix délibéré de l'Allemagne, redoublait notre tare secrète, à ma mère et à moi' (p.206). Faced with such a painful action by her parent, Le Garrec could not fail to bear him a considerable grudge, nor could she fail to experience an urgent need for exorcism, so this is the first explanation of her venture – an obsessive attempt at self-purging, the roots of which can be traced back to the very start of her literary career: 'Quand j'ai commencé à écrire, je l'ai fait sous un nom d'emprunt, celui de mon mari. Pour me débarrasser de l'héritage paternel, de la part allemande qui m'était léguée par mon père français' (p.48).

This conscious rejection of the family name leads on nicely to the second cause of Le Garrec's quest – her wish to discover her identity. 'J'ai rejeté le nom de mon père et [. . .] je suis devenue une femme sans identité', she candidly admits (pp.47–8), and as a result of this she has had to spend most of her life acting out a series of roles. But in *La Rive allemande de ma mémoire* she is evidently breaking with such a dishonest *mode de vie*: 'Puisque me sont coupées mes fausses racines, identités usurpées – à moins de m'en construire d'autres, mais je n'en ai pas le courage et puis [. . .] il est trop tard –, il faut bien que j'affronte les vraies. L'Allemagne' (p.27). Beneath this symbolic 'Allemagne', it is, more specifically, her negative emotions that she must confront, because as she readily concedes: 'Ma culpabilité, ma honte, ma haine pour mon père, c'est moi. Elles m'ont faite telle que je suis. J'y tiens, je veux les conserver, les nourrir, aussi longtemps du moins que je n'y verrai pas plus clair' (p.26). So her aim could hardly be more explicit – it is most definitely self-knowledge that she is pursuing.

Not unexpectedly, perhaps (given the modernity of *La Rive allemande de ma mémoire* in matters of form), this exorcistic search for an identity is placed within the (no less modern) framework of psychoanalytical theory. 'Le catéchisme psychanalytique nous apprend que nous devons "tuer le père"', we are reminded (p.211), and Le Garrec at one stage eagerly takes this remark at face value. Imagining her young self making up stories about her father in school, she suggests she could well have contributed to, if not actually started, the rumours which would help bring about his death. 'C'est sur la dénonciation de sa propre fille qu'ils l'ont condamné', she insists (p.175), and although her absolute certainty here soon subsides, even in her more moderate conclusion – 'Je ne saurai pas si j'ai participé concrètement à la mort de mon père ou si je l'ai tué en rêve' (p.178) – the element of Freudian wish fulfilment is still paramount.

This dramatic confession to the crime of parricide, whether symbolic or actual, takes us to the very heart of *La Rive allemande de ma mémoire*; so to discover its cause will be to find out exactly why, deep down, Le Garrec detests her father so violently. Fortunately, this cause is not especially difficult to unearth – what motivates the author, it is increasingly apparent, is her inveterate feminism, for in her eyes, the vital failing of the man who helped bring her into the world was that he was, precisely, a man. 'Il est le premier à avoir introduit dans notre histoire familiale le pouvoir masculin', she observes, and continues:

> Nous sortions du matriarcat pour entrer dans le patriarcat. Domination de l'homme sur ma mère et moi. Il entendait régner absolument sur 'ses' femmes. J'étais peut-être marquée inconsciemment par toute une lignée d'aïeules-reines. Toujours est-il que je ne supportais pas cette domination. Il était l'intrus dans notre famille de femmes. (p.186)[15]

Hence: 'Pour que notre famille de femmes renaisse et vive, il doit disparaître de notre communauté' (p.211).

This is all very well, but if, as is now clear, Le Garrec hates her father simply because he is a man, does this mean that his wartime collaboration is not as important as was first thought? The answer to this question is a resounding 'yes', because as we are informed towards the end of the quest:

> Ce n'est pas parce qu'il était collaborateur, et donc dans une situation historique particulière, que j'ai souhaité la mort de mon père, mais parce qu'il était mon père, tout simplement, incarnation d'une virilité autoritaire que je ne supportais pas. [. . .] Eût-il été dans l'autre camp, résistant, mort au champ d'honneur, héros à titre posthume, ma haine pour lui n'aurait pas été moins vive. Mais elle aurait été plus dure à assumer, car sans circonstances atténuantes. (p.212)

This does not imply, however, that the paternal *engagement* is totally irrelevant. Not at all. There are at least two ways in which it manifestly comes into play. The first of these is that, in Le Garrec's own words,

> l'idéologie de l'Allemagne nazie coïncidait avec le caractère de mon père et sa conception de l'autorité. Chez lui, il y avait adéquation parfaite entre l'idéologie politique et l'idéologie familiale. [. . .] s'il avait été résistant, il y aurait eu en lui, pour moi, contradiction entre l'exercice de son pouvoir sur nous et sa désobéissance au pouvoir en place. Despote à la maison, rebelle au-dehors. Le cas n'est certes pas exceptionnel, mais j'aurais pu, il me semble, creuser cette faille et me battre contre lui sans peut-être souhaiter sa mort, car une possibilité de gagner m'aurait été ouverte. En tout cas, je l'aurais cru. Peut-être. (p.213)

The second reason why collaboration is a relevant factor is that, thanks to the mythification which surrounds it, it demands a certain, stereotyped response from all those who come into contact with it. After the war, as has been seen, the response required was one of revulsion, and this was ideal for Le Garrec, since her feelings towards her father were already intensely negative:

> La situation historique, son engagement politique particulier, ont permis que [. . .] mon règlement de compte personnel et familial se fonde dans le gigantesque règlement de compte qui a résulté de la guerre. [. . .] L'adhésion de mon père à la Collaboration m'a permis d'étayer ma haine par un motif extérieur, objectif, indiscutable. Un motif politique et historique non contestable par qui que ce soit. J'étais dans mon bon droit. (pp.212–13)

But a good thirty years later the climate had changed. France and Germany were now partners in Europe and, furthermore, the domestic view of the Occupation, as embodied by the *mode rétro*, had turned through a full one hundred and eighty degrees. So all of a sudden, Le Garrec was no longer in tune with events. 'J'ai été baisée par l'Histoire', she sadly confirms,

> [. . .] moi, avec mes trente années de culpabilité, de honte, de mensonges, de déguisements, de clandestinité, je me retrouve comme une idiote, grosse Jeanne comme devant dans cette réhabilitation générale. Je ne comprends plus rien aux règles du jeu. On les a changées pendant que je dormais et je ne sais plus où je dois me mettre, quels gestes on attend de moi. (p.25)

What is expected of her, of course, is that she fall into step with the new orthodoxy and view the Collaboration – and along with it her father – far less severely.

But this she is unwilling to do, preferring instead to carry on exactly as before. Consequently, if she now sets off in search of her long-lost, much-hated parent, it is not to try and find reasons to love him, but rather to reaffirm and justify her existing antipathy, for by her own admission:

> J'avais peur [. . .] de ce qu'une enquête pourrait m'apporter. Mais ce que je redoutais de voir établie, irréfutable, avec preuves à l'appui, ce n'était pas la culpabilité de mon père. C'était son innocence. Car, s'il s'avérait que ses activités politiques ne méritaient pas la peine capitale, que me resterait-il pour justifier ma haine et la punition que je m'étais imposée au nom de l'Allemagne? (p.79)

This wish – almost determination – to prove the justice of the wartime killing suggests that Le Garrec is, to say the least, a less than impartial observer of the paternal past, and that this is indeed the case is demonstrated on numerous other occasions throughout her book. For example, discovering that her father tended to spoil her when she was young, she sees in this fact not a redeeming feature of his character, but rather another overpowering reason to detest him: 'Je crois que je l'aurais mieux supporté indifférent, lointain. Contre sa présence trop lourde, trop violente ou trop attentive, je n'avais aucun autre moyen de défense que la haine' (p.203). Such readiness to see no good at all in the man confirms, it would appear, what was said earlier about the mythopoeic nature of *La Rive allemande de ma mémoire*. Yet at the same time it also takes the debate one stage further, for by seeking – whether consciously or unconsciously – to condemn her father out of hand, Le Garrec is patently at odds with the new, revisionistic mythification of the *mode rétro*. In other words, what she is creating, ultimately, is not so much a myth as, more precisely, a countermyth – or even a counter-countermyth.

In this roundabout manner, therefore, Le Garrec falls neatly into line behind her orphan-writer colleagues. For at the end of the day she too, like them, can be said to have just one basic goal: to subvert the current social status of her collaborator-father, and thereby justify her own, heretical feelings towards him – a goal which, by a process of countermythification, and again like her predecessors, she plainly achieves to perfection.

Having now analysed the work of Jardin, Chaix, Le Garrec and, earlier, Bonny, Maxence and Gatard, what emerges as striking about these six authors is the uncanny resemblance which binds them together. As has been seen, all of them suffer from the absence of a father, a father who, if not always dead, is nevertheless lost to them because of the collective myth – of one sort or another – which has grown up around the Occupation, and so to try and overcome this orphanage they all set off in search of their missing parents. Plagued by a lack of relevant source material, however, these searches never culminate in faithful portraits of the person sought, but rather in collages of small fragments of fact held together by the glue of invention. In short, they result in the creation of personal myths, or to be more precise, given the unorthodoxy involved, in the creation of personal countermyths. Evidently, such a consistent recourse to mythification can hardly be explained away as mere coincidence; there must be more to it than that, and it is not hard to see what: cut off from their parents, the six authors are also cut off from facets of their identity. Hence, if they embark on filial quests of rediscovery, it is to re-establish contact, beneath the various myths surrounding the *années noires*, with their roots and with their 'lost' selves. This, then, is why they are so significant within the *mode rétro*: by seeking, openly, to repossess the heritage of which they have been deprived, they constitute the visible tip of a very considerable iceberg – the iceberg composed of their generation as a whole; the iceberg formed by a generation of orphans.

Notes

1. To facilitate the giving of references, a shorthand form of each book's title will hereafter be incorporated into the main text alongside the relevant page numbers. The abbreviations used will be *GNA*, *GAG*, *NJ* and *BBD* respectively.
2. As is frequently the case with members of the young generation, Jardin is in no way innovating here. In 1948, for instance, Claude Jamet had written in *Fifi Roi*: 'Nous parlons de Pétain, de Laval. Sans aucun doute, ils étaient sages en juin 40; ils avaient la raison pour eux [. . .]. L'Histoire cependant ne le reconnaîtra pas. [. . .] *Vae Victis*! Ils avaient tort, puisqu'ils ont perdu' (p.52). In the same year, Maurice Sachs, in *La Chasse à courre*, had also argued that collaboration with Germany was the sensible option in 1940 (p.62). In fact, this argument was one commonly used by collaborators in their defence, with some justification, it would appear – see Jacques Delperrié de Bayac, *Histoire de la milice, 1918–1945*, p.41.
3. Cf. *GNA*, p.34, *NJ*, pp.19, 149.
4. Cf. Jean-Luc Maxence, *L'Ombre d'un père*. Like Jardin, Maxence too sees his father as 'mon hérédité despotique suspendue au-dessus de tous mes faits et gestes' (p.11); he too distances himself from the paternal *prises de position* ('J'aime à le crier, je n'adhère ni de près ni de loin aux options fondamentales de ton existence' – p.15); and he too eventually admits: 'Mon père, [. . .] je t'aime autant que je te hais' (p.31).
5. Again, cf. Maxence: 'La famille, justement, ne se choisit pas, on la subit ou on l'assassine comme on peut! [. . .] Il va me falloir te régler ton compte, mon père, ma race' (ibid., pp. 15–16).
6. 'Préface', in *La Guerre à neuf ans*, Rombaldi, 1975, p.15.

7. Ibid., pp.11–12.
8. See, e.g., Jean Jardin's reaction to *La Guerre à neuf ans*: 'C'est le contraire d'un roman dont on dit que tout y est vrai sauf les noms: chez Pascal, seuls les noms sont vrais; tout le reste est faux!' (cit. in François Nourissier, 'Tel père, tel fils', p.78).
9. Founded by Doriot in June 1936, the PPF had, according to Pascal Ory, a 'fonction de pédagogie fasciste: culte du chef, exaltation de l'autorité virile, refus symétrique du capitalisme et du bolchevisme' (*Les Collaborateurs, 1940–1945*, p.26). Albert's wartime role within the movement was to take charge of its secret *service de renseignement*, of which historian Marcel Hasquenoph noted, rather disturbingly: 'Cet organisme [. . .] livre à l'*Abwehr* et à la Gestapo tout ce qui peut être utile aux Allemands' (*La Gestapo en France*, p.176).
10. So fundamental is this quest for an inheritance in Chaix's eyes that she has since recounted the lives of her two other 'parents': her mother (in *Les Silences ou la vie d'une femme*) and her 'seconde mère', the maid Juliette (in *Juliette, chemin des Cerisiers*). Both of these works cover some of the same ground as *Les Lauriers du lac de Constance*, but contain little of relevance that is new, and so have been omitted from the present study. (With regard to the 'adoption' of the maid as a second mother, however, cf. Maxence and his governess, 'cette minuscule Yvonne qui fut en quelque sorte pour moi une "maman-bis"' – *L'Ombre d'un père*, p.222.)
11. This obsession with the burden posed by a stigmatised family name was, understandably, common to a large number of collaborators in post-Liberation France. See, e.g., Jean-H. Roy, 'Les Deux Justices', which refers (albeit sceptically) to an *épuré* who writes under a pseudonym because 'il a peur, nous dit son éditeur, de livrer à notre justice boiteuse un nom qu'après sa mort portent encore sa femme et son fils' (p.2262).
12. Cf. also Jacques Bonny, Marie Gatard and Jean-Luc Maxence, as demonstrated in Part I.
13. To appreciate just how great an excuse these words became for the Beugras family, see Chaix's later work, *Juliette*, pp.116–17.
14. Cf. Maxence: 'Je commence à peine à te connaître quand tu disparais, à peine à t'aimer, à te craindre' (*L'Ombre d'un père*, p.234).
15. Cf. Chaix's comments on Albert's release from prison, as described in *Juliette*: 'Notre famille a son chef, intrus malgré lui dans un univers féminin qui tournait assez bien autour de son absence' (p.190).

–5–

Patrick Modiano

> La vie réelle ne suffit pas [. . .] à me satisfaire.
>
> *Patrick Modiano*

> Moi j'avais la *manie* de regarder en arrière, toujours ce sentiment de quelque chose de perdu, pas comme le paradis, mais de perdu, oui.
>
> *Patrick Modiano*

> Comme tous les gens qui n'ont ni terroir ni racines, je suis obsédé par ma préhistoire. Et ma préhistoire, c'est la période trouble et honteuse de l'Occupation.
>
> *Patrick Modiano*

Of all the young authors whose problems were to crystallise into the *mode rétro*, the one who stands out head and shoulders above the rest is Patrick Modiano. Born into the France of 1945 of a half-Hungarian, half-Belgian, Flemish-speaking actress and a mysterious, Mediterranean, Jewish *apatride*, Modiano was, from birth, a cultural orphan, an intricate mixture of differing, and often contradictory impulses. This, in itself, would no doubt have been enough to colour his future development, but a childhood plagued by upheaval and solitude – his father abandoned him, then his brother (and close friend) Rudy died – served to compound his predicament by infusing him with an acute sense of deprivation and loss.[1] The result of all this was that, at a precociously early age, he found himself drawn into fiction writing, attracted, amongst other things, by the freedom it gave him to reconstruct his past and hence establish an alternative life history for himself. As he revealed in 1976, following his interview with Emmanuel Berl: 'En face de Berl, je retourne à mes préoccupations: le temps, le passé, la mémoire. Il les ravive, ces préoccupations. Il m'encourage dans mon dessein: me créer un passé et une mémoire avec le passé et la mémoire des autres.'[2] It is in the light of this declaration, then, and, of course, in the light of the identity crisis which subtends it, that Modiano's portrayal of the *années noires* can best be elucidated.

Modiano's first plunge into the depths of the Occupation came in his début novel, which won two literary prizes and a great deal of critical acclaim. The title of this highly-praised work was *La Place de l'Étoile* (1968), a reference both to the celebrated Paris landmark and to the place where Jews wore the star of David during the war – over the heart. This is significant, for the book is essentially a French Jew's *cri de cœur*, an intense examination of Jewish identity, and although Modiano is hardly the first novelist to tackle this troublesome subject, what sets him apart from his predecessors is that he deals with the old topic in a startlingly new way, namely by creating Raphaël Schlemilovitch. A composite of many different, stereotyped personalities, Schlemilovitch is the bizarre embodiment of *Le Juif* in the abstract, an archetypal token of his people as a whole, as one perceptive journalist instantly recognised: 'Qu'ils s'aiment ou non, qu'ils s'acceptent ou non, tous les juifs de ce monde sont un seul juif, qui s'appelle toujours Raphaël Schlemilovitch – et un seul juif, hélas! porte le poids de tous les autres, présents, passés et à venir.'[3] In other words, to draw a comparison based on the novel itself, he is just like one of the kaleidoscopes which his father makes: 'un visage humain composé de mille facettes lumineuses et qui change sans arrêt de forme' (pp.109–10).

Because of this fragmentation of its narrative voice, *La Place de l'Étoile* cannot be analysed according to traditional criteria. It must be judged on its own terms and accepted for what it is: an incongruous, comical voyage in space and time, where the primary logic to which Raphaël adheres is the logic of Jewish precedent. For example, he emulates Fleg, Blum and Henri Franck by working hard to get into the École Nationale Supérieure; he becomes a pimp partly because, as he says, 'quand Apollinaire parlait du "maquereau juif, roux et rose", il pensait à moi' (p.106); and he even proceeds to take Kafka's tuberculosis as his own. In fact, surprising as this may seem, his 'retour à la terre' phase can also be accounted for in this manner, since Pétain's famous saying which he adapts and appropriates – 'Je hais les mensonges qui m'ont fait tant de mal. La terre, elle, ne ment pas' (p.83) – was, in reality, formulated by Emmanuel Berl, a Jew.[4]

This flirtation with the Victor of Verdun, that is to say with the man who, as figurehead of *la Révolution nationale*, came to be associated with institutionalised anti-Semitism, is not the only occasion on which Schlemilovitch sides with his apparent persecutors, for in yet another astonishing metamorphosis, and in imitation this time of Maurice Sachs and Joanovici, he willingly takes on the mantle of a 'juif collabo'. Furthermore, pushing such a contradictory stance to its limit, and no doubt recalling as well that Jewish blood was said to flow in the veins of Hitler and Heydrich, he continues down this avenue, becomes a Nazi and takes Eva Braun as his lover.

The Jewish connection cannot explain all of his relationships with renowned anti-Semites, however. There are many instances when this link just does not apply, as when he mingles with Maurras and his companions on the extreme Right, or when he joins the team of *Je suis partout*. Does this consequently mean that he is ignoring his own logic and acting incomprehensibly? Not at all. There is, despite appearances, considerable method in his madness, since by frequenting these Fascist milieux he is able, quite rationally, to kill three sizeable birds with one stone. First, he can make, as it were, a pre-emptive, defensive strike against his enemies, 'pour court-circuiter la menace', as Modiano himself agrees.[5] Second, he can indulge the other half of his schizophrenic character, establish himself as truly *French*, and accept the *antidreyfusard* heritage which this entails. And finally, he can obtain an anti-Semite's-eye view of the world and thereby gain a better, more informative insight into the social identity he has as a Jew.

This last concern is arguably the most important of the three, for Raphaël feels he has a duty to fulfil every anti-Semitic expectation of him, and as early as the opening paragraph he is to be found putting this conviction into practice – his reference to his 'héritage vénézuélien' plays on 'well-known' Jewish internationalism (a point taken up later when he mentions his cousins in Cairo, London, Paris, Caracas, Trieste and Budapest), and his very name would satisfy most people as being 'typical' of his race.[6] Indeed, the longer the novel goes on, the clearer it becomes that he is moulding himself on popular prejudice. 'Oui, je dirige le complot juif mondial à coups de partouzes et de millions', he proclaims. 'Oui, la guerre de 1939 a été déclarée par ma faute. Oui, je suis une sorte de Barbe-Bleue, un anthropophage qui dévore les petites Aryennes après les avoir violées. Oui, je rêve de ruiner toute la paysannerie française et d'enjuiver le Cantal' (p.35).

This penchant for laying claim to the roles allotted – more explicitly seen in statements such as 'Je jouerai à ma façon le rôle du jeune milliardaire' (p.34), or 'Je jouerai à la perfection mon rôle de persécuté' (p.62) – is again displayed when Schlemilovitch meets Charles Lévy-Vendôme, who is the Jew-as-seen-by-the-anti-Semite *par excellence*. As his name suggests, Lévy-Vendôme personifies the Semitic 'threat' to France, for not only does he 'export' young French women to work abroad in brothels, he transforms the country's literary classics into erotica. 'Non content de débaucher les femmes de ce pays, j'ai voulu aussi prostituer toute la littérature française', he confesses (p.68). Needless to say, Raphaël has no qualms at all about emulating this behaviour, and he quickly agrees to become part of the white slave trade himself. What is more, he then crowns his subversive activities by having an affair with a *marquise*, who, by dressing up as a different historical figure each time they make love, allows him to complete his assumed mission in a strikingly symbolic manner – with her help, it is unambiguously stated, 'il souilla la France à loisir' (p.95).[7]

Given that, as may perhaps now be apparent, Schlemilovitch has a certain existentialist air about him, a distinct colouring of *existence pour autrui*, it is highly appropriate that he should further be influenced by Jean-Paul Sartre's *Réflexions sur la question juive* (1954). Strangely enough, what he finds useful in this work is not, it would seem, the rightly famous philosophical argument, which is dismissed out of hand along with its author – 'Il affirmait que le juif n'existerait pas si les goyes ne daignaient lui prêter attention. Il faut donc attirer *leurs* regards aux moyens d'étoffes bariolées' (p.48) – but rather the mention of 'la mythologie antisémite', and the typical character traits which it ascribes to the Jew: a love of money, constant self-analysis and the inability to assimilate, among others.

Not surprisingly, all of these points are eagerly taken on board by Raphaël. 'Je suis JUIF. Par conséquent, seuls l'argent et la luxure m'intéressent', he notes (p.34), highlighting his avarice with his own, peculiar brand of logic. Fifty pages later, it is the tendency towards intense, personal criticism which manifestly comes to the fore:

> Après avoir été un juif collabo, façon Joanovici-Sachs, Raphaël Schlemilovitch joue la comédie du 'retour à la terre' façon Barrès-Pétain. A quand l'immonde comédie du juif militariste, façon capitaine Dreyfus-Stroheim? Celle de juif honteux façon Simone Weil-Céline? Celle du juif distingué façon Proust-Daniel Halévy-Maurois? Nous voudrions que Raphaël Schlemilovitch se contente d'être un juif tout court. (p.84)[8]

Where Raphaël most visibly follows Sartre, though, is in his feeling of cultural orphanage, his total failure to integrate himself into French society. Part of his trouble here derives from his family background, for although he occasionally refers to his mother and does actually meet up with his father, these two characters soon disappear from his life to leave him completely rootless, as he readily – and compositely – admits: 'Notre mère était morte ou folle. Nous ne connaissions pas l'adresse de notre père à New York' (p.103). The other source of his problem is no less traumatic, if somewhat more predictable – the painful knowledge that, as he says, 'Je ne suis pas un enfant de ce pays' (p.12), and that this makes him 'une fleur artificielle au milieu de la France' (p.47).[9]

Yet it is not through want of trying that Schlemilovitch finds himself isolated and adrift. He is continually doing his utmost to blend in and establish himself, using two ploys in particular to seek out the ties he lacks. On the one hand: marriage. He has fiancées in every province when working *la traite des blanches*, and he seems quite eager to wed any woman he encounters, whether it be Rebecca, the Israeli soldier, or Hilda, whose father is a strict SS disciplinarian. On the other hand, there is his constant invention of surrogate relatives: he thinks nothing of claiming to be 'le frère jumeau du juif Süss' (p.113), nor does he hesitate to speak of 'mon père, le vicomte Lévy-Vendôme' (p.85), 'Des Essarts, mon frère' (p.105), 'mon cousin, le peintre juif Modigliani' (p.113), 'mon grand-père, le colonel Aravis' (p.75) or 'mon grand-oncle Adrien Debigorre' (p.75). His view of Maurras and his helpers at *L'Action Française* further reflects this state of affairs: 'Depuis mon enfance je rêvais à des grands-pères de ce genre. Le mien, juif obscur d'Odessa, ne savait pas parler français' (p.25).[10]

This search for some sort of anchorage culminates, naturally, in a pilgrimage to Israel, 'la terre ancestrale' (p.122). But no sooner does Raphaël arrive in Tel Aviv (having first played the wandering Jew by travelling to Cairo and Vienna) than his expectations are once again dashed to the ground. To his great discomfort, he is made to feel every bit as unwelcome there as he was in France, for the Israelis, he discovers, are a nation of Fascistic strong men, and have nothing but disdain for their effete European counterparts, announcing: 'Nous ne voulons plus entendre parler de l'esprit critique juif, de l'intelligence juive, du scepticisme juif, des contorsions juives, de l'humiliation, du malheur juif et patati et patata' (p.133). Such a bizarre depiction of the Jewish homeland stems, no doubt, from the popular belief that Israel is a state full of militarists, all determined to assert their power and ensure that they are never victimised again. Nevertheless, there is also a night-club in the capital where German uniforms must be worn, so the stereotyped 'couple éternel du SS et de la juive' (p.22) has by no means been overlooked.[11]

On a more abstract, non-geographical level, there is one final way in which Raphaël tries to lay down roots – through the process of writing, which enables him to attach himself to a whole literary and cultural tradition. As he confesses: 'J'avais voulu m'approprier les stylos de Proust et de Céline, les pinceaux de Modigliani et de Soutine, les grimaces de Groucho Marx et de Chaplin' (p.118), and these are only a few of the models he draws upon. Indeed, as long as he plays the role of Franco-Jewish-author-in-search-of-an-identity, he can be seen to occupy exactly the same position that Modiano does, so it comes as no surprise to find that he also owes a debt to the man who invented him. For example, in at least one of his incarnations, he too, like his creator, was born in Boulogne-Billancourt and was just under two metres tall, he too had family origins in Thessalonika and he too lived on the quai Conti in Paris. There is another, more significant area of contact as well. 'Comment se fait-il que vous vous rappeliez tout cela', the great Sigmund Freud asks him in the closing pages,[12] amazed at his familiarity with the Second World War, 'vous n'étiez pas né' (p.150). It is a remark which could just as pertinently be addressed to Modiano himself, for he was not born until after VE Day either (not until 30 July 1945 to be exact). Because of this, then, *La Place de l'Étoile* can perhaps best be interpreted as an apocryphal autobiography, a therapeutic exercise in which the memories recounted are almost wholly fictitious – in short, a work designed to assuage the anguish of narrator and novelist alike.

Modiano's second novel, *La Ronde de nuit* (1969), shows a strong sense of continuity with his first, taking up more or less where its predecessor left off – in the gruesome company of the same band of French *gestapistes* – and having as narrator a man who plainly harks back to Raphaël Schlemilovitch, as the nature of his reading matter illustrates: 'Quelques livres: *Anthologie des traîtres, d'Alcibiade au capitaine Dreyfus*, *Joanovici tel qu'il fut*, *Les Mystères du Chevalier d'Éon*, *Frégoli, l'homme de nulle part*, m'éclairèrent sur mon compte' (p.122).[13] Furthermore, the theme of identity which pervaded *La Place de l'Étoile* is still very much in evidence, for as Modiano explains: 'Dans les deux livres, c'est toujours la recherche d'une identité: l'identité juive, pour le premier et dans le second plutôt une fuite instinctive devant toute identification.'[14]

This summary of *La Ronde de nuit* is immensely helpful, because the central character of the work certainly is extremely hard to pin down. At first (if the chronology of events is re-created), his position is obvious enough – he is Swing Troubadour, a *gestapiste* working at 3bis square Cimarosa for le Khédive and M. Philibert. Things become more problematic, however, after he has been asked by his employers to infiltrate the Resistance. He successfully completes his mission, assuming the *nom de guerre* Princesse de Lamballe, but is then sent to join the Gestapo as an undercover agent. It is at this juncture that confusion rains down about him, for his affiliation to both sides means, in effect, that he belongs to neither. Whenever he is a *résistant*, his persona of Swing Troubadour is negated and vice versa: 'Agent double? ou triple? Je ne savais plus qui j'étais. Mon lieutenant, JE N'EXISTE PAS' (p.132).[15] Similarly, when he denounces Lamballe as the head of the underground network, he is both asserting his own identity (bestowing upon himself the status of a leader) and simultaneously nullifying it (earmarking himself for execution). It is consequently quite natural that he should conclude: 'A ce jeu-là, on finit par se perdre soi-même. De toute façon, je n'ai jamais su qui j'étais' (p.175), which would, in turn, partly explain why he often dresses up as a woman, and why he can claim to be Judas's elder brother, Maxime de Bel-Respiro, Marcel Petiot, Philippe Pétain, Landru and King Lear.[16]

The same personality crisis colours his treatment of Coco Lacour and Esmeralda, his two imaginary friends. Being to all intents and purposes an orphan – his mother is far away in Lausanne and his father (Alexandre Stavisky!)[17] is dead – he finds in these extraordinary comrades a sort of compensatory presence, a necessary palliative to his deficient family background: 'Nous menions, square Cimarosa, une vie de famille', he overtly affirms (p.163). Moreover, by using his ill-gotten gains to cocoon this vulnerable couple, he can justify his crimes to himself and establish his personal importance:

> Coco Lacour et Esmeralda. Misérables. Infirmes. Toujours silencieux. Un souffle, un geste aurait suffi pour les briser. Que seraient-ils devenus sans moi? Je trouvais enfin une excellente raison de vivre. Je les aimais, mes pauvres monstres. Je veillerais sur eux . . . Personne ne pourrait leur faire de mal. Grâce à l'argent que je gagnais square Cimarosa, en qualité d'indic et de pillard, je leur assurerais tout le confort possible. (p.160)

Yet in spite of this apparent benevolence, he sometimes feels the urge to abandon his helpless companions, or far worse, push them under the métro.[18] Given that the couple provide him, as he acknowledges, with 'une excellente raison de vivre', their symbolic murder (which, in typically paradoxical fashion, also allows him to dominate others and thereby procure a sense of identity) once again highlights his manic drive towards self-destruction.[19]

This unstable, schizophrenic approach to life permeates every aspect of Swing Troubadour/Lamballe's behaviour, for not even his treachery is as clear-cut as is generally the case. First of all, his enlistment by the Gestapo in no way corresponds to a commitment on his part. Having, by his own admission, 'pas assez de force d'âme pour me ranger du côté des héros. Trop de nonchalance et de distraction pour faire un vrai salaud' (p.40), he joins up not by conscious choice, but entirely by accident:

> Quelle drôle d'idée de m'être assis à la terrasse du *Royal-Villiers*, place Pereire, moi si discret, si précautionneux et qui voulais à tout prix me faire oublier. Mais on doit débuter dans la vie. On n'y coupe pas. Elle finit par vous envoyer ses sergents recruteurs: en l'occurrence le Khédive et M. Philibert. Un autre soir, sans doute, je serais tombé sur des personnages plus honorables qui m'auraient conseillé l'industrie des textiles ou la littérature. Ne me sentant aucune vocation particulière, j'attendais de mes aînés qu'ils me choisissent un emploi.[. . .] Le plus curieux avec les garçons de mon espèce: ils peuvent aussi bien finir au Panthéon qu'au cimetière de Thiais, carré des fusillés. On en fait des héros. Ou des salauds. On ignorera qu'ils ont été entraînés dans une sale histoire à leur corps défendant. (pp.101–2)[20]

Once he has drifted into the Gestapo in this equivocal, half-hearted manner, he finds it impossible not to speed on down the road to ruin, for his lack of will power means that he will do absolutely anything his masters require of him: 'Mouchard. Je deviendrai même assassin, s'ils le veulent', he maintains (p.21). Yet no matter how many crimes he commits, he is still able to convince himself: 'Je n'étais pas plus méchant qu'un autre. J'ai suivi le mouvement, voilà tout. Je n'éprouve pour le mal aucune attirance particulière' (p.141). Such an overtly brazen statement can mean but one thing, as Modiano himself was quite happy to point out – 'l'action se situe dans un contexte moral, mais elle est vécue par un être dépourvu de tout sens moral.'[21] In other words, Swing Troubadour/Lamballe is doubly ambiguous. Not only does he have no permanent physical identity; he has no moral identity either.

The corollary of this dilemma is that he finds himself trapped in an ever more distressing *ronde* of mental anguish. Initially, it is because of the pressure placed on him to be decisive for once that he is tormented, the *gestapistes* – like his head – seeming to spin as they encourage him to betray the Resistance: 'Une ronde autour de moi, de plus en plus rapide, de plus en plus bruyante, et je finirai par céder pour qu'ils me laissent tranquille' (p.90). Then, after the act of treachery has taken place, there is a different reason why he is in a whirl – he falls victim to pangs of remorse, the impact and effects of which he readily admits to himself: 'Le REMORDS. Ces visages n'en finiront pas de tourner et, désormais, vous dormirez mal' (pp.54–5).[22]

But the narrator's *vertige* is not simply stated explicitly, as is the case here; it is, above all, *evoked*. The entire text is suffused with echoes of what has gone before, and so systematically that the novel, as its title suggests, follows a circular and not a linear course. For instance, the very first section of the book turns back in on itself, commencing and ending with laughter in the darkness, and numerous leitmotival phrases are employed, with only slight variations, if any: 'un beau coup de filet en perspective' (pp.15, 49, 68, 118, and 123); 'Aucune importance' (pp.133, 155, 156, 163, and 168); 'J'ai des billets de banque plein les poches' (pp.22, 73, 98, and 174); 'une place calme comme il en existe dans le XVIe arrondissement' (pp.29, 77, and 83). Furthermore, there is frequent mention of the rotating caterpillar at Luna-Park and, more importantly, of the Princesse de Lamballe's downfall, whether it be the execution of the historical figure (p.61), the tipping of someone from a bed at a fairground stall (p.92) or Goya's painting of her demise (p.140). Princesse de Lamballe is, of course, the pseudonym the narrator uses in his role of *résistant*, so his death is allusively forecast once more.

A similar sense of impending doom is conveyed by other aspects of the text, not least among which are predictions such as 'je ne sortirais pas vivant de toute cette histoire' (p.157) and 'après des rondes et des rondes, mille et mille allées et venues, je finirais par me perdre dans les ténèbres' (p.125). It is in the closing pages of the book, however, that the impression of imminent disaster is at its most intense. Having failed in an attempt to kill le Khédive, Swing Troubadour/Lamballe is trying desperately to effect his escape, but to no avail. The *gestapistes* are hot on his heels, tracking him and teasing him, letting him pull away slightly, and then quickly hauling him back in. 'Le Khédive, Philibert, tous les autres forment une ronde autour de moi', he had earlier remarked, '[. . .] Il faut que je trouve une oasis, sous peine de crever: mon amour pour Coco Lacour et Esmeralda' (p.73). There is no such oasis for him now – with his former colleagues waiting to pounce at any moment, he has resigned himself to the fact that 'Coco Lacour et

Esmeralda n'existaient pas' (p.175), and thereby accepted that he is merely living on borrowed time. His fate, quite clearly, is well and truly sealed.

Or is it? Elsewhere in the text considerable doubt is thrown on this assumption, for there are strong indications that, in reality, Swing Troubadour/Lamballe is simply *remembering* the nightmare he describes.[23] Probably the best demonstration of this is the incident which occurs, significantly, at roughly the mid-point of the narrative (pp.83–4). On a day when, again significantly, the sun is shining brightly, he looks at the house at 3*bis* and reveals that, although strange things happened when he used to live there, the shutters have been closed for a long time. This admission, fascinatingly, sets up a totally different time-scale within the work – the narrator's treachery and remorse, originally taken to belong to the present, are, it would now appear, part of the past, which a stroll round Paris forces him to re-enact, for as he observes at one stage: 'Vous voudriez oublier le passé mais votre promenade vous ramène sans cesse aux carrefours douloureux' (p.118).[24] Indeed, in this interpretation of the work, the fact that he chances upon '*La Ronde de nuit*, une opérette bien oubliée' (p.105) during his walk is eminently appropriate; the operetta comes to symbolise his own *ronde de nuit, forgotten* in the sense that it belongs to a bygone era, yet still running, still plaguing him at the current moment.[25]

This is not to say, though, that memory is cast purely in an unfavourable light in the novel; there is another, more positive role it performs as well – that of a powerful antidote to the ravages of time. Throughout the book Swing Troubadour/Lamballe is constantly noting how people and objects disappear, leaving behind them no proof at all of ever having existed. 'De tant de frénésie, tumulte, violences, que reste-t-il?' he wonders, thinking back to the funfair at Luna-Park, 'Une esplanade vide en bordure du boulevard Gouvion-Saint-Cyr', is his painful reply (p.92). But he refuses to sit back and simply accept this beckoning obscurity; instead, he determines to keep a record of his experiences, recognising that, by preserving his unique memories in print, he can at least rescue something from the jaws of oblivion: 'Le temps a passé. Si je n'écrivais pas leur nom: Coco Lacour, Esmeralda, il n'y aurait aucune trace de leur séjour en ce monde' (p.91).[26] That these two characters are, in truth, just figments of his imagination does not affect him in the slightest, since their inclusion in his text emphasises – reassuringly – the ability of the written word to give lasting, concrete existence to even the most fictitious of recollections. But it *does* affect the reader, who must consequently realise that, like *La*

Place de l'Étoile before it, Modiano's second work takes on a particular, well-defined form – the form of an unreliable, frequently invented memoir.

With this point now firmly established, the obvious parallel between *La Ronde de nuit* and Rembrandt's famous canvas of the same name (*The Night Watch* in English) most tellingly comes into play. Like its literary counterpart, the old master's painting depicts a company of military men and has an atmosphere of dreamy unreality, but more notably, to the left of the picture, doused in bright light, stands a young girl. Many critics see in this figure a personal intervention by the artist, the evocation of somebody close to him, and this suggests that in the book, too, the illuminated character can be linked back directly to his creator. This being the case, it seems reasonable to deduce that, behind the walker of the sunlit streets of Paris, it is Modiano himself who is penning the false autobiography.[27]

Modiano's next venture into the realms of the Occupation, *Les Boulevards de ceinture* (1972), brings a marked refinement to the atmosphere of hallucinatory anguish found in *La Place de l'Étoile* and *La Ronde de nuit*, but in most other respects continuity with the two previous novels is maintained. The focus of the narrative – the world of collaborationist journalism – plainly derives from Schlemilovitch's stint at *Je suis partout*; incidents mentioned earlier, like the journey in Bordeaux from the Hôtel Splendid to the gare Saint Jean, are repeated and elaborated upon; established characters such as Odicharvi, Violette Morriss and Jean Le Houleux return to take up their old roles again; and numerous well-worn phrases and images hauntingly reappear.[28] Moreover, the prime concern of the work remains the troublesome question of identity, although the topic is now approached in a slightly different manner – via the search for a missing parent.

It is narrator Serge Alexandre who feels compelled to embark on this quest, but his task is by no means an easy one, for it requires an enormous input on his part:

> On s'intéresse à un homme, disparu depuis longtemps. On voudrait interroger les personnes qui l'ont connu mais leurs traces se sont effacées avec les siennes. Sur ce qu'a été sa vie, on ne possède que de très vagues indications souvent contradictoires, deux ou trois points de repère. Pièces à conviction? un timbre-poste et une fausse Légion d'honneur. Alors il ne reste plus qu'à imaginer. (p.148)[29]

By using his powers of invention in this fashion, Serge manages to journey back in time to the *années noires* and successfully make contact there with his father, who is passing himself off as Baron Chalva Deyckecaire. But this success, understandably, is anything but permanent. At the end of the book, the baron ages by thirty years as the temporal perspective is re-established, and his son acknowledges that he is in no better position than he was at the start: 'Qui êtes-vous? J'ai beau vous avoir suivi pendant des jours et des jours, je ne sais rien de vous. Une silhouette devinée sous la veilleuse' (p.198). Like the ring roads of the title and, indeed, like the structure of the narrative itself, he has gone round and round in circles, because the only relevant details he has 'discovered' have been entirely of his own making.[30] He has, in fact, unwittingly followed in the footsteps of Marcheret: 'Orphelin, Marcheret l'avait toujours été. Et s'il s'engagea à la Légion, ce fut peut-être pour retrouver la trace de son père. Mais il n'y avait au rendez-vous que la solitude, le sable et les mirages du désert' (p.75)[31]

One of the many qualities of *Les Boulevards de ceinture* is that the text itself acknowledges this failure of the quest to be inevitable, with numerous techniques being used to undermine the 'reality' of the fiction almost as soon as it is created. Well to the fore in this respect are Serge's constant admissions that nothing permanent can ever come of his endeavours. 'Au milieu de tant d'incertitudes', he states on page 105, 'mes seuls points de repère, le seul terrain qui ne se dérobait pas, c'était les carrefours et les trottoirs de cette ville où je finirais sans doute par me retrouver seul'. Later on, when baron Deyckecaire is addressed directly, the point is made even more explicit: 'Que seriez-vous, sans moi? Sans ma fidélité, ma vigilance de saint-bernard? Si je lâchais prise, vous ne feriez pas plus de bruit, en tombant, qu'une outre vide' (p.130)[32] This persistent, intentional distancing of the reader from the narrative is further achieved on the stylistic level. Events seem to take place in slow motion; characters and settings slide in and out of focus; voices sound as if they are heard on the telephone; and whole passages reveal themselves to be little more than snapshots brought to life.[33] In short, the contact between parent and child is, from start to finish, infused with a sense of vagueness, unreality and, ultimately, transience.

To conclude from this, however, that Serge's efforts have been a complete waste of time would be to make a grave mistake, for something positive and important *has* been accomplished by his search. Although he may not have been able to find out what his father was *actually* like, he has at least managed to select a specific *type* of father for himself, one who conforms to his emotional requirements: 'Pourquoi avais-je voulu, si tôt, être votre fils?' he revealingly remarks (pp.142–3). And it matters not in the slightest that the profile he concocts for his parent cannot be verified, because he feels it to be correct, and that is the essential thing: 'Je n'invente rien. Non, ça n'est pas cela, inventer . . . Il existe certainement des preuves, une personne qui vous a connu, jadis, et qui pourrait témoigner de toutes ces choses. Peu importe. Je suis avec vous et je le resterai jusqu'à la fin du livre' (pp.161–2).[34] Clearly, then, the mere act of pursuing the quest has brought him a measure of psychological relief, and it is not all that difficult to see why – by 'adopting' the parent of his choice, he has, albeit momentarily, procured for himself the identity which he lacks. For as he overtly confesses: 'C'était *moi* que je traquais sans relâche' (p.166).

Yet it is not just the issue of who he is that preoccupies Serge, since he is well aware that this particular problem is tied in with a much more general one, namely the ability of time to consume everything and everyone in its path. Were it not for this inexorable destruction wrought over the years, he knows, he would have no trouble at all in finding out about his father and his origins, and he would not now be in the hopeless predicament that he is. Consequently, whatever else his quest may represent, it is, primarily, an endeavour on his part to save the past for posterity, as his obsession with curricula vitae indicates:

> Je sais bien que le curriculum vitae de ces ombres ne présente pas un grand intérêt, mais si je ne le dressais pas aujourd'hui, personne d'autre ne s'y emploierait. C'est mon devoir, à moi qui les ai connus, de les sortir – ne fût-ce qu'un instant – de la nuit. C'est mon devoir et c'est aussi, pour moi, un véritable besoin. (pp.68–9)[35]

This pressing need to transfer information from perishable memory into durable print seems, on the face of it, innocuous enough in the circumstances. Yet, as already noted, there is something decidedly strange about the content of Serge's memoirs – despite such reassuring statements as 'Il suffit que je frappe du talon sur certains points sensibles de Paris pour que les souvenirs jaillissent en gerbes d'étincelles' (p.98), or 'Bien des années ont passé, mais les visages, les gestes, les inflexions de voix restent gravés dans ma mémoire' (p.172),[36] the experience recalled is largely invented and eminently questionable. For this reason, *Les Boulevards de ceinture* must be approached with care. The work is not the simple autobiography it appears to be at first glance; it is, on the contrary, an imaginative fiction. The recollections evoked are *not* those of the narrator. And more pointedly perhaps, they are not those of the author either.

La Place de l'Étoile, *La Ronde de nuit*, and *Les Boulevards de ceinture* thus show a tremendous amount of overlap when examined one after the other, so much so, in fact, that an entirely new line of attack becomes possible. While these texts can be read and analysed individually, as perfectly self-contained fictions, they nevertheless call out to be tackled as a kind of unconventional trilogy, for by Modiano's own admission:

> On pourrait dire qu'il s'agit d'un seul livre. On retrouve à travers les trois romans les mêmes thèmes, tantôt esquissés, tantôt amplifiés (ainsi le thème du père est esquissé dans le premier roman puis développé dans le troisième). Ces trois romans ne constituent pas une suite chronologique mais un enchevêtrement, une sorte de miroir dont les trois faces se renvoient les mêmes images.[37]

Some of these reflected images are plainly the themes of identity, time, memory and the past, all of which have been highlighted in the preceding pages. But as may be apparent by this stage, there is another key leitmotif in evidence as well, a leitmotif which it will now be useful to study in far greater detail – the focus on the dark and dreadful years of the Occupation.

Modiano's ability to re-create the *années noires* has continually astounded both critics and public alike, and rightly so, because although he himself has no direct experience of the war, his knowledge of the period is so intimate as to be almost incredible. Take, for example, *La Ronde de nuit*. Behind the *gestapistes* of 'la bande du square Cimarosa' it is not difficult to discern the real-life *bande de la rue Lauriston*.[38] Henri Normand, alias 'le Khédive', has followed the same course as Henri Laffont (a deprived childhood with little teaching, work in *Les Halles*, detention centres and then a rise to prominence under the Germans); Monsieur Philibert – once 'le premier flic de France' (p.35), but now sacked and helping Normand with the administrative side of his practice – bears a striking resemblance to Pierre Bonny;[39] Mickey de Voisins harks back to Guy de Voisin; le mage Ivanoff, Lionel de Zieff, Pols du Helder, Gouari l'Américain and Magda d'Andurian are no doubt reflections of le mage Popov, Lionel de Wiett, Paulo du Helder, Riri l'Américain and Marza d'Andurian; and this is not to mention characters such as Violette Morris, Armand le Fou and Danos (alias 'le mammouth'), who appear with no change to their names at all.[40]

Les Boulevards de ceinture further demonstrates Modiano's impressive grasp of the Occupation, for once again historical references and allusions proliferate throughout the text. Celebrities such as Jean Drault, Costantini, Darquier de Pellepoix, Professor Montandon, Eddy Pagnon, Mag Fontanges and Lionel de Wiet are introduced with absolutely no attempt to hide their identity; Sézille, Suarez, Alain Laubreaux and Bouly de Lesdain can easily be spotted in the guises of Seyzille, Suaraize, Alin-Laubreaux and Mouly de Melun; press baron Jean Luchaire, his actress daughter Corinne and her husband, the ex-legionnaire Guy de Voisin, have obviously served as models for Jean Muraille, Annie Muraille and Guy de Marcheret;[41] and there are echoes too of an infamous article published in *Je suis partout* on 27 June 1942 (P. A. Cousteau's 'Savez-vous jouer au tennis juif?'), and of the conference which the same newspaper held in the Salle Wagram on 15 January 1944 ('Nous ne sommes pas des dégonflés').

Despite all this, however, *La Ronde de nuit* and *Les Boulevards de ceinture* are far from being *des romans à clé*. They do, undeniably, have a definite historical aspect to them, as has just been shown, but this does not serve to supply the reader with a ready-made interpretative grid, for as Modiano himself explains:

> J'ai employé un processus de mythomanie qui permet de mélanger réalité et fiction. En même temps j'ai l'impression que cette interférence crée un certain malaise qui n'aurait pas lieu si le lecteur était sûr de se trouver soit dans l'imaginaire pur, soit dans la réalité historique. J'ajoute que beaucoup des personnages historiques cités relèvent presque pour moi de la légende. Je les ressens comme une espèce de mythe.[42]

Modiano's Occupation, therefore, is not realistic in the generally accepted sense of the word, but belongs rather to the less concrete, more atmospheric domain of mythology.[43]

Yet that said, perhaps not even the term *myth* is an entirely satisfactory one to use here, because Modiano has also confided in interview: 'Quand je pense à la période de l'Occupation, ce qui me retient, ce n'est pas l'héroïsme de quelques-uns, mais ce qu'il y a eu chez le plus grand nombre de pourrissement et de lâcheté.'[44] This is an exact reversal of the orthodox outlook, and the portrayal of the *années noires* in the 'trilogy' is coloured accordingly. Serge and Raphaël do not participate in resistance, only in collaboration, and the so-called *réprouvés*, when presented, are never directly criticised, but are instead accepted if not rehabilitated, as one of Schlemilovitch's comments indicates: 'La Milice m'avait déçu. Je n'y rencontrais que des boy-scouts qui ressemblaient aux braves petits gars de la Résistance. Darnand était un fieffé idéaliste' (p.117). Admittedly, a number of *résistants* are depicted in *La Ronde de nuit*, but their appearance is never anything more than fleeting, and in any case they strike the reader as being unheroically insipid and lifeless when compared to the bustling *gestapistes*; they are certainly nothing like the extraordinary figures normally associated with the *armée de l'ombre*. This, then, is why Modiano's rendering of the war years is not fully conveyed by the adjective 'mythical' – the downgrading of the Resistance, coupled to the overt focus on the Collaboration, ensures that a much more appropriate word to use would be 'countermythical'.

So, from the firm foundations offered by an acute grasp of historical fact, Modiano lets his imagination go to work on the Occupation and ends up producing a countermyth. But why? Why should he choose to home in on the *années noires* in the first place? There are, it would appear, a variety of possible reasons for this. The first of these relates to the fact that, as a novelist, he recognises the period's great literary – and essentially symbolic – potential. 'L'époque ne m'intéresse pas pour elle-même. J'y ai greffé mes angoisses', he has asserted,[45] and that is not all. He has also pointed to links between the early 1940s and the present, and hence argued that, while superficially seeming to re-enact the past, he is, in reality, broaching topics which are relevant to his own day. This claim is manifestly justified, for although the main concerns of his first two novels – *la question juive* and treachery – were most visibly and poignantly spotlighted under Pétain, hardly anyone would deny that they remain matters of moment today. And the same applies to *Les Boulevards de ceinture*, because

> Ce père minable et fantomatique que recherche le narrateur peut être le symbole de beaucoup de choses. Symbole de l'effritement des Valeurs (avec un grand V), de la disparition de tout principe d'autorité et de toute assise morale, etc. . . . toutes choses qui étaient liées à l'image traditionnelle du Père. Le père des *Boulevards de ceinture* est une sorte de dérision désespérée du Père dans l'absolu.[46]

One reason for Modiano's interest in the war years is thus a purely professional one – they provide him with an evocative, metaphorical setting in which a whole host of timeless problems can be explored at one remove. But this is not his only stimulus for looking back to the 1940s; there is an intensely personal, exorcistic side to his retrospection as well.

This need for self-purging is due in large part to the behaviour of his father during the *années noires*. As a Jew, Modiano senior was plainly in a vulnerable position after the Germans had invaded France, and yet in spite of this, in spite of the *rafles* and deportations which permanently threatened, he still mingled with people he knew to be collaborators.[47] For him, such an apparent venture into the lion's den was extremely successful, since he was not denounced and so lived to fight another day. But for his son the consequences were a lot less positive – the future novelist became so haunted by what his parent had done that he had to seek therapy in fiction. 'Ma mère est absente de mon œuvre', he would later confess,

> car je cherche à la préserver de l'impureté. L'affaire se situe entre mon père et moi. Mon père a pu préserver sa vie grâce à une attitude trouble, grâce à de multiples concessions. Ce qui alimente mon obsession, ce n'est pas Auschwitz, mais le fait que dans ce climat, pour sauver leur peau, certaines personnes ont pactisé avec leurs bourreaux. Je ne réprouve pas pour autant la conduite paternelle. Je la constate.[48]

In the light of this admission, it comes as no surprise to find Modiano adding that, in both the novels he had written up to that point, 'le fils se charge des faiblesses et de la lâcheté du père. Il y a une culpabilisation du fils qui endosse la veulerie du père, son comportement pendant l'occupation.'[49]

The target of Modiano's exorcism is not restricted to this 'veulerie du père', though, for in each of his first three texts other aspects of the Occupation are purged from his system too. *La Place de l'Étoile* allows him to exteriorise the nightmare of the Holocaust and to exact a measure of revenge for this so-called 'final solution' (Raphaël kills Gérard le Gestapiste and then puts the best-known collaborators and Nazis on show in Port Said); *La Ronde de nuit* gives him the chance to decide whether he would have been a *collabo* or a martyr had he been alive during the war;[50] and *Les Boulevards de ceinture* finds him endeavouring not so much now to put the *années noires* themselves firmly behind him as to overcome his own, obsessive *infatuation* with the period, for as he intimates through his narrator, this book is intended to be 'le dernier concernant [son] autre vie' (p.162).

His next novel, *Villa Triste* (1975), demonstrates that this remark was not made in idle jest – set principally in the 1960s, the text gives clear notice that the other, prenatal life the author 'lived' has indeed been jettisoned. But this is not to say that a radical change of direction has taken place. A less circular, more linear narrative notwithstanding, continuity with the 'trilogy' has been rigorously maintained, since there is 'un climat trouble qui rappelle l'Occupation par as teinte crépusculaire',[51] and, moreover, all the well-established leitmotifs recur. The (anti-)hero, Victor Chmara, is again a frightened, rootless individual in search of family ties; secondary characters (such as Pulli and Yvonne's uncle) once more fill the role of father-figures; and, most striking of all, the essence of the work has not altered in the slightest: 'C'est la nostalgie de quelqu'un qui se fabrique des souvenirs imaginaires, parce qu'il en a le temps', the novelist himself acknowledges, 'c'est la nostalgie de quelqu'un qui puise dans cette vie rêvée les ressources qui manquent à la sienne.[. . .] J'essaie simplement de montrer comment le temps passe et recouvre tout, choses et gens.'[52] So, at the end of the day, Modiano's approach remains very much the tried and tested one. He is still able to confess: 'C'est moi, mais à travers une autobiographie complètement rêvée.'[53]

The work which follows *Villa Triste* – a deftly unified collection of *récits* entitled *Livret de famille* (1977) – similarly harks back to Modiano's previous fictions, most notably through its continued use of paternal surrogates. The man in the registry office, with his 'regard très doux, presque paternel' (p.20), Marignan, 'l'une des multiples incarnations de mon père' (p.23) and Le Gros, who discloses, 'J'ai envie de vous adopter' (p.125), are some of the more obvious examples of these, but in reality the list is virtually endless, for innumerable members of the film world also have to be included, as Georges Rollner unwittingly implies:

> 'Vous êtes parent avec Stocklin?'
> 'Je . . . je ne crois pas', lui dis-je.
> Il me souriait et me tapotait le crâne, d'une main paternelle.
> 'De toute façon . . . Nous sommes tous parents entre nous . . . Le cinéma est une grande famille . . .' (p.90)

Yet for all these undoubted echoes of what has gone before, *Livret de famille* is anything but a mere reworking of old material. On the contrary. For the first time in his *œuvre* Modiano abandons his former reliance on 'une autobiographie complètement rêvée', and punctuates his fiction with extensive, detailed references to his own real-life family background. Pages are devoted to his grandmother, his mother, his wife and his daughter, and there is mention, too, of his father, his grandfather and his brother Rudy. Furthermore, the narrator is even identified as Patrick or Modiano at certain moments. This sudden movement towards a more (traditionally) autobiographical mode of writing may, on the face of it, appear somewhat surprising, but there would seem to be at least two very good reasons for this development. First, as incontestable facts, the personal revelations give the book a psychological *vraisemblance*, and hence make it, as its title suggests, a convincing substitute for the 'normal' *livret de famille* after which the author hankers. Second, it could well be that courtship and marriage have transformed Modiano's outlook on life, and that he has now become more confident – and therefore more forthcoming – about the constitution of his *état civil*. Certainly, when he describes his trip to Tunisia with his future wife, he does tend to imply that, at long last, he has discovered the roots he longs for:

> On entendait le ressac de cette mer et le vent m'apportait les derniers échos d'Alexandrie et de plus loin encore, ceux de Salonique et de bien d'autres villes avant qu'elles n'aient été incendiées. J'allais me marier avec la femme que j'aimais et j'etais enfin de retour dans cet Orient que nous n'aurions jamais dû quitter. (p.162)

This new-found sense of stability further emerges from his depiction of his daughter Zénaïde, whose birth plainly represents another great step forward to him. 'Cette petite fille serait un peu notre déléguée dans l'avenir', he notes. 'Et elle avait obtenu du premier coup le bien mystérieux qui s'était toujours dérobé devant nous: un état civil' (p.22). In other words, the family heritage is assured for the future, no matter how tenuous it may have been in the past.

The theme of inheritance exemplified here is again well to the fore when Modiano, reiterating remarks he had already made in interview, goes on to reveal his most compulsive reason of all for looking back to the Second World War – the *années noires*, he writes, are the 'terreau d'où je suis issu' (p.169), because 'sans cette époque, sans les rencontres hasardeuses et contradictoires qu'elle provoquait, je ne serais jamais né' (p.173). The Occupation, then, is the source of his identity, and as such it must inevitably feature strongly every time he investigates his origins. Yet although this fact would, in itself, be sufficient to explain his obsession with the period, there is obviously much more to the matter than this, for as he confides elsewhere, the actions of his father – once again – severely exacerbated the issue. 'C'est juste au moment où je ne l'ai plus vu', he says of his parent, 'que j'ai appris ce qu'était cette époque, et que je n'ai pas pu lui poser les questions.'[54] With this confession, the full extent of Modiano's problem becomes clear – he is not just a child and heir of the early 1940s, he is, more specifically, their *orphan*. And it is precisely to counteract this orphanage, of course, that he laces his *œuvre* with paternal surrogates.

So, when Modiano portrays the war years in his fiction, associating them, as has been seen, with torment, a need for exorcism and the theme of the father-figure, what he is ultimately doing is evoking, in his own words, 'la lumière incertaine de mes origines'.[55] But he is also doing something more besides, as has likewise been seen – he is re-enacting a past which in reality is not his. The question accordingly arises as to how he manages to pull off this feat, and here, once more, *Livret de famille* supplies a fascinating insight: 'Ma mémoire précédait ma naissance. J'étais sûr, par exemple, d'avoir vécu dans le Paris de l'Occupation puisque je me souvenais de certains personnages de cette époque et de détails infimes et troublants, de ceux qu'aucun livre d'histoire ne mentionne' (p.96). Such an amazing statement cannot, in all honesty, be said to be particularly credible, but it does have a certain significance nonetheless. If we accept that, as is his wont, Modiano has again channelled his own thoughts into the mind of his narrator, then he has patently come a long way since he observed in 1968:

> Il y a longtemps que je baignais dans cette atmosphère, elle a fini par s'intégrer à moi [. . .]. Ce n'est qu'*a posteriori*, en réfléchissant à cette époque, que j'ai vécu de manière hallucinatoire la période 35–45. J'en ai fait mon paysage naturel que j'ai nourri de lectures appropriées: Mémoires, pamphlets, romans, études historiques.[56]

Obviously, the fruits of this early reading have been spiced with family anecdotes, enhanced by his imagination and then moulded into the prenatal remembrance with which he now claims to be endowed. His stated objective has thus most strikingly been secured – he has indeed forged a new memory for himself out of the memories of his elders.

Modiano gets no satisfaction, however, from this uncanny ability to 'remember' things experienced by others. As *Livret de famille* again suggests, the power of recollection (like the Occupation, to which it relates) is synonymous with anguish in his eyes, and he would happily unburden himself of the faculty if only he actually could: 'J'essayais de lutter contre la pesanteur qui me tirait en arrière, et rêvais de me délivrer d'une mémoire empoisonnée. J'aurais donné tout au monde pour devenir amnésique' (p.96). After such a candid *cri de cœur*, it can hardly be pure coincidence that his next novel, the Prix-Goncourt-winning *Rue des Boutiques Obscures* (1978), is narrated by a man who has, in effect, lost his memory.

The amnesiac in question is Guy Roland, or rather that is the name he has chosen to go under, for he has no inkling at all of who he really is. Nevertheless, with ten years' service as a private detective behind him, he is ideally placed to track down his unknown self, so duly sets out to do so. And as the enigma slowly unravels (with the linearity required by a *roman policier*), Modiano's perennial leitmotifs resurface. The search for an identity through the reconstruction of the past, the use of imagination to supplement remembrance, the acknowledged importance of documents and keepsakes, the tendency of time to leave nothing in its wake – such themes are already so familiar as to need no further analysis here. There are, however, two other features of *Rue des Boutiques Obscures* whose resonance is not immediately apparent, and which it *will* therefore be useful to elaborate upon.

The first of these is an incident which occurs when, almost inevitably, the temporal setting switches from the mid-1960s to the troubled years of the German occupation. In 1943, it emerges, the future Guy Roland had tried to flee France and illegally cross into Switzerland, only to be abandoned in the mountains by his treacherous *passeur*. He had somehow managed to extricate himself from this predicament – obviously – but his companion, Denise Coudreuse, had not been so lucky: she had never been seen or heard of again. This unfortunate tragedy proves to be the dramatic high point of the novel, but to avid readers of Modiano's work it comes as no real surprise, for in other texts, too, Switzerland had represented a longed-for haven that was never actually reached. In *La Ronde de nuit*, for example, Swing Troubadour/Lamballe had thought he could dispel his anguish by running away to Lausanne, but had eventually had to concede: 'Lausanne ne me suffirait pas' (p.174), while in *Villa Triste* Victor Chmara had confided, more explicitly:

> Moi, j'avais peur, encore plus qu'aujourd'hui et j'avais choisi ce lieu de refuge parce qu'il était situé à cinq kilomètres de la Suisse. Il suffisait de

> traverser le lac, à la moindre alerte. Dans ma naïveté, je croyais que plus on se rapproche de la Suisse, plus on a de chance de s'en sortir. Je ne savais pas encore que la Suisse n'existe pas. (pp.14–15)

Livret de famille had further articulated this theme, although initially Modiano had seemed to depart from his established practice, allowing his narrator – for once – to set foot on Swiss soil and declare: 'J'étais heureux. Je n'avais plus de mémoire. [. . .] J'avais atteint cet état que j'appelais: "la Suisse du cœur"' (p.98). But D., 'le personnage le plus hideux du Paris de l'Occupation' (p.105), had soon turned up to shatter the illusion of happiness, and so, yet again, relief had ultimately proved to be unattainable: 'Il n'y avait plus qu'à se laisser submerger par cette léthargie que je m'obstinais à appeler: la Suisse du cœur' (p.120). The use of the phrase 'la Suisse du cœur' here is extremely revealing, and it serves to confirm what may, by this stage, already have been inferred, namely that Modiano is using Switzerland symbolically, as a token of emotional tranquillity and contentedness – in short, as a counterweight (where appropriate) to the metaphorical, anguish-laden Occupation.[57]

The second feature of *Rue des Boutiques Obscures* whose resonance deserves to be spelled out is the presence of Denise Coudreuse. Plainly and simply, Denise generates an impression of *déjà vu* because she is a model, for as such she immediately calls to mind the countless other mannequins and starlets who grace the pages of Modiano's fiction. From the unnamed film star who is sent the 'Courrier du cœur', on through Yvonne Jacquet in *Villa Triste* to, say, Arlette d'Alwyn in 'Johnny', the cast list is so extensive as to have no apparent end. Why should this be? Why should the world of high fashion and the cinema so captivate Modiano? The reason can, no doubt, be traced back directly to the position of his mother, who was not only an actress and a model herself, but was also frequently away from home, on tour, while her adolescent son was growing up – just as paternal surrogates are deployed to replace the missing father, so too, it can be argued, does the mannequin/starlet figure help compensate for maternal absence. This being the case, Modiano's early observation on his work (see p.160 above) is an unhelpful guide to his *œuvre* as a whole, for as can now confidently be asserted, once he begins to move his settings forward in time and out of the *années noires*, he comes, most patently, to evoke *both* of his parents in his fiction.[58]

In the context of this cult of parental substitutes, *Rue des Boutiques Obscures* proves to be a watershed in Modiano's development as a writer. Being his first – and only – text to carry the dedication

'Pour mon pere', it can rightly be said to mark his final, valedictory attempt to investigate his origins, all the more so in that shortly after its publication he divulged: 'A 33 ans je ne peux pas rechercher toute ma vie l'image de mon père. Quand on a des enfants, on est père à son tour, et l'on peut oublier un peu le passé. [. . .] je ne crois pas que je vais parler tout le temps de la guerre.'[59] Sure enough, in his next novel, *Une jeunesse* (1981), he visibly translates these words into action. Out goes the once omnipresent narrator character, forever solitary and traumatised, and in come Louis and Odile, a happily married couple with two children. Furthermore, although the key themes of time, memory and the past remain, the basic temporal setting has now been brought unequivocally up to date. The Occupation is scarcely given a mention at all.

The same deliberate intention to break new ground is also a feature of Modiano's subsequent work. *De si braves garçons* (1982) has two primary narrators, both of whom look back over the last twenty years of their lives, recalling their days at school together in the early 1960s and revealing what has since become of their old classmates and teachers. Embodying a largely negative view of parenthood in general, and of motherhood in particular, this collection of doom-laden *récits* finds the novelist at his most melancholic. *Quartier perdu* (1984) and *Dimanches d'août* (1986) similarly indicate that some sort of page has been turned, for like their predecessor, they too have a time-scale that is firmly entrenched in the 1980s. And that is not all. The protagonist of the first of these novels, Ambrose Guise, is a totally contented husband and father (in spite of the disquieting 'vie antérieure' which he led up until 1965), while his counterpart in the second, Jean, is denied police aid when his girlfriend disappears because, as is made perfectly clear to him (pp.124–5), the missing person he is trying to locate is not one of his relatives. In this latter instance especially, the contrast with the earlier texts is quite blatant. *Remise de peine* (1988) takes the reader even further into uncharted territory, and almost into the realms of pure autobiography. Published not now by Gallimard, but by the Éditions du Seuil (another new departure!), this intimate, confessional piece allows Modiano finally to purge himself of what he calls the 'période de ma vie dont je ne pouvais parler à personne' (p.141): that time in the 1950s when, at the age of ten and in the company of his younger brother Rudy, he first met with the dubious parental stand-ins who would later figure so prominently in his fiction. His most recent work to date, *Vestiaire de l'enfance* (1989) shows just how refreshing this exorcism has been. Situating the main narrative in the 1980s and, moreover, on foreign soil for the first time, he now depicts a narrator full of 'fibre paternelle' (p.103) who claims to have escaped from '[le passé] des quelques personnes dont je m'inspirais pour mes livres, du temps où j'habitais la France' (p.37). The break with Guy Roland and his forerunners here could hardly be more pointed.

This is not to imply, though, that previous practice has been abandoned in its entirety, for the books Modiano has produced since 1978 still show great affinities with those that came before them. The use of familiar characters and settings persists (both Stioppa de D. and the mysterious garage in *Remise de peine*, like the Collège run by M. Jeanschmidt in *De si braves garçons*, had first cropped up in *Rue des Boutiques Obscures*); the authorial presence is as uninhibited as ever; the function of retrospection retains its centrality; false identities continue to abound – and this is to highlight only the principal constants.

Collectively, then, *Une jeunesse*, *De si braves garçons*, *Quartier perdu*, *Dimanches d'août*, *Remise de peine* and *Vestiaire de l'enfance* constitute an essential and well-integrated part of Modiano's universe. Yet no matter how much they may overlap with their companion volumes in the *œuvre*, one vital characteristic irrevocably sets them apart: they centre on the author's own life and times, not on somebody else's. This movement away from fake autobiography marks a distinct, if partial, change of direction, and nowhere is the reason for such a development better seen than in a remark made by Modiano himself. 'Il vient un moment', he observes, 'où on peut parler de soi-même, où l'on commence à posséder un passé à soi et où l'on n'a plus besoin de celui des autres.'[60] His initial plan, therefore, has most perceptibly been cast aside, and not without good cause. Marriage and fatherhood have woven their spell. He no longer has to put down roots through his fiction.

The preceding pages of this chapter may already have given some idea of why Modiano, in his portrayal of the *années noires*, can be said to tower above the rest of his orphaned colleagues in the 'innocent' generation. The full extent of his distinctiveness, however, will probably not have been appreciated, so it will be useful at this juncture to spell out exactly what it is that so sets him apart within the *mode rétro*.

The most obvious of Modiano's distinguishing traits here is, undoubtedly, his refusal to ignore the pioneering work of the *nouveaux romanciers* and the Structuralists. As may by now be apparent, *La Place de l'Étoile*, *La Ronde de nuit* and *Les Boulevards de*

ceinture, taken together, depend heavily upon devices which were very much the trademarks of Robbe-Grillet and his companions – devices such as the abandonment of traditional chronology and the fragmentation of the narrative voice, for instance, not to mention the use of circularity or 'un double mouvement de création et de gommage'.[61] Indeed, even the format of the detective novel – used to such great effect in *Rue des Boutiques Obscures* – had long been a favourite with the author of *Dans le labyrinthe*. So the debt to the New Novel 'movement' would appear to be unquestionable. And so would the influence of Saussure, for after all, what does Modiano's avowed objective – a false autobiography – represent if not the creation of (a new) reality through the mere use of language?

Yet Modiano is most definitely not a New Novelist, and even less a Structuralist, for as early as 1968, he can be found maintaining: 'Je ne m'intéresse à aucune école expérimentale et je reproche notamment au Nouveau Roman de n'avoir ni ton ni vie. Je suis étranger à la littérature désincarnée. Car [. . .] je suis hanté par le souci du ton et du style.'[62] A few years later he was to be even more precise about his literary aims: 'La littérature pour la littérature, les recherches sur l'écriture, tout ce byzantinisme pour chaires et colloques, ça ne m'intéresse pas: j'écris pour savoir qui je suis, pour me trouver une identité.'[63] Hence there is nothing theoretical about the stance which Modiano takes up. His formal modernism derives not from a commitment on his part to give the writer a new horizon, but rather from an identity crisis which can only be articulated through vagueness and incertitude. And the fact that his novels become less complicated and more linear as his *état civil* strengthens serves, of course, as the most visible and powerful confirmation of this.

But there is another side to Modiano's modernism as well: the legacy of Saussure, Robbe-Grillet et al. is simply part of the much wider literary heritage which is consciously being assimilated and exploited. Take *La Place de l'Étoile*, for example. This highly eclectic novel draws, quite openly, on a whole host of well-known writers (among others: Jean-Paul Sartre, François Mauriac, Valéry Larbaud, Pierre Drieu la Rochelle and F. Scott Fitzgerald), and often goes so far as to offer a faithful pastiche their styles, as the ramblings of le docteur Bardamu (Céline) demonstrate:

> . . . Schlemilovitch? Ah! la moisissure de ghettos terriblement puante!. . . pâmoison chiotte!. . . Foutriquet prépuce!. . . arsouille libano-ganaque!. . . rantanplan. . . Vlan!. . . Contemplez donc ce gigolo yiddish. . . cet effréné empaffeur de petites Aryennes!. . . avorton

> infiniment négroïde!. . . cet Abyssin frénétique jeune nabab!. . . A l'aide!. . . Montjoie-Saint-Denis!. . . Tralalilonlaire!. . . qu'on l'étripe. . . le châtre!. . . Délivrez le docteur d'un pareil spectacle. . . qu'on le crucifie, nom de Dieu!. . . Rastaquouère des cocktails infâmes. . . youtre des palaces internationaux!. . . des partouzes *made in Haifa*!. . . Cannes!. . . Davos!. . . Capri et *tutti quanti*!. . . grands bordels extrêmement hébraïques!. . . Délivrez-nous de ce circoncis muscadin!. . . ses Maserati rose salomon!. . . ses yachts façon Tibériade!. . . Ses cravates Sinaï!. . . que les Aryennes ses esclaves lui arrachent le gland!. . . avec leurs belles quenottes de chez nous. . . leurs mains mignonnes. . . lui crèvent les yeux!. . . sus au calife!. . . Révolte du harem chrétien!. . . Vite!. . . Vite. . . refus de lui lécher les testicules!. . . lui faire des mignardises contre des dollars!. . . Libérez-vous!. . . du cran, Madelon!. . . autrement, le docteur, il va pleurer!. . . se consumer!. . . affreuse injustice!. . . Complot du Sanhédrin!. . . On en veut à la vie du Docteur!. . . croyez-moi!. . . le Consistoire!. . . la Banque Rothschild!. . . Cahen d'Anvers!. . . Schlemilovitch!. . . aidez Bardamu, fillettes!. . . au secours!. . . . (pp.9–10)

As admirers of Céline will readily admit, it could almost have been the master stylist himself who penned these words. The foreign language borrowings, the crudely vituperative tone, the use of slang and onomatopoeia, the *points de suspension*, the neologisms, the exclamations, the redundancy, the ellipsis, the rhythm – Modiano has captured nearly every facet of his predecessor's technique. And when he then goes on briefly to parody Proust (*Du côté de Fougeire-Jusquiames*), the result is scarcely any less impressive: 'C'était, ce Fougeire-Jusquiames, comme le cadre d'un roman, un paysage imaginaire que j'avais peine à me représenter, et d'autant plus le désir de découvrir, enclavé au milieu de terres et de routes réelles q .i tout à coup s'imprégnaient de particularités héraldiques' (p.93).

Imitation is the sincerest form of flattery, it is said, and this old adage is certainly borne out here. Modiano so respects the authors of *Voyage au bout de la nuit* and *A la recherche du temps perdu* that, from his very early days as a writer, he has set out to develop a 'style émotionnel' as personal as theirs.[64] That he has succeeded, most spectacularly, in achieving this goal can easily be ascertained by a quick glance at the French press, for there is hardly a reviewer of his work to be found who does not now acknowledge – and commend – 'l'atmosphère Modiano'.

This consecration by the journalists is by no means at all

unwarranted. Each of Modiano's texts does have its own distinctive atmosphere, as the following extract from *Les Boulevards de ceinture* shows:

> Au-dessus de la silhouette rigide de Grève, une tête de chevreuil se détache du mur comme une figure de proue et l'animal considère Marcheret, Murraille et mon père avec toute l'indifférence de ses yeux de verre. L'ombre des cornes dessine au plafond un entrelacs gigantesque. La lumière s'affaiblit. Baisse de courant? Ils demeurent prostrés et silencieux dans la pénombre qui les ronge. De nouveau cette impression de regarder une vieille photographie, jusqu'au moment où Marcheret se lève, mais de façon si brutale qu'il bute parfois contre la table. Alors, tout recommence. Le lustre et les appliques retrouvent leur éclat. Plus une ombre. Plus de flou. Le moindre objet se découpe avec une précision presque insoutenable. Les gestes qui s'alanguissaient deviennent secs et impérieux. Mon père lui-même se dresse comme à l'appel d'un 'garde-à-vous'. (pp.17–18)

Note how the changes in sentence length produce an evocative rhythm, a rhythm which is in perfect harmony with the narrative it underlies, undynamic and featureless at first, but then gaining both in certainty and momentum. Note too how there is a musical arrangement of long and short, soft and harsh sounds, from the lulling 'silencieux dans la pénombre qui les ronge' to the jarringly abrasive 'brutale qu'il bute'. And above all note how the combination of these two devices creates an impression of dreamlike ebb and flow. It is this indefinite, fragile half-light that is Modiano's trademark.

Such vagueness, though, could never have been generated without a special kind of formal approach, as Modiano himself is the first to concede. 'J'écris dans la langue française la plus classique', he declares,

> non par une insolence droitière, non plus par un goût des effets surannées, mais parce que cette forme est nécessaire à mes romans: pour traduire l'atmosphère trouble, flottante, étrange que je voulais leur donner, il me fallait bien la discipliner dans la langue la plus claire, la plus traditionnelle possible. Sinon, tout se serait éparpillé dans une bouillie confuse.[65]

Given this linguistic conservatism, and given also, as mentioned above, the ever more linear and straightforward nature of his novels, it is hardly surprising that Modiano should now be classified in the way that he is – as a novelist who, broadly speaking, is very much in tune with the classical tradition.

Drawing the threads of the preceding argument together, the achievement of Modiano as a writer instantly becomes clear. Starting from a near-encyclopedic grasp of his cultural heritage, and endowed with a startlingly precocious talent, as the pastiches of *La Place de l'Étoile* demonstrate, he builds on these qualities to create a universe and a style which are as artistically impressive as they are totally distinctive. In a word, he is an author who is most decidedly *literary*. And it is this literariness which, more than anything else, distinguishes him from the other 'innocent' novelists in post-Gaullist France.

The apparent exclusiveness of this remark notwithstanding, there is one final reason why Modiano stands out so markedly in the current context: his first two novels were published in 1968 and 1969, that is to say just before the *mode rétro* came into being. Consequently, like the calibre of his writing, his relationship to the fashion is most manifestly unique. He is not so much part of the overall trend – and he himself has constantly underlined his detachment from it – as, to use the colourful phrase of Dominique Jamet, 'celui qui en fut sans l'avoir prémédité comme l'archange annonciateur'.[66] Or put another way, he is to the *mode rétro* in its written form what Ophüls was to become to it in its cinematographic expression – the influential trail-blazer for his generation as a whole.

In sum, then, Modiano is an author who has gradually worked himself through a state of crisis, without for one moment ceasing to exploit the same rich literary vein. At the start of his career, he uses his fiction as a means of self-discovery, a method of acquiring the roots he lacks but so desires. It is certainly not for nothing that, during this early period, his work is dotted with parental substitutes, nor is it any coincidence that he should choose to turn his texts into false autobiographies – by acting in this manner he is able to secure an appealing, custom-built identity for himself. But this harnessing of literature to therapeutic ends proves, understandably, to be far from enduring. As he finds stability in engagement, marriage and fatherhood, his initial turmoil subsides, and he comes to relinquish his previously obsessive soul-searching. This improved outlook on life filters through into his later novels quite noticeably – in the form of greater linearity and the appearance of more modern settings – yet in spite of this, there is no fundamental change of tack in his writing, for the thematic emphasis on time, memory and the past is retained, and so too is that special atmosphere that can only be described as *modianesque*. In the final analysis, therefore, Modiano has compiled an *œuvre* that is essentially harmonious and cohesive. He may, from time to time, move the spotlight from one aspect of his fictional universe to another, but the actual universe itself is never abandoned.

Within this overall picture of consistency-despite-innovation, the importance of the *années noires* for Modiano is plain for all to see: being the time when his mother and father met, these 'dark years' form an indispensable part of the heritage he seeks to appropriate, the obligatory backdrop for his early pursuit of his origins. Furthermore, thanks to the effects of *le résistancialisme*, and more particularly to the portrayal of the *collabos* as extraordinary, larger-than-life monsters, the Occupation provides him with a ready-made symbol of nightmarish anguish, the use of which allows him to exorcise his problematic family background. Such close association of two different inheritances – the one individual and the other national – is, of course, by no stretch of the imagination unique, as previous chapters of this survey have endeavoured to show. But that said, a sense of perspective must be maintained. Of all the 'innocent' writers active in the 1970s, it was Modiano who first found a palliative to the postwar legacy crisis, Modiano who, by usurping the memories of his elders, first reaped the benefits of personal mythification, and Modiano who, in the most literary of manners, reminded his fellow 'orphans' that writing could prove refreshingly curative. In brief, it was Modiano who set the standard for others to follow. And in so doing, albeit unwittingly, he achieved a feat which no one else could emulate – he ushered in the *mode rétro*.

Notes

1. See Marie-Françoise Leclère, 'Il a vingt-deux ans et il méritait le Goncourt': 'Au fond, ce qui m'a le plus manqué', he admits, 'c'est ce que les autres rejettent: une enfance bourgeoise, une maison provinciale et une sœur fiancée à un officier de marine' (p.139).
2. Emmanuel Berl, '*Interrogatoire par Patrick Modiano' suivi de 'Il fait beau, allons au cimetière*', p.9. It is interesting to note that Pascal Sevran,

another creator of a 'passé supplémentaire', was also mı
by Berl.

3. Josane Duranteau, 'Un début exceptionnel: *La Place* Patrick Modiano', p.II.
4. See Berl, '*Interrogatoire par Patrick Modiano*', p.88. Regarding Raphaël's dependence on precedents, cf. Pascal Sevran's *Le Passé supplémentaire*, which also features a narrator who, in order to establish an identity for himself, takes on a whole variety of guises.
5. Jean-C. Texier, 'Rencontre avec un jeune romancier: Patrick Modiano', p.8. Cf. Janine Chasseguet-Smirgel, *Pour une psychanalyse de l'art et de la créativité*: 'L'identification au persécuteur peut [. . .] avoir [. . .] pour fonction de le désarmer, de le rendre inopérant (c'est-à-dire, dans l'inconscient, de le châtrer), voire de l'anéantir' (p.235).
6. Cf. Chasseguet-Smirgel: 'Le nom du héros est à lui seul révélateur de l'acceptation de l'identité juive et de ses racines: il est plus juif que nature' (*Pour une psychanalyse*, p.231n.).
7. Cf. Louis Malle's film, *Lacombe Lucien*, the screenplay of which Modiano helped write, and whose main female character, France, can similarly be seen in symbolic terms.
8. Céline, who is widely recognised as an anti-Semite, appears to be jarringly out of place in this company. There is, however, at least one possible reason for his inclusion, since Modiano has said of him in interview: 'En lisant son œuvre romanesque, j'ai été frappé par le caractère assez juif de son esprit et de son style [. . .]. D'ailleurs, Céline avoue lui-même dans *Bagatelles pour un massacre*: "Dans le fond mon œuvre est assez juive"' (Jean Montalbetti, 'La Haine des professeurs: instantané Patrick Modiano', p.2).
9. Cf. Alain Spiraux, *Une fleur juive dans un jardin à la française*. Here too the narrator is 'en mal d'enracinement' (p.28), plagued by the question 'Qui suis-je?' (p.30) and very much aware that the Jewish element of his Franco-Jewish identity is a composite one: 'Je suis une foule où l'on parle autant de langues qu'à la tour de Babel [. . .]. Tous ces gens, mes ancêtres, dont je suis le petit dernier, se pressent surtout dans ma tête, voulant voir par mes yeux, entendre par mes oreilles' (pp.15–16).
10. Once again cf. Sevran's *Le Passé supplémentaire*, the parentless narrator of which, having mingled with well-known literary and show-business personalities because, as he avows, 'ils étaient un peu ma famille inventée' (p.77), tells himself: 'Toutes les femmes du monde sont ta mère' (p.177) and then receives 'un conseil paternel' from Drieu la Rochelle (p.186).
11. Cf. the relationship between France and Lucien in *Lacombe Lucien*.
12. Philip Roth's famous novel, *Portnoy's Complaint* similarly ends with its Jewish narrator on a psychoanalyst's couch. This, and numerous other resemblances with *La Place de l'Étoile*, would make a comparison of the two works extremely rewarding.

13. Alcibiades (450–404 BC) was the Athenian statesman and general who, having first called for an expeditionary force to be sent to Sicily, then turned traitor and ensured the venture ended in failure. Alfred Dreyfus (1859–1935) was a Jewish captain in the French army. Falsely accused of treachery, he became the focal point of the (in)famous Dreyfus Affair. Joseph Joanovici, the 'juif collabo' of *La Place de l'Etoile*, was one of the key *trafiquants* in the French black market during the Occupation. Perfectly at home in the company of Germans and members of the *Gestapo française*, he nevertheless set aside some of his profits in order to finance a Resistance network. Arrested after the Liberation, he was tried and sentenced (in 1949) to five years' imprisonment. The Chevalier d'Éon worked in the French embassy in London in the second half of the eighteenth century. Originally a thorn in the side of his government (he regularly threatened to leak the documents he held to the British), he was perceived as less of a threat when he began to dress as a woman and claim to be a lady. Leopoldo Fregoli (1867–1936) was an Italian actor, singer, dancer, mime artist and illusionist. Famous the world over, he is still remembered in France as a *comédien à transformations*.
14. Jean Montalbetti, 'Patrick Modiano ou l'esprit de fuite', p.42.
15. Cf. Roger Nimier's *Les Épées*, in which François Sanders joins the Resistance and, in order to kill Darnand, then goes on to become a *milicien*, with the predictable result that he too begins to lose track of his identity: 'Je me suis demandé si j'étais simplement un milicien ou un résistant camouflé en milicien. Ou encore un fasciste qui jouait à la résistance sous un uniforme bleu marine' (p.104).
16. The fictional and real-life characters listed here need no introduction, apart, perhaps, from Petiot and Landru, both of whom were notorious mass murderers in France. As regards Swing Troubadour/Lamballe's tendency to don female attire, see the reference to the Chevalier d'Éon above (p.149, and especially note 13).
17. Alexandre Stavisky (1886–1934) was the infamous swindler at the centre of the Stavisky Affair in France. His death, in suspicious circumstances, was one of the great *causes célèbres* of a moribund Third Republic.
18. Cf. *La Place de l'Étoile*, in which Raphaël wanted to kill his father, Tania and Des Essarts because: 'Moi, les gens que j'aime, je les tue. Alors je les choisis bien faibles, sans défense' (p.104).
19. Cf. Pascal Jardin's *Guerre après guerre*: 'Je tue tout ce que j'aime. J'ai commencé par moi lorsque j'étais enfant' (p.19). Cf. also Horn's suicidal visit to the Gestapo HQ in *Lacombe Lucien*.
20. Again, cf. *Lacombe Lucien* (see pp.57–8 above). Cf. also Alphonse Boudard's analysis of Alex: 'Ses convictions profondes? L'impression surtout qu'il s'amuse dans un rôle, [. . .] mais que pourtant il est capable d'aller jusqu'au bout. C'est-à-dire de tuer ou de se faire tuer.

Le final de tous les engagements. . . martyr ou bourreau. . . selon les circonstances!' (*CJ*, p.243).

21. Montalbetti, 'Patrick Modiano ou l'esprit de fuite', p.42.
22. Cf. Solange Fasquelle, *Les Falaises d'Ischia*: 'Je rêvais d'échapper à cette ronde d'ombres que j'avais moi-même réveillées et animées, de quitter ce lieu maléfique où seule me retenait une vengeance dont l'accomplissement me libérerait à jamais [. . .] de la culpabilité d'une petite fille, contrainte à assister au drame et à demeurer impuissante' (pp.163–4).
23. Unless, of course, he is *anticipating* remembering! Cf. *La Place de l'Étoile*, in which there is similar uncertainty as to the narrator's fate: 'Ma tête éclate, mais j'ignore si c'est à cause des balles ou de ma jubilation' (p.149).
24. Cf. Modiano's own assessment of *La Ronde de nuit*: 'Le principal personnage de ce livre: Paris. Paris dont les avenues, les carrefours, les maisons évoquent des souvenirs pour le promeneur solitaire' (Patrick Modiano, 'Un roman sur Paris en été. . .', p.5). It is also worth noting that the first sentence of the novel to be written was: 'Le mois d'août à Paris provoque l'afflux des souvenirs' (p.83).
25. The symbolism here seems all the more flagrant in that the novel too has a distinctive musical element: snippets of songs from the early 1940s punctuate the text, and the *ronde* of the title could refer to the dance of the same name.
26. Cf. his earlier statements: 'Je voudrais laisser quelques souvenirs: au moins transmettre à la postérité les noms de Coco Lacour et d'Esmeralda' (p.72) and 'Il faut bien que je donne ces détails puisque tout le monde les a oubliés' (p.83). Pascal Jardin likewise believed that literature could 'fixer quelques fragments du temps' (*GAG*, p.149): 'Si j'éprouve le besoin impérieux de parler de tous ces gens pour la plupart disparus, et que je n'ai moi-même pas tous connus, c'est que je ne peux me résoudre à ce que tout s'efface [. . .] je suis peut-être aujourd'hui le seul homme au monde qui sache que ces personnes ont existé' (*NJ*, p.46). Cf. also Sevran, *Le Passé supplémentaire*: 'Qui, à part moi, se soucie de Maxence Bibié, André Cointreau, Dutertre de la Coudre, Thureau Dangin de Tinguy du Pouet, Paul Fleurot, François de Saint-Just?' (p.159).
27. Cf. Robert Kanters, 'La Nuit de Patrick Modiano', p.24. Further support for this contention is given by the narrator's claims to be Stavisky's son – Modiano himself said of the infamous swindler: 'Il ne serait pas exagéré de dire que je voyais en lui une sorte d'image paternelle' (Josane Duranteau, 'L'Obsession de l'anti-héros', p.13).
28. See e.g. p.58, where the familiar theme of the *ronde* recurs ('La tête me tourne. Mon père m'apparaît à chaque fois que je vire et volte') and p.199, where Grève, in the paraphrase given, blatantly echoes Freud's comment to Raphaël ('Oui, il a connu les gens dont je lui cite les noms. Mais moi, si jeune, comment se fait-il que je lui parle de ces gens-là').

29. Cf. Pascal Jardin, p.128 above, and Pascal Sevran, *Un garçon de France*, p.71. Cf. also Jean Bloch-Michel's *Daniel et Noémi*. Apart from the obvious difference that Bloch-Michel's narrator is writing about himself and not his father, his objective is still similar to Serge's: 'Il s'agit de reconstruire une vie' (p.82), 'essayer de réinventer mon enfance et ma jeunesse' (p.29).
30. Cf. Bloch-Michel: 'Mon entreprise consistait précisément à reconstruire une vie qui [. . .] n'existait peut-être que dans un quotidien dont toute trace a disparu. Ramener toute une existence à ce que la mémoire en garde [. . .] c'était peut-être une entreprise condamnée par avance à l'échec' (*Daniel et Noémi*, p.43).
31. Cf. Modiano's own description of *Les Boulevards de ceinture*: 'L'histoire d'une quête qui ne peut déboucher sur rien de stable, aucune terre ferme, aucune terre promise, mais sur du sable mouvant, un climat de désarroi et d'inquiétude' (Victor Malka, 'Patrick Modiano: un homme sur du sable mouvant', p.2). Cf. also the novels of Pascal Sevran, in which imaginative searches for absent parents similarly end in disappointment.
32. Cf. Bloch-Michel: 'C'est sans doute pour être seul, encore une fois, [. . .] que j'ai entrepris ce récit [. . .], puisque tous ceux que j'évoque et qui apparaissent dans ce récit n'y existent que par le fait de ma mémoire: c'est-à-dire qu'ils ont perdu toute existence et qu'ils ne procèdent que de moi' (*Daniel et Noémi*, pp.222–3).
33. See e.g. p.38: 'Il laissait pendre sa cigarette au coin des lèvres comme elle y pend pour l'éternité.' Cf. Alphonse Boudard, *Les Combattants du petit bonheur*, pp.314–15, and José-André Lacour, *Le Rire de Caïn*, pp.10–11.
34. Cf. Bloch-Michel: 'Bien entendu, je ne me rappelle pas ces détails. Mais je sais qu'en les ajoutant [. . .] je n'invente rien, à proprement parler. C'est bien comme cela que les choses se sont passées, j'en suis sûr' (*Daniel et Noémi*, p.14). Cf. also Pascal Jardin: 'Rien de ce que je raconte n'est inventé' (*GNA*, p.78).
35. Cf. Bloch-Michel: 'Ce n'est pas pour comprendre [. . .] que j'ai entrepris d'écrire ce récit, mais pour figer en une matière que le temps ne pourra pas user des souvenirs [. . .]. Je ne sais même pas si les mots que j'écris seront lus demain [. . .]. Du moins [. . .] demeureront-ils quelque part où on les retrouvera peut-être un jour' (*Daniel et Noémi*, p.163).
36. Cf. *La Ronde de nuit*: 'Je ferme les yeux pour retrouver les parfums et les chansons de ce temps-là' (p.124).
37. Malka, 'Patrick Modiano: un homme sur du sable mouvant', p.2.
38. Modiano himself acknowledges this debt to history – see Patrick Modiano, 'Un roman sur Paris en été. . .', p.5. For a good idea of the extent of Modiano's familiarity with the gang, see Philippe Aziz, *Tu trahiras sans vergogne*, Marcel Hasquenoph, *La Gestapo en France* and , of

course, Jacques Bonny, *Mon père, l'inspecteur Bonny*, all of which, significantly, were published after *La Ronde de nuit*.

39. Aziz, in *Tu trahiras sans vergogne*, reveals where Modiano probably found the name for his character, referring to 'Georges Garance, dit "Monsieur Philibert", tenancier de maisons closes, organisateur attitré des soirées mondaines et des orgies de la rue Lauriston' (p.69). One of the *gestapistes* in *Lacombe Lucien*, Pierre Tonin, was also an inspector and 'un policier exceptionnel' (p.37) before he was dismissed from the force.
40. The use of 3bis square Cimarosa as the gang's address is no coincidence either. 3bis place des États-Unis was another of Laffont's haunts, and one of the streets leading towards it from the rue Lauriston is the rue Cimarosa.
41. See Françoise Jaudel, 'Quête d'identité', p.61, and cf. *Lacombe Lucien* in which the Corinne Luchaire–Guy de Voisin couple is reincarnated as Betty Beaulieu and Jean-Bernard de Voisins. Modiano may also have been thinking here of Annie Mouraille, the actress who was involved in the killing of Marx Dormoy (see Philippe Bourdrel, *La Cagoule*, pp.251–4).
42. Montalbetti, 'Patrick Modiano ou l'esprit de fuite', p.43.
43. Cf. *Lacombe Lucien*, apropos of which Modiano remarked: 'C'est d'une occupation un peu rêvée qu'il s'agit, comme déformée à travers une glace, revue par l'imaginaire. Nous avons moins cherché la véracité historique pure que la restitution d'une certaine atmosphère' (Jean Libermann, 'Patrick Modiano: *Lacombe Lucien* n'est pas le portrait du fascisme mais celui de sa piétaille', p.3).
44. Montalbetti, 'Patrick Modiano ou l'esprit de fuite', p.42.
45. Dominique Jamet, 'Patrick Modiano s'explique', p.36.
46. Malka, 'Patrick Modiano: un homme sur du sable mouvant', p.2.
47. Cf. one of his famous acquaintances, Maurice Sachs, whom Modiano consequently sees as a sort of substitute father.
48. Texier, 'Rencontre avec un jeune romancier: Patrick Modiano', p.8. Modiano is not alone in evoking the bizarre linking of victim and torturer – see Liliana Cavani's film, *The Night Porter* (1974); Brigitte Friang, *Regarde-toi qui meurs*, p.117; or Yves Darriet, *Pibale*, p.194. François Nourissier's *Bleu comme la nuit* (p.125) and Jean-Paul Sartre's play *Morts sans sépulture* both show that, here as elsewhere, the writers and *cinéastes* of the *mode rétro* are by no means innovating.
49. Texier, 'Rencontre avec un jeune romancier: Patrick Modiano', p.8. Cf. Gilles Perrault's 'Les Sanglots longs' (in *Les Sanglots longs*), at the end of which a son again exorcises the past by acting out the role his father played during the war.
50. This problem was somewhat of an *idée fixe* for him at the time. See e.g. Bernard Pivot, 'Demi-juif, Patrick Modiano affirme: "Céline était un véritable écrivain juif"', p.16.

51. J. J., 'Patrick Modiano à la question', p.14.
52. Jean-Louis Ezine, 'Sur la sellette: Patrick Modiano ou le passé antérieur', p.5.
53. Jamet, 'Patrick Modiano s'explique', p.27.
54. Ibid., p.32.
55. Ezine, 'Sur la sellette', p.5.
56. Montalbetti, 'La Haine des professeurs', p.2. Modiano's movement away from this initial standpoint is further demonstrated in Jean-Louis de Rambures, 'Comment travaillent les écrivains. Patrick Modiano: "apprendre à mentir"': 'Comment je procède pour retrouver cette période? Pas en recourant aux ouvrages historiques', he paradoxically insists (p.24).
57. An echo of this procedure can be found in *Lacombe Lucien*, in which Horn makes costly arrangements to flee to the safety of another neutral country – Spain – only to realise in the end: 'l'Espagne! Ça n'existe pas l'Espagne' (p. 114). Towards the end of the film, Lucien too is unable to escape across the border – his car breaks down en route.
58. The two actresses who *are* associated with the Occupation – Annie Murraille (*Les Boulevards de ceinture*) and Betty Beaulieu (*Lacombe Lucien*) – are modelled not, it may be recalled, on his mother, but rather on Corinne Luchaire.
59. Patrick Modiano, 'Patrick Modiano', p.79. This statement may have been prompted in part by the recent death of his father.
60. Gilles Pudlowski, 'Modiano le magnifique', p.28.
61. Alain Robbe-Grillet, *Pour un nouveau roman*, p.127.
62. Montalbetti, 'La Haine des professeurs', p.2.
63. Ezine, 'Sur la sellette', p.5.
64. See Montalbetti, 'La Haine des professeurs', p.2, and Duranteau, 'L'Obsession de l'anti-héros', p.13.
65. Ezine, 'Sur la sellette', p.5.
66. 'Patrick Modiano s'explique', p.23.

Conclusion

As the preceding pages have attempted to demonstrate, reactions to the *années noires* in France have changed quite radically in the course of the past forty-five years or so. From 1944 to 1969, thanks to the not inconsiderable efforts of the Parti Communiste Français and, more particularly, of General Charles de Gaulle, the Occupation was seen in terms which were excessively optimistic, for the disturbing fissures within the nation – a direct consequence of the 'dark years' – were effectively papered over by a far less realistic, more heroic version of events in which defiance of the occupant, rather than *attentisme* or collaboration, was deemed to have been the order of the day under the Germans. This collective myth of a *France résistante*, for that is what it amounted to, showed itself to be so appealing that, for a full quarter of a century, it was to prove immune to all attacks upon it. But by 1970 its powerful defences were down. More and more visibly a *mode rétro* began to establish itself, and hand in hand with this new fashion came demythification of the war years. The Resistance was brought crashing down from its lofty pedestal and, conversely, the Collaboration was elevated from its postwar purgatory. The break with the past could hardly have been more striking, but one thing was lacking in this long-awaited *remise en cause*: a sense of proportion. Mythification had given way to countermythification.

This was, however, no bad thing for the French, for as has been seen, although in the short term they simply moved from one extreme to the other, in the longer term something much more positive and beneficial was achieved. 'Je crois, moi, profondément', Jean-Paul Sartre has remarked, 'que toute démystification doit être en un sens mystifiante. Ou plutôt que, devant une foule en partie mystifiée, on ne peut se confier aux seules réactions critiques de cette foule. Il faut lui fournir une contre-mystification.'[1] This was precisely what happened in post-Gaullist France, and from the conflict between myth and countermyth enlightenment slowly emerged.

The reason why this enlightenment suddenly became possible, as has likewise been seen, was essentially twofold. Firstly, the demise of de Gaulle made re-evaluation of the *années noires* far simpler, since the general's authority and prestige had long served as an impenetrable shield for *le résistancialisme*. And secondly, the 1970s saw the maturing of a mass of French people having no adult experience of the war years at all. This young, 'innocent' generation, aware that a national myth and the silence of their parents had denied them access to the Occupation, and thereby cut them off from their roots, felt themselves to be cultural orphans, and so to overcome this predicament they set off in search of their lost origins. The quests which resulted, more often than not, took one of two forms: either an attempt to discover an absent, real-life parent (as was the case for Pascal Jardin, Marie Chaix and Evelyne Le Garrec), or the fabrication of a 'passé supplémentaire' replete with parental surrogates (the greatest exponent of which has been seen to be Patrick Modiano). Before such personal, individual myths could be produced, though, it was first necessary to subvert the prevailing collective myth, and the sole means of doing this was to usurp the closely-guarded memories of the older generation. Needless to say, this act of violation did not pass off without consequence. Numerous *anciens combattants* reacted vigorously, defending a past *engagement* which was now under threat of devaluation, while others, realising why their children were turning their gaze backwards, spoke up to pass on the information which had not previously filtered down. Eloquence thus replaced silence, and the effect of this abrupt volte-face was immediate: the young 'innocents' at long last acquired parents (figuratively speaking), and along with this 'adoption' came something much more fundamental besides – a heritage and an identity; a heritage and an identity both personal and national.

Such total dependence on the memories of their parents suggests, of course, that the young generation conducted their quests along fairly traditional lines, and this was indeed how things turned out. Every point they made to demythify the war years had already been made at some stage prior to 1969, albeit without success, and the nature of their quests was hardly innovative either, for with only a handful of notable exceptions (Jardin, Le Garrec and Modiano instantly spring to mind) they shunned the techniques of Structuralism, the New Novel and every other modern movement on which they could have built. The novelty of the *mode rétro*, then, if novelty there can be said to be, must be sought elsewhere – neither in the domain of content, nor in that of form, but rather in the fact that, for the first time ever, demythification was so widespread as to develop into a fashion.

How effective has this fashion proved to be? How permanently has the ghost of the *années noires* been laid to rest? These are questions which, in conclusion, it would be extremely helpful to answer, but unfortunately it is still far too early to do so, for where mythification is involved nothing is ever instantly certain.[2] Only time will tell if France has come to terms with her past, only time will confirm that the *réconciliation nationale* has been achieved. Nobody yet knows how the next generation will view the Occupation. Perhaps the myth of the Resistance will suddenly spring up again. Perhaps the seeds of a new *mode rétro* have already been sown. Who is to say? For the sake of the French, though, let us hope not.

Notes

1. *Un théâtre de situations*, p.77.
2. In the nineteenth century, for instance, a Napoleonic myth grew up and was then discredited, only to re-emerge years later under Napoleon III.

Select Bibliography

To list every text consulted during the preparation of this book would result in a Bibliography which was inordinately long, so details will only be given here of those works which were found to be of especial interest.

Unless otherwise stated, the place of publication in all cases is Paris.

BOOKS

Historical Background

Amouroux, Henri, *La Vie des Français sous l'Occupation*, Fayard, 1961

——, *La Grande Histoire des Français sous l'Occupation*, 8 vols to date, Laffont, 1976–

Aron, Robert, *Histoire de Vichy*, Fayard, 1954

——, *Histoire de l'épuration*, 3 vols, Fayard, 1967–75

Assouline, Pierre, *L'Épuration des intellectuels*, Brussels, Complexe, 1985

——, *Une éminence grise: Jean Jardin (1904–1976)*, Balland, 1986

Azéma, Jean-Pierre, *La Collaboration, 1940–1944*, PUF, 1975

——, *De Munich à la Libération, 1938–1944*, Seuil, 1979

Aziz, Philippe, *Tu trahiras sans vergogne*, Fayard, 1970

Bourdrel, Philippe, *La Cagoule*, Albin Michel, 1970

——, *L'Épuration sauvage, 1944–1945*, 1 vol. to date, Perrin, 1988

Bower, Tom, *Blind Eye to Murder*, London, Deutsch, 1981

——, *Klaus Barbie, Butcher of Lyons*, London, Corgi, 1985

Chambrun, René de, *Pierre Laval devant l'histoire*, France Empire, 1983

Defrasne, Jean, *Histoire de la Collaboration*, PUF, 1982

——, *L'Occupation allemande en France*, PUF, 1985

Delarue, Jacques, *Histoire de la Gestapo*, Fayard, 1962

——, *Trafics et crimes sous l'Occupation*, Fayard, 1968

Delperrié de Bayac, Jacques, *Histoire de la milice, 1918–1945*, Fayard, 1969

Dioudonnat, Pierre-Marie, *'Je suis partout', 1930–1944: les maurrassiens devant la tentation fasciste*, Table Ronde, 1973

Durand, Pierre, *Vivre debout: la Résistance*, La Farandole, 1974

Études sur la France de 1939 à nos jours, Seuil, 1985

Ganier-Raymond, Philippe, *Une certaine France: l'antisémitisme, 1940–44*, Balland, 1975
Halimi, André, *La Délation sous l'Occupation*, Moreau, 1983
Hasquenoph, Marcel, *La Gestapo en France*, de Vecchi, 1975
Kedward, H. R., *Occupied France: Collaboration and Resistance, 1940–1944*, Oxford, Blackwell, 1985
Kupferman, Fred, *Le Procès de Vichy: Pucheu, Pétain, Laval*, Brussels, Complexe, 1980
Le Boterf, Hervé, *La Vie parisienne sous l'Occupation*, 2 vols, France Empire, 1974–5
Michel, Henri, *Histoire de la Résistance en France*, PUF, 1980
——, *La Libération de Paris*, Brussels, Complexe, 1980
Novick, Peter, *The Resistance versus Vichy*, London, Chatto and Windus, 1968
Ory, Pascal, *Les Collaborateurs, 1940–1945*, Seuil, 1977
——, *La France allemande*, Gallimard/Julliard, 1977
——, *De Gaulle, ou l'ordre du discours*, Masson, 1979
Paxton, Robert O., *Vichy France: Old Guard and New Order, 1940–1944*, London, Barrie and Jenkins, 1972
Pryce-Jones, David, *Paris in the Third Reich: A History of the German Occupation, 1940–1944*, London and Glasgow, Collins, 1981
Rioux, Jean-Pierre, *La France de la Quatrième République*, 2 vols, Seuil, 1980–3
Rousso, Henry, *Le Syndrome de Vichy 1944–198. . .*, Seuil, 1987
Siclier, Jacques, *La France de Pétain et son cinéma*, Veyrier, 1981
Touchard, Jean, *Le Gaullisme, 1940–1969*, Seuil, 1978
Tournoux, Raymond, *Le Royaume d'Otto*, Flammarion, 1982
Veillon, Dominique, *La Collaboration: textes et débats*, Livre de Poche, 1984
La Vie de la France sous l'Occupation, 1940–1944, Plon, 1957

The Heritage, 1940–1969

Aymé, Marcel, *Le Chemin des écoliers*, Gallimard, 1946
——, *Uranus*, Gallimard, 1948
Bardèche, Maurice, *Lettre à François Mauriac*, La Pensée libre, 1947
Beauvoir, Simone de, *La Force de l'âge*, Gallimard, 1960
——, *La Force des choses*, Gallimard, 1963
Bernanos, Georges, *Français si vous saviez, 1945–1948*, Gallimard, 1969
Boisdeffre, Pierre de, *Les Fins dernières*, Table Ronde, 1952
Bordonove, Georges, *La Toccata*, Laffont, 1968
Bory, Jean-Louis, *Mon village à l'heure allemande*, Flammarion, 1945
——, *La Sourde Oreille*, Julliard, 1958
Cassou, Jean, *La Mémoire courte*, Minuit, 1953
Castillo, Michel del, *Tanguy*, Julliard, 1957

Céline, Louis-Ferdinand, *Féerie pour une autre fois II: Normance*, Gallimard, 1954
——, *D'un château l'autre*, Gallimard, 1957
——, *Nord*, Gallimard, 1960
——, *Rigodon*, Gallimard, 1969
Chardonne, Jacques, *Détachements*, Albin Michel, 1969
Curtis, Jean-Louis, *Les Forêts de la nuit*, Julliard, 1947
Dutourd, Jean, *Au bon beurre*, Gallimard, 1952
——, *Le Demi-solde*, Gallimard, 1965
Fabre-Luce, Alfred, *Au nom des silencieux*, L'Auteur, 1945
——, *Le plus illustre des Français*, Julliard, 1960
Fréville, Jean, *Les Collabos*, Flammarion, 1946
Frison-Roche, Roger, *Les Montagnards de la nuit*, Arthaud, 1968
Frossard, André, *Histoire paradoxale de la IVe République*, Grasset, 1954
Garas, Félix, *Charles de Gaulle: seul contre les pouvoirs*, Julliard, 1957
Gary, Romain, *Éducation européenne*, Libraires associés, 1961
Gaulle, Charles de, *Mémoires de guerre*, 3 vols, Plon, 1954–9
——, *Discours et messages*, 5 vols, Plon, 1970
——, *Mémoires d'espoir*, 2 vols, Plon, 1970–1
Genet, Jean, *Pompes funèbres*, A. Bikini, aux dépens de quelques amateurs, 1947
Guéhenno, Jean, *Journal des années noires*, Gallimard, 1947
Guimard, Paul, *L'Ironie du sort*, Denoël, 1961
Higgins, Ian, ed., *Anthology of Second World War French Poetry*, London, Methuen, 1982
Jamet, Claude, *Fifi Roi*, Élan, 1948
——, *Le Rendez-vous manqué de 1944*, France Empire, 1964
Lanoux, Armand, *Le Commandant Watrin*, Julliard, 1956
——, *Le Rendez-vous de Bruges*, Julliard, 1958
——, *Quand la mer se retire*, Julliard, 1963
Laurent, Jacques, *Le Petit Canard*, Grasset, 1954
——, *Mauriac sous de Gaulle*, Table Ronde, 1964
Luchaire, Corinne, *Ma drôle de vie*, Sun, 1949
Mauriac, Claude, *Un autre de Gaulle: journal 1944–1954*, Hachette, 1970
Mauriac, François, *Bloc-Notes, 1952–57*, Flammarion, 1958
——, *De Gaulle*, Grasset, 1964
Nettelbeck, Colin, ed., *War and Identity: The French and the Second World War: An Anthology of Texts*, London, Methuen, 1987
Nimier, Roger, *Les Épées*, Gallimard, 1948
Nourissier, François, *Bleu comme la nuit*, Grasset, 1958
——, *Un petit bourgeois*, Grasset, 1963
Paulhan, Jean, *Lettre aux membres du CNE*, 69, quai d'Orsay, 1947
——, *Lettre aux directeurs de la Résistance*, Minuit, 1952
Perret, Jacques, *Bande à part*, Gallimard, 1951
Peuchmaurd, Jacques, *La Nuit allemande*, Laffont, 1967

Peyrefitte, Roger, *La Fin des ambassades*, Flammarion, 1953
Reiner, Sylvain, *Après la guerre*, Laffont, 1966
Sachs, Maurice, *La Chasse à courre*, Gallimard, 1948
Saint-Lô, Michèle, *Les Inséparables*, Albin Michel, 1969
Sanitas, Jean, *Un jour et une nuit*, EFR, 1969
Sartre, Jean-Paul, *Morts sans sépulture*, Gallimard, 1947
——, *Situations III*, Gallimard, 1949
Simenon, Georges, *La Neige était sale*, Presses de la Cité, 1948
Spade, Henri, *Le Temps des cerises*, France Empire, 1968
——, *La Renaissante*, France Empire, 1969
Triolet, Elsa, *Le Premier Accroc coûte deux cents francs*, Laffont, 1965
Vailland, Roger, *Drôle de jeu*, Corrêa, 1945
Vercors, *La Bataille du silence*, Presses de la Cité, 1967

La Mode Rétro

Audiard, Michel, *La Nuit, le jour et toutes les autres nuits*, Denoël, 1978
Blancpain, Marc, *La Grande Nation*, Denoël, 1970
Bloch-Michel, Jean, *Daniel et Noémi*, Gallimard, 1971
Bonny, Jacques, *Mon père, l'inspecteur Bonny*, Laffont, 1975
Bood, Micheline, *Les Années doubles: journal d'une lycéenne sous l'occupation*, Laffont, 1974
Boudard, Alphonse, *Bleubite*, Table Ronde, 1975
——, *Les Combattants du petit bonheur*, Table Ronde, 1977
——, *Le Corbillard de Jules*, Table Ronde, 1979
Bourgeade, Pierre, *Deutsches Requiem*, Gallimard, 1973
——, *Le Camp*, Gallimard, 1979
Buhler, Alain, *Enfer et ses fils*, Mercure de France, 1980
Cavanna, *Les Russkoffs*, Belfond, 1979
——, *Bête et méchant*, Belfond, 1981
Chaix, Marie, *Les Lauriers du lac de Constance*, Seuil, 1974
Chamson, André, *La Reconquête*, Plon, 1975
——, *Suite guerrière*, Plon, 1975
Croussy, Guy, *La Tondue*, Grasset, 1980
Daninos, Pierre, *La Composition d'histoire*, Julliard, 1979
Darriet, Yves, *Pibale*, Denoël, 1971
Deforges, Régine, *La Bicyclette bleue*, 3 vols, Ramsay, 1981–5
Dreyfus, Paul, *Histoires extraordinaires de la Résistance*, Fayard, 1977
Elgey, Georgette, *La Fenêtre ouverte*, Fayard, 1973
Fasquelle, Solange, *Les Falaises d'Ischia*, Albin Michel, 1977
Fernandez, Adèle, *Le Fruit sans douceur*, EFR, 1972
Frenay, Henri, *La Nuit finira*, Laffont/Opéra Mundi, 1973
Friang, Brigitte, *Regarde-toi qui meurs*, Laffont, 1970
——, *Comme un verger avant l'hiver*, Julliard, 1978
Ganier-Raymond, Philippe, *Les Chanteurs de cordes*, Balland, 1974

Garnier, Dominique, *Nice, pour mémoire*, Seuil, 1980
Gatard, Marie, *La Guerre, mon père*, Mercure de France, 1978
Giovanni, José, *Mon ami le traître*, Gallimard, 1977
Haedrich, Marcel, *Le Maréchal et la dactylo*, Laffont, 1977
Heller, Gerhard, *Un Allemand à Paris*, Seuil, 1981
Ikor, Roger, *Pour une fois, écoute mon enfant. . .*, Albin Michel, 1975
Jardin, Pascal, *La Guerre à neuf ans*, Grasset, 1971
——, *Guerre après guerre*, Grasset, 1973
——, *Le Nain Jaune*, Julliard, 1978
——, *La Bête à bon Dieu*, Flammarion, 1980
Joffo, Joseph, *Un sac de billes*, Lattès, 1973
Jouhandeau, Marcel, *Journal sous l'Occupation*, Gallimard, 1980
Lacour, José-André, *Le Rire de Caïn*, Table Ronde, 1980
Lagorce, Guy, *La Raison des fous*, Grasset, 1980
——, *Le Train du soir*, Grasset, 1983
Lalanne, Denis, *Le Devoir de Français*, Table Ronde, 1974
La Mazière, Christian de, *Le Rêveur casqué*, Laffont, 1972
Lanzmann, Jacques, *Tous les chemins mènent à soi*, Laffont, 1979
Laurent, Jacques, *Histoire égoïste*, Table Ronde, 1976
Le Garrec, Evelyne, *La Rive allemande de ma mémoire*, Seuil, 1980
Mabire, Jean, *La Brigade Frankreich*, Fayard, 1973
Malle, Louis, and Patrick Modiano, *Lacombe Lucien* (filmscript), Gallimard, 1974
Maxence, Jean-Luc, *L'Ombre d'un père*, Éditions Libres-Hallier, 1978
Modiano, Patrick, *La Place de l'Étoile*, Gallimard, 1968
——, *La Ronde de nuit*, Gallimard, 1969
——, *Les Boulevards de ceinture*, Gallimard, 1972
——, *Livret de famille*, Gallimard, 1977
——, *Rue des Boutiques Obscures*, Gallimard, 1978
Moret, Frédérique, *Journal d'une mauvaise Française*, Table Ronde, 1972
Noirot, Paul, *La Mémoire ouverte*, Stock, 1976
Nourissier, François, *Allemande*, Grasset, 1973
Ophüls, Marcel, *Le Chagrin et la pitié* (filmscript), Moreau, 1980
Orsenna, Erik, *La Vie comme à Lausanne*, Seuil, 1977
Perrault, Gilles, *Les Sanglots longs*, Fayard, 1970
Pierrard, André, *On l'appelait Tamerlan*, Julliard, 1970
Poulet, Robert, *La Conjecture*, Table Ronde, 1980
Rabiniaux, Roger, *Les Bonheurs de la guerre*, Buchet-Chastel, 1973
Rachline, Michel, *Le Bonheur nazi, ou la mort des autres*, Malakoff, Authier, 1972
Rebatet, Lucien, *Les Mémoires d'un fasciste. . .*, 2 vols, Pauvert, 1976
Robida, Michel, *Le Déjeuner de Trieste*, Julliard, 1974
Serval, Pierre, *Une boule de neige en enfer*, Albin Michel, 1980
Sevran, Pascal, *Le Passé supplémentaire*, Orban, 1979
——, *Vichy-Dancing*, Orban, 1980

Sorel, Marie-Reine, *Les Roses de sel*, Gallimard, 1972
Spade, Henri, *Et pourquoi pas la patrie?*, Julliard, 1974
Tournier, Michel, *Le Vent paraclet*, Gallimard, 1977
Vercors, *Le Piège à loups*, Galilée, 1979
Werrie, Paul, *La Souille*, Mercure de France, 1970
——, *Les Chiens aveugles*, Mercure de France, 1972

Other Books Referred to

Ajar, Émile, *L'Angoisse du roi Salomon*, Mercure de France, 1979
Barthes, Roland, *Mythologies*, Seuil, 1957
Bell, Michael, ed., *The Context of English Literature, 1900–30*, London, Methuen, 1980
Berl, Emmanuel, *'Interrogatoire par Patrick Modiano' suivi de 'Il fait beau, allons au cimetière'*, Gallimard, 1976
Chaix, Marie, *Les Silences ou la vie d'une femme*, Seuil, 1976
——, *Juliette, chemin des Cerisiers*, Seuil, 1985
Chasseguet-Smirgel, Janine, *Pour une psychanalyse de l'art et de la créativité*, Payot, 1971
Culler, Jonathan, *Structuralist Poetics*, London, Routledge and Kegan Paul, 1975
Drieu la Rochelle, Pierre, *État civil*, Gallimard, 1921
Eagleton, Terry, *Literary Theory: An Introduction*, Oxford, Blackwell, 1983
Écrire, lire et en parler, Laffont, 1985
Jefferson, Ann, and David Robey, eds, *Modern Literary Theory: A Comparative Introduction*, second edition, London, Batsford, 1986
Lane, Michael, ed., *Structuralism: A Reader*, London, Cape, 1970
Lévi-Strauss, Claude, *Mythologiques*, 4 vols, Plon, 1964–71
Lièvre, Pierre, and Roger Caillois, eds, *Théâtre complet de Pierre Corneille*, 2 vols, Gallimard, 1950
Modiano, Patrick, *Villa Triste*, Gallimard, 1975
——, *Une jeunesse*, Gallimard, 1981
——, *De si braves garçons*, Gallimard, 1982
——, *Quartier perdu*, Gallimard, 1984
——, *Dimanches d'août*, Gallimard, 1986
——, *Remise de peine*, Seuil, 1988
——, *Vestiaire de l'enfance*, Gallimard, 1989
Ory, Pascal, *L'Entre-deux-mai*, Seuil, 1983
Robbe-Grillet, Alain, *Dans le labyrinthe*, Minuit, 1959
——, *Pour un nouveau roman*, Minuit, 1963
——, *Le Miroir qui revient*, Minuit, 1984
Roth, Philip, *Portnoy's Complaint*, London, Cape, 1969
Sachs, Maurice, *Le Sabbat*, Corrêa, 1946
Sartre, Jean-Paul, *Réflexions sur la question juive*, Gallimard, 1954

——, *Un théâtre de situations*, ed. by Michel Contat and Michel Rybalka, Gallimard, 1973

Saussure, Ferdinand de, *Cours de linguistique générale*, Payot, 1916

Sevran, Pascal, *Un garçon de France*, Orban, 1982

Simon, Claude, *La Route des Flandres*, Minuit, 1960

Spiraux, Alain, *Une fleur juive dans un jardin à la française*, Julliard, 1973

Stendhal, *Le Rouge et le noir*, in H. Martineau, ed., *Stendhal: romans et nouvelles*, 2 vols, Gallimard, 1959

Sturrock, John, ed., *Structuralism and since: From Lévi-Strauss to Derrida*, Oxford, Oxford University Press, 1979

ARTICLES, INTERVIEWS, ETC.

The Heritage, 1940–1969

'Après Céline Rebatet!', *Les Lettres Françaises*, 14 February 1952, p.2

Arland, Marcel, 'Sur les *mémoires* du général de Gaulle', *NRF*, 24 (December 1954), 1073–9

Aron, Raymond, 'Les Désillusions de la liberté', *Les Temps Modernes*, 1 (October 1945), 76–105

——, 'De la trahison', *La Table Ronde*, 47 (November 1951), 48–69

Blanzat, Jean, 'Les Romans de la semaine: *Le Chemin des écoliers* de Marcel Aymé', *Le Figaro Littéraire*, 6 July 1946, p.4

Bloch-Michel, Jean, 'Les Grandes Circonstances', *Les Temps Modernes*, 9 (June 1946), 1642–56

Boegner, Marc, 'Contre la violence et la haine', *Le Figaro*, 31 August 1944, p.1

Braspart, Michel, 'L'œil d'Uranus', *La Table Ronde*, 9 (September 1948), 1544–7

Cassou, Jean, 'Corps mystique de la France', *Domaine Français*, Geneva, *Messages* (1943), 87–92

Daix, Pierre, 'Du culte de la personnalité', *Les Lettres Françaises*, 12–18 November 1959, pp.1, 10

Delas, Paul, 'Fresnes 1948', *Les Temps Modernes*, 35 (August 1948), 314–24

——, 'A propos de "Fresnes 1948"', *Les Temps Modernes*, 37 (October 1948), 766–8

Duché, Jean, 'Jean Paulhan et Vercors disputent de l'épuration chez les écrivains', *Le Figaro Littéraire*, 18 January 1947, pp.1–2

Duhamel, Georges, 'Tout jugement sera jugé', *Le Figaro*, 12 January 1945, p.1

Fouchet, Max-Pol, 'Une seule Patrie', *Fontaine*, Algiers, 4, no.25 (1942), 489–94

Fumet, Stanislas, '"Qui" est la France?', *Fontaine*, Algiers, 5, no.29 (1943), 355–66

Garçon, Maurice, 'De l'indignité', *Le Figaro*, 9 November 1944, pp.1–2

——, 'De la liberté individuelle', *Le Figaro*, 14 December 1944, pp.1–2
——, 'La Juste Mesure', *Le Figaro*, 18 January 1945, p.1
Henriot, Émile, 'Les *Mémoires de guerre* du général de Gaulle', *Le Monde*, 20 June 1956, pp.8–9
——, '*Le Salut*, troisième tome des *Mémoires* du général de Gaulle', *Le Monde*, 29 October 1959, p.9
Higgins, Ian, 'Tradition and Myth in French Resistance Poetry: Reaction or Subversion?', in *The Second World War in Literature*, ed. by Ian Higgins, Edinburgh, Scottish Academic Press, 1986, pp.45–58
Jankélévitch, Vladimir, 'Dans l'honneur et la dignité', *Les Temps Modernes*, 33 (June 1948), 2249–60
Kedward, H. R., 'Patriots and Patriotism in Vichy France', *Transactions of the Royal Historical Society*, London, 5, vol. 32 (1982), 175–92
Latreille, André, 'Les Mémoires du général de Gaulle', *Le Monde*, 13 November 1954, p.9
Lebreton, Yves, 'Les Silencieux parlent', *Les Temps Modernes*, 33 (June 1948), 2291–2
Lecache, Bernard, 'Fabre-Luce ou le Juvénal clandestin', *Les Lettres Françaises*, 11 August 1945, p.2
L[escure]., J[ean]., 'Présentation', *Domaine Français*, Geneva, *Messages* (1943), 13–14
Maast, 'Morceaux choisis: épurés', *Les Temps Modernes*, 9 (June 1946), 1696–7
Marceau, Félicien, 'Plaies et bosses', *La Table Ronde*, 59 (November 1952), 144–8
Martin-Chauffier, Louis, 'Ma Patrie, la langue française', *Domaine Français*, Geneva, *Messages* (1943), 63–70
Mauriac, Claude, 'Nous n'avons pas voulu cela', *La Table Ronde*, 10 (October 1948), 1747–8
Mauriac, François, 'La Vraie Justice', *Le Figaro*, 8 September 1944, p.1
——, 'La Vocation de la Résistance', *Le Figaro*, 3–4 December 1944, p.1
——, 'Justice', *Le Figaro*, 12 December 1944, p.1
——, 'L'Année de la réconciliation', *Le Figaro*, 2 January 1945, p.1
——, 'Les Conséquences politiques de l'épuration', *Le Figaro*, 12 January 1945, p.1
——, 'Le Procès d'un seul homme', *Le Figaro*, 26 July 1945, p.1
——, 'La Question de l'amnistie', *Le Figaro*, 7 March 1946, p.1
——, 'L'Esprit de la Résistance', *Le Figaro*, 18 May 1946, p.1
——, 'Le Tome III des *Mémoires* de Charles de Gaulle', *Le Figaro Littéraire*, 31 October 1959, pp.1–2
Morgan, Claude, 'L'Armée du crime', *Les Lettres Françaises*, 9 September 1944, p.1
——, 'Droit d'injustice', *Les Lettres Françaises*, 1 September 1945, p.1
——, 'Le droit au crime', *Les Lettres Françaises*, 31 January 1947, p.1
——, 'Nazis sans uniforme', *Les Lettres Françaises*, 14 February 1947, p.1

——, 'Paulhan ou la fausse ingénue', *Les Lettres Françaises*, 1 August 1947, pp.1–2

Nourissier, François, 'Roger Peyrefitte: *La Fin des ambassades*', *NRF*, 10 (October 1953), 720–1

Ormesson, Wladimir d', 'Justice de guerre', *Le Figaro*, 27 January 1945, p.1

Parrot, Louis, 'Les Livres et l'homme: documents', *Les Lettres Françaises*, 22 March 1946, p.5

——, 'Prix littéraires', *Les Lettres Françaises*, 18 December 1947, p.5

Paulhan, Jean, 'Trois notes à propos de la patrie', *La Table Ronde*, 1 (January 1948), 20–41

Pouillon, Jean, 'Notes: *Lettre à François Mauriac*, par Maurice Bardèche', *Les Temps Modernes*, 26 (November 1947), 949–55

——, 'Offres de Collaboration', *Les Temps Modernes*, 33 (June 1948), 2267–83

'Premier Maurrassien de France', *Les Lettres Françaises*, 16 October 1947, pp.1–2

Roire, Jean, 'Après la mise en liberté de Lucien Rebatet', *Les Lettres Françaises*, [22] July 1952, p.4

Rousseaux, André, '*Journal des années noires* de Jean Guéhenno', *Le Figaro Littéraire*, 5 July 1947, p.2

——, '*Les Forêts de la nuit*', *Le Figaro Littéraire*, 13 December 1947, p.2

——, 'Les *Mémoires* du général de Gaulle', *Le Figaro Littéraire*, 30 October 1954, p.2

——, 'Les *Mémoires* du général de Gaulle', *Le Figaro Littéraire*, 7 July 1956, p.2

Roy, Jean-H., 'Les Deux Justices', *Les Temps Modernes*, 33 (June 1948), 2261–6

Schumann, Maurice, 'De Gaulle écrivain', *Les Nouvelles Littéraires*, 5 November 1959, pp.1, 8

Soustelle, Jacques, 'Les *Mémoires* de guerre du général de Gaulle', *La Table Ronde*, 83 (November 1954), 113–15

T[avernier]., R[ené]., 'La Victoire en chantant', *Confluences*, Lyons, 34 (August 1944), 115–26

Tournier, Jacques, 'Jean-Louis Curtis: *Les Forêts de la nuit*', *La Table Ronde*, 1 (January 1948), 128–33

Triolet, Elsa, 'Jean Paulhan successeur de Drieu la Rochelle', *Les Lettres Françaises*, 7 February 1952, p.1

'Vie d'un légionnaire', *Les Temps Modernes*, 9 (June 1946), 1657–76

Villefosse, Louis de, 'Les Petites Iles de la liberté', *Les Temps Modernes*, 49 (November 1949), 868–95

Wurmser, André, 'Hommage au déshonneur', *Les Lettres Françaises*, 30 October–6 November 1952, p.3

The Mode Rétro

General

Billard, Pierre, 'L'Occupation: pourquoi tout le monde en parle', *Le Point*, 11 March 1974, pp.84–9

B[onitzer]., P[ascal]., and S[erge]. T[oubiana]., 'Entretien avec Michel Foucault', *Les Cahiers du Cinéma*, 251–2 (July–August 1974), 5–15

Chadwick, Kay, '*Collabos, révisos*: même combat', *Strathclyde Modern Language Studies*, Glasgow, 9 (1989), 51–68

Chambrun, René de, 'Pierre Laval et les Israélites', *Le Monde*, 11 September 1971, p.8

Denuzière, Maurice, 'L'Imprescriptible Honte', *Le Monde*, 29 October 1975, p.12

Derogy, Jacques, '*L'Express* a retrouvé le bourreau de Lyon', *L'Express*, 5–11 June 1972, pp.68–9

Duquesne, Jacques, 'Marchais: les énigmes', *Le Point*, 23 February 1981, pp.38–43

Even, Martin, 'Les Ambiguïtés de la mode "rétro": les créateurs font marche arrière', *Le Monde*, 18 April 1974, pp.18–19

Frossard, André, 'Occupation: le temps de mes 20 ans', *Le Point*, 11 March 1974, p.89

Ganier-Raymond, Philippe, 'Un entretien avec Darquier de Pellepoix', *L'Express*, 4 November 1978, pp.164–99

Giard, Luce, 'La Honte', *Esprit*, 25, no.1 (January 1979), 71–8

Nettelbeck, Colin, 'Getting the Story Right: Narratives of World War II in Post-1968 France', *Journal of European Studies*, Chalfont St Giles, 58 (June 1985), 77–116

Nourissier, François, 'Le Cadavre dans le placard', *Le Point*, 11 March 1974, pp.86–7

——, 'Les Français étaient-ils des veaux en 40?', *Réalités*, 342 (July 1974), 18–25

Ory, Pascal, 'Comme de l'an quarante: dix années de "rétro satanas"', *Le Débat*, 16 (November 1981), 109–17

Ozouf, Mona, 'Sans Chagrin et sans pitié', *Le Nouvel Observateur*, 25–31 March 1974, pp.54–6

Planchais, Jean, 'Le Vilain', *Le Monde*, 4 November 1978, pp.1, 10

Poirot-Delpech, Bertrand, '1978, Année des "collabos": à quand le procès de Jean Moulin?', *Le Monde*, 29 December 1978, p.11

Raczymow, Henri, 'L'Écoute d'un silence', *Le Monde*, 19 September 1980, p.19

'Réponses à M. de Chambrun: Pierre Laval et les Israélites', *Le Monde*, 23 September 1971, p.6

Siclier, Jacques, 'Depuis trente-cinq ans le cinéma raconte le nazisme', *Le Monde*, 18 April 1974, p.18

Le Chagrin et la pitié

Gérard, Andrée, '*Le Chagrin et la pitié* ou l'histoire en polyphonie', *La Revue Nouvelle*, 56, no.9 (September 1972), 170–2

Harris, André, and Alain de Sédouy, 'A propos d'une fresque', *L'Avant-Scène du Cinéma*, 127–8 (July–September 1972), 11

Heymann, Danièle, 'Français, vous saurez', *L'Express*, international edition, 4 September 1981, pp.18–19

Hoffmann, Stanley, 'Dans le miroir: *Le Chagrin et la pitié*', *Contrepoint*, 10 (April 1973), 101–17

Langlois, Gérard, 'Entretien: *Le Chagrin et la pitié* de Marcel Ophüls, véritable histoire de la France occupée', *Les Lettres Françaises*, 14–20 April 1971, pp.10–11

Loubière, Pierre and Gilbert Salachas, 'Libre cours: Marcel Ophüls', *Télé-Ciné*, 171–2 (July–September 1971), 22–33

——, 'Libre cours: André Harris', *Télé-Ciné*, 171–2 (July–September 1971), 34–41

Manceaux, Michèle, 'A la recherche du temps honteux', *Le Nouvel Observateur*, 12–18 April 1971, pp.39–40

Ophüls, Marcel, '60 heures de 16 mm. . .', *Le Monde*, 15 April 1971, p.15

——, 'Regardez donc dans vos greniers', *L'Avant-Scène du Cinéma*, 127–8 (July–September 1972), 9–10

Zissler, Albert, '*Le Chagrin et la pitié*', *Télé-Ciné*, 171–2 (July–September 1971), 2–18

Lacombe Lucien

Baroncelli, Jean de, 'Un nouveau film de Louis Malle: *Lacombe Lucien*, un adolescent dans la Gestapo', *Le Monde*, 31 January 1974, pp.1, 13

Billard, Pierre, 'Louis Malle: l'enfant et ses sortilèges', *Le Point*, 5 October 1987, pp.97–101

Bonitzer, Pascal, 'Histoire de sparadrap', *Les Cahiers du Cinéma*, 250 (May 1974), 42–7

Capdenac, Michel, 'Révolte dévoyée, film fourvoyé', *Europe*, 540–1 (April–May 1974), 264–8

Delain, Michel, 'Louis Malle: dernier zigzag', *L'Express*, 14–20 January 1974, p.48

E., M., 'Revue de presse: faut-il voir *Lacombe Lucien*?', *Le Monde*, 14 February 1974, p.13

Jacob, Gilles, 'Entretien avec Louis Malle (à propos de *Lacombe Lucien*)', *Positif*, 157 (March 1974), 28–35

Malcolm, Derek, 'Turning fascist', *The Guardian*, Manchester, 31 July 1974, p.10

Malle, Louis, '*Lacombe Lucien*: un enfant perdu dans un monde chaotique', *France-Soir*, 31 January 1974, p.13

Olivier, Jean-Jacques, 'L'Engagement de Louis Malle', *Le Figaro*, 26 January 1974, p.V [p.15]
Viansson-Ponté, Pierre, 'Au fil de la semaine: *Lacombe Lucien* ou l'ambiguïté', *Le Monde*, 17–18 February 1974, p.7

Pascal Jardin

'A bout portant: Pascal Jardin', *Paris-Match*, 13 October 1978, p.57
Gombault, Charles, 'La Honte à héritage', *Le Monde*, 17 November 1978, p.20
G[oury]., G[érard].-H[umbert]., 'Le fils de chronos', *Magazine Littéraire*, 142 (November 1978), 37–8
Nourissier, François, 'Tel père, tel fils', *Le Figaro-Magazine*, 28 June 1980, p.78
Ormesson, Jean d', 'Ah! que la guerre est jolie', *Les Nouvelles Littéraires*, 23 July 1971, p.6
Pivot, Bernard, 'Pourquoi ce livre sur votre père?', *Lire*, 39 (November 1978), 77–81
'Préface', in Pascal Jardin, *La Guerre à neuf ans*, Rombaldi, 1975, pp.6–20
Viansson-Ponté, Pierre, 'A Vichy, un petit garçon écoutait', *Le Monde*, 10 September 1971, pp.13, 15

Marie Chaix

Boisdeffre, Pierre de, 'La Revue littéraire', *Nouvelle Revue des Deux Mondes*, 4 (April 1974), 162–70 (pp.162–6)
Brisac, Geneviève, 'Les Confessions cruelles de Marie Chaix', *Le Monde*, 2 February 1985, p.21
Chavardès, Maurice, 'Histoire d'un "collabo"', *La Quinzaine Littéraire*, 15–31 March 1974, pp.6–7
Grisolia, Michel, '*Les Lauriers du lac de Constance*, par Marie Chaix', *Magazine Littéraire*, 86 (March 1974), 30–1
Josselin, Jean-François, 'Le Charme discret de la collaboration', *Le Nouvel Observateur*, 11–17 February 1974, p.54

Patrick Modiano

Bersani, Jacques, 'Patrick Modiano, agent double', *NRF*, 298 (November 1977), 78–84
Chalon, Jean, 'Patrick Modiano: le dernier promeneur solitaire', in Patrick Modiano, *La Ronde de nuit*, Tallandier (Cercle du nouveau livre), 1970, *postface*, 6–23
Dumur, Guy, '*La Polka*, de Patrick Modiano', *Le Nouvel Observateur*, 1–9 June 1974, pp.72–3

Duranteau, Josane, 'Un début exceptionnel: *La Place de l'Étoile*, de Patrick Modiano', *Le Monde*, 11 May 1968, p.II

——, 'L'Obsession de l'anti-héros', *Le Monde*, 11 November 1972, p.13

Ezine, Jean-Louis, 'Sur la sellette: Patrick Modiano ou le passé antérieur', *Les Nouvelles Littéraires*, 6–12 October 1975, p.5

J. J., 'Patrick Modiano à la question', *Le Figaro*, 20 September 1975, pp.I–II [pp.13–14]

Jamet, Dominique, 'Patrick Modiano s'explique', *Lire*, 1 (October 1975), 23–36

Jaudel, Françoise, 'Quête d'identité', *L'Arche*, October–November 1972, p.61

Kanters, Robert, 'La Nuit de Patrick Modiano', *Le Figaro Littéraire*, 27 October–2 November 1969, pp.23–4

Leclère, Marie-Françoise, 'Il a vingt-deux ans et il méritait le Goncourt', *Elle*, 8 December 1969, p.139

Libermann, Jean, 'Patrick Modiano: *Lacombe Lucien* n'est pas le portrait du fascisme mais celui de sa piétaille', *Presse Nouvelle Hebdo*, 8 March 1974, pp.3, 9

Malka, Victor, 'Patrick Modiano: un homme sur du sable mouvant', *Les Nouvelles Littéraires*. 30 October–5 November 1972, p.2

Modiano, Patrick, 'Un roman sur Paris en été. . .', in Patrick Modiano, *La Ronde de nuit*, Tallandier (Cercle du nouveau livre), 1970, *postface*, 3–5

——, 'Patrick Modiano répond au questionnaire Marcel Proust', in Patrick Modiano, *La Ronde de nuit*, Tallandier (Cercle du nouveau livre), 1970, *postface*, 24–6

——, 'Courrier du cœur', *Les Cahiers du Chemin*, 20 (January 1974), 35–40

——, 'Johnny', *NRF*, 307 (August 1978), 1–5

——, 'Patrick Modiano', *Paris-Match*, 1 December 1978, p.79

Montalbetti, Jean, 'La Haine des professeurs: instantané Patrick Modiano', *Les Nouvelles Littéraires*, 13 June 1968, p.2

——, 'Patrick Modiano ou l'esprit de fuite', *Magazine Littéraire*, 34 (November 1969), 42–3

Pivot, Bernard, 'Demi-juif, Patrick Modiano affirme: "Céline était un véritable écrivain juif"', *Le Figaro Littéraire*, 29 April 1968, p.16

Pudlowski, Gilles, 'Modiano le magnifique', *Les Nouvelles Littéraires*, 12–19 February 1981, p.28

Rambures, Jean-Louis de, 'Comment travaillent les écrivains: Patrick Modiano: "apprendre à mentir"', *Le Monde*, 24 May 1973, p.24

Rolin, Gabrielle, 'Patrick Modiano: le dernier enfant du siècle', *Le Point*, 3–9 January 1983, pp.63–4

Texier, Jean-C., 'Rencontre avec un jeune romancier: Patrick Modiano', *La Croix*, 9–10 November 1969, p.8

Index

Index

Of Related Interest

The Silence of the Sea/Le Silence de la mer

A Novel of French Resistance during World War II by "Vercors"

Edited by James W. Brown and Lawrence D. Stokes

During the spring of 1942 the novel *Le Silence de la mer*, clandestinely published in Nazi-occupied Paris and written by the then little known cartoonist Jean Bruller – alias Vercors, impressed contemporaries as 'the most moving, the most deeply human that we have had the opportunity to read since the beginning of the German occupation' (*Les Lettres françaises*) and as 'not only a distinguished piece of fiction but also a brilliant piece of reporting on French resistance' (*Life*). Its message, appropriate to the early stage of French resistance, was that French people should abstain from communicating with the Germans. It has been praised by historians for its realism and has found enthusiastic readers around the world.

This bilingual edition is intended to introduce Vercors's famous tale to a generation without personal experience of the Second World War, who may or may not be able to read it in its original language. They are assisted by historical and literary introductions provided by the editors, explanatory notes, a glossary of French terms and a select bibliography.

James W. Brown is Professor of French and **Lawrence D. Stokes** is Professor of Modern European and German History, both at Dalhousie University, Halifax, Nova Scotia.

112p
Published in 1991
ISBN 0 85496 671 4

Collaboration in France

Politics and Culture during the Nazi Occupation, 1940–1944

Edited by
Gerhard Hirschfeld and Patrick Marsh

The French response to the Nazi occupation during the Second World War remains one of the most fascinating and controversial chapters of the recent political and cultural history of Continental Europe. While a good deal of research has been done on the French Resistance, it is only more recently that attention has focused on the phenomenon of collaboration. The contributors to this volume, all of them well-known experts in the field, are particularly interested in the cultural and political aspects of collaboration and have joined forces in these original papers to explore to what extent the French gave active support to the Nazi vision of a 'New Europe'.

Gerhard Hirschfeld is Director of the Bibliothek für Zeitgeschichte. Stuttgart and **Patrick Marsh** is in the Department of French, University College, Dublin.

336pp
Published in 1989
ISBN 0 85496 237 9

The Berg French Studies Series
Recent Publications

The Use of Abuse

The Polemics of the Dreyfus Affair and its Aftermath

Richard Griffiths

This book closely examines the techniques used by the polemicists of the Dreyfus Affair as found in the newspapers, journals and books of the period. In the process, much is learned not only about the Affair itself but also about the nature of polemic and of the French press at the time which, with its complete lack of concern for libel and obscenity laws, gave rise to particularly vivid examples of the art. We are shown how authors' choice of stylistic techniques and of words and images reveal their innermost aims and how words and concepts subtly change their meaning with certain notions such as Truth and Justice becoming completely devalued.

By using a wide range of material of the period the author combines the techniques of the historian, the literary scholar and the linguist. In this way he arrives at a completely new approach which leads us to a greater knowledge of contemporary attitudes and to new insights into the Affair itself.

Richard Griffiths is Professor of French at King's College, London.

224pp
Published in 1991
ISBN 0 85496 626 9

Voices from the North African Immigrant Community in France

Immigration and Identity in Beur Fiction

Alec G. Hargreaves

Well over a dozen members of the so-called Beur generation, a popular name in France for the sons and daughters of first-generation North African immigrants, have so far published narrative works. This study combines careful analysis of the formal structures of Beur fiction with a wealth of insights derived from interviews with the authors and extensive access to unpublished writings.

Alec G. Hargreaves is Senior Lecturer in French at Loughborough University.

192pp
Published in 1991
ISBN 0 85496 649 8

Forever French

Exile in the United States 1939–1945

Colin W. Nettelbeck

The French emigration to the United States during the Second World War was a phenomenon of notable cultural and political significance. While a crushed and occupied France could project little of its former grandeur, the emigration involved many of pre-war France's most influential and creative people in all fields. The French community in the United States was divided by political opinion and beset by the abrasive efforts of the Gaullists to impose their leader's supremacy, even against explicit opposition from the US administration. Nevertheless, not only did the presence and activity of so many exiled artists and writers contribute to the rise of New York as cultural capital of the West, members of the emigrant community also succeeded in maintaining an image of an independent and democratic France as an indispensable partner in the reconstruction of Europe, and hence played a significant role in the shaping of post-war France.

Colin W. Nettelbeck is Associate Professor in the Department of Romance Languages at Monash University.

224pp
Published in 1991
ISBN 0 85496 632 3

Victor Serge

The Uses of Dissent

Bill Marshall

This study introduces the reader to Victor Serge's life and extraordinary novels, locating them amidst crucial debates about revolution, communism and anarchism, literature and representation, and in comparison with his contemporaries. From the prisons of France and Siberia, through the Russian Civil War and the purges of Stalin to the Second World War and the last exile in Mexico, the voice of Serge speaks out with authority and compassion. Bill Marshall demonstrates that the voice of Serge, in all its contexts, is unified by a notion of dissent – an active dissent far removed from the quietism and conservatism of other dissidents.

Bill Marshall is Lecturer in French at the University of Southampton.

January 1992
224pp
ISBN 0 85496 766 4

Printed in the United Kingdom
by Lightning Source UK Ltd.
110616UKS00001B/99

9 780854 966349